DOG DAYS

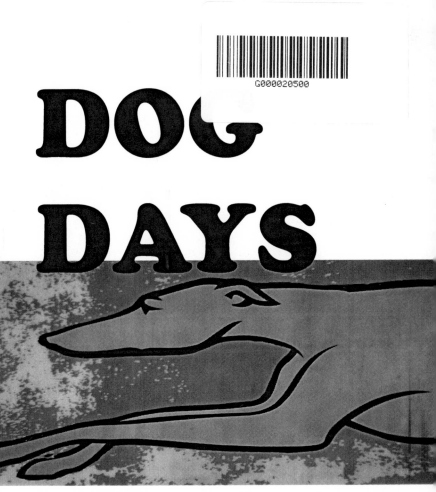

TALES FROM AN AMERICAN ROAD TRIP

Andrew Thompson

FINGERPRESS LTD
LONDON

Dog Days – Tales From an American Road Trip

ISBN (pbk): 978-1-908824-44-8

Published by Fingerpress Ltd

Production Editor: Matt Stephens
Production Manager: Michelle Stephens
Copy Editor: Madeleine Horobin

Photo attributions:
Greyhound on wall—by 'ilovememphis'
Bus in parking lot—by Mark aka 'eggrole', San Diego, USA

www.fingerpress.co.uk

facebook.com/fingerpress
twitter.com/FingerpressUK

The high-visibility vested Dog employee stood in the doorway again, making herself as large as possible. She was large.

'It is time to board the bus,' she yelled. 'Board the bus. Ensure you do so in an orderly fashion, following the yellow line. You must follow the yellow line.'

'A few of this mob should be quite used to that,' I mumbled to Lucy.

'Follow the yellow line,' the employee added for clarity.

'This is the last time,' Lucy said.

I nodded and we walked up the steps and onto the Dog.

Born in Australia in 1972, Andrew Thompson lived and practised Law in London for 12 years, before embarking on a three year world tour that has taken him to 32 countries, including all of the habitable continents. He thought he knew a lot about America and its culture, but during a three-month road trip around the United States, he found it to be vastly different to what he expected.

Spawned from the American road trip, *Dog Days* is his first travel memoir.

www.andrewthompsonwriter.co.uk

Also by Andrew Thompson

Trivia Books:
WHY SKIES ARE BLUE AND PARROTS TALK
WHY DO KAMIKAZE PILOTS WEAR HELMETS?

'Alternate History' Novel:
THE HEMINGWAY SOLUTION

To Lucy

DOG DAYS

1

Purgatory

'This ain't exactly Hell. It sure as Hell ain't
Heaven...I guess I'll do my waitin' in this
purgatory line.'

—'The Purgatory Line', Drive-By Truckers

Christ, he looked tough. They all did, but he looked especially tough. Tough and dangerous. As though he'd been designed for violence. A genuine Mustang Man.

He was sitting on the hard and cold floor. It looked like he'd been there all night. He was about thirty-five, I suppose. His faded jeans were torn and he wore almost knee-length boots that were scuffed and haggard. Those boots had seen a few things, done a few things. I don't even know what sort of shirt he had on. It was probably a ripped lumberjack, but my eyes were drawn to his tattoos. He was covered in them. And not designer type ones, but ones that looked like they'd been done by crude hand-fashioned implements in the blazing sun of some hot prison yard. Of course, his face was stubbled—it wasn't designer either—and he had a strong, unkempt moustache and goatee beard. There were tattoos on his face;

specifically under his eyes. They were very rudimentary in design. On one upper cheek there were some intersecting lines in a 'noughts and crosses' pattern. The opposite side held a tear drop coming down from under his eye. Not a real tear drop, but a tattooed one. I remembered being told by someone who seemed to know, that a tattooed tear drop meant that you'd been in jail or had killed someone or both. I'm not sure which. Either way, I've always been firm in my view that any man who gets his face tattooed is pretty tough. Tougher than me, anyway.

'Christ, he looks tough,' I whispered to Lucy, looking away from the subject and trying to act casual.

'Which one?' she mumbled back, immediately falling in with my pantomime.

'The really tough one. Any tougher and he'd rust.'

'Yeah,' she said. 'I've noticed him. How do you find the tattoos?'

'Tough. I think that tear one means…'

'That he's killed someone,' she said, cutting me off.

'Yeah, that's what I thought. Don't make eye contact, whatever you do.'

'I won't,' she replied. 'He's one of those guys who could just go berserk at any minute'.

'Yeah. I'm pretty sure he's done some time. And I'm pretty sure it wasn't white collar.'

I looked at the list of stations on the sign above the man's head as a distraction, then quickly down to his face again. He had his right index finger well up his nostril and was staring directly at me, a blank emotionless expression on his face; an expression so cold that it effortlessly conveyed 'I'll happily gut you like a pig without raising my heart beat one iota'.

I averted my eyes as quickly as I could, without appearing obvious, an effect I'm sure I didn't come close to achieving.

Another gaze around the station to show blasé, before turning back to Lucy.

'He's staring right at me,' I said.

'He's been staring at me too.'

'Christ, I hope he's not sitting anywhere near us.'

'Mmmm.'

'I'm going to sleep for a week when I get home,' a young and fit-looking black man said loudly to nobody in particular. 'A fucking week.'

'The first thing I'msa gunna do is shower,' replied a white man who was standing nearby. He spoke with a southern drawl and was wearing a wide-brimmed cowboy hat.

'Shower. What a beautiful word. Beautiful word, shower.'

Sitting on a metal wire chair against the window a few metres away was an obese white woman with bedraggled straw-like hair. She was alone. Most of the people seemed alone, but an unsavoury camaraderie appeared to be developing.

Standing next to us was a short, bald white man in his mid-twenties. He had a black T-shirt on that advertised a heavy-metal band that I didn't know. He looked fairly tough in his own right.

'I've got a three year old daughter,' he opened with, completely non-sequitur. Perhaps we'd missed the back story. He was standing with a trailer-park skank, presumably not the mother. Her age was difficult to determine. Very hard to tell with the skanks.

He went to speak again.

'I wonder where this synaptic misfire will land,' I said to

Lucy under my breath.

'Actually,' he went on. 'I had better stop talking now. Right now. Whatever I say will offend somebody for sure.'

'Man, an uppercut is no good as a punch,' he continued, in what I gathered he considered a less offensive subject. 'Just no good.'

'Totally,' agreed the young black man, seizing on some common ground.

'Yeah,' said Bald Man, as he demonstrated his right uppercut in a fast and repeated cadence. 'You're just in way too close. I prefer the straight.' He threw three straight rights, then began pacing like a frustrated animal in a zoo cage.

It was 8.25am and there were about thirty people ahead of us in the queue. My meagre wealth undoubtedly exceeded the collective of theirs. We were waiting for the 9.25am Greyhound bus to Nashville, Tennessee; the 'Dog' or 'Dawg', as it's affectionately known by the scourge of the earth that ride it.

'Will everybody listen up now?' yelled a burly woman from the entrance to gate 6 in front of us. She was wearing a high-visibility yellow vest. 'Anybody who has bags to go under the bus, bring them forward now. But we are not boarding at this time.' Always so many rules on the Dog. 'I repeat, we are not boarding at this time.'

'You wait here,' I said to Lucy. 'I'll get these bags up. We don't want to lose our place in the line.'

I wheeled our suitcases to the doorway.

'Sorry,' I said, as I hit into somebody's elbow. It was Mustang Man.

He turned around with an economy of motion. You could tell that he definitely knew how to handle himself.

'Did I hit you?' he said in an accusatory manner.

'No, no,' I said. 'You're right. You're right.'

I moved forward, trying to seem self-assured.

'Where are you going, sir?' the burly lady asked me.

'Nashville.' You use few words with the Greyhound staff. They're angry and they don't enjoy chit chat.

'Leave your bags here and go back in line.'

I did. Lucy had held firm on our place in the queue and we hadn't lost any ground. In fact, we'd gained some. Not that I was happy about that. Now standing behind us were the bald man and his skank, the fit black man, the cowboy hat man, Mustang Man and a drug-addled worm who had joined their party. They were in front of us before the bag drop.

'We've been hosed,' said Drug Boy, the vile little newcomer. 'Fucking hosed.'

'Shhhooooss.' The fit guy mimicked the noise of a hose. It was directed towards us.

'They're onto us,' I said to Lucy. 'And,' appraising us both, 'we really need to reassess our outfits for the Mid-West leg.'

I was in bright pink, flowery Abercrombie & Fitch board shorts, green Havaiana flip-flops, a Tiger Beer T-shirt and Ray-Ban Wayfarer sunglasses. Lucy was wearing leopard-print ballet pumps with a red trim, as well as a tight-fitted vest. Her brown hair was flowing past her shoulders and her olive skin glowed, her dark eyes mesmerized. Aubin & Wills terracotta preppie shorts showed off her smooth, toned and tanned legs. God, she looked good. She always looked good. The most beautiful girl in the room, in every room, she could brighten an entire place with her smile, that heart-breaking smile. She was like a supernova in this hovel of bottom feeders.

'I know,' she said. 'We look like we've just stepped out of a Harvard Law School tutorial. You should at least rethink the watch.' It was a Daytona Rolex, albeit a knock-off, but a very good one.

We stood out like dogs' balls.

'Yeah, the watch has to go,' I said. 'And I'm thinking cargo shorts from now on. Or faded jeans and boots.'

I also had $1,200 in cash in a clear freezer packet in my pocket. The bastards would have inhaled me if they'd known that.

The high-visibility vested Dog employee stood in the doorway again, making herself as large as possible. She was large.

'It is time to board the bus,' she yelled. 'Board the bus. Ensure you do so in an orderly fashion, following the yellow line. You must follow the yellow line.'

'A few of this mob should be quite used to that,' I mumbled to Lucy.

'Follow the yellow line,' the employee added for clarity.

'This is the last time,' Lucy said.

I nodded and we walked up the steps and onto the Dog.

2

HELL

'On a Greyhound bus, Lord I'm travelling this morning…It's been making me lonesome, on'ry and mean.'

—'Lonesome On'ry and Mean', Waylon Jennings

'Grab the first set of two seats you see,' I said to Lucy, sliding my watch off and putting it into my pocket as we boarded the bus. It was crowded. We were lucky to get a seat in the first place. We had arrived at the station at 8am for the 9.25 bus. I asked the rarely-seen male ticket counter employee for two tickets to Nashville, handing over our Discovery Passes. The Discovery Pass is a good and bad thing to have. It only costs $564 for sixty days, whereas one-off Greyhound tickets are absurdly expensive for the crap service that is offered, usually costing around $100 for one five hour journey. The Pass also gives unlimited journeys in that sixty day period. The downside is that you can't book seats ahead, but other people can. In fact, you aren't allowed to reserve a seat on a bus apart from at the station of departure and no more than one hour before departure. There are many rules for the Dog, and most of them are fucking absurd. I tried to reserve a seat in St. Louis the night before and, when I told her I had a Discovery Pass, the ticket woman just screamed, 'Well, there's nothing for me to do. Come back in the morning.' What this means is that a lot of buses are full or almost full when the Discovery Pass holder tries to get a ticket. It was only the day before in Chicago that we were turned away and forced to pay for the far superior Texas Eagle train.

'I don't think that will be possible,' said the man, shaking his head and starting the ridiculous five minute typing charade that goes on at bus and airport check-in counters. I can only think that the morons are emailing friends to pass the time and piss off the customers. 'I'll see what I can do,' he said, still typing away. He was doing fuck all. Just checking if there were any seats left. Without saying anything more, he then printed out baggage tickets and put them on our suitcases and motioned for me to take the bags away.

'Did we only just make it?' I asked.

'Yes,' he said.

'How close?'

'There are forty-seven seats taken out of fifty.'

'Thanks.' I walked off. No more chatting with him.

So we got tickets, had endured the pain and danger of the pre-bus queue, and were now on the Dog.

We ended up getting a pair of seats together. There were three sets of two left. As we got our iPods out and settled in, the remaining seats filled up. The Dog set off. The configuration was not pretty. Directly in front of us was the fit guy and a girl, whose name turned out to be Ash. Across the aisle from her was the bald man, behind us was Drug Boy and across the way from us was a black woman with a crying newborn baby. Next to her was Mustang Man. It couldn't have been worse. It was as if the good Lord had created Earth and all its beings, done Noah's Ark and all that shit, had life exist for 5,000 years or whatever the claim is, and waited for that exact moment for the planets and stars to align and everything to come together perfectly to culminate in this, the ultimate test for me. 'Hell is other people,' as Jean-Paul Sartre said.

'We'll be alright,' I said to Lucy. 'At least we got a seat together.'

She didn't respond.

As we rolled out of St. Louis for the six hour trip to Nashville, a man in the seat behind propped up on my headrest and said, 'Miss Ashley. Miss Ashley,' to the girl in front of me. There was an implication in the deep voice of the man that I was to get Ashley's attention, who was oblivious. I ignored the appeal, but the fit guy heard it and alerted her. Ash turned around.

'I've got some gum for you,' the man said, reaching out past my seat and handing something to Ash, who cupped it secretively and put it in her pocket. It probably wasn't gum. A few minutes later, Ash got up and went to the toilet. When she returned I got a better look at her. She had bright pink hair and was wearing pink tights. They were torn at the back, revealing six inches of her panties, a brightly-coloured striped number. She was a skinny skank as well. As she sat back down, Bald Man saw his opening.

'Where you heading?' he said to her from across the aisle.
'Nashville.'
'That's a shame,' he said. 'I'm off in Kentucky.'
She opened a packet of crisps and offered some to him,

tossing him a bone anyway.

'Are you hungry?' she said.

'No,' he said. 'I've got my meal right here.' He opened his mouth to reveal a large wad of well-chewed tobacco. I could smell the pungent odour from my seat. To complete the courtship ritual, he smiled, exposing a gap from a missing front tooth, presumably a consequence of the habit.

But despite the futile nature of his pursuit, he continued poking her to get her attention and talking to her for the next three hours. He was, however, in competition with the fit guy who was preaching about his work in the army and his 'strong belief in keeping our country safe'. 'It is my responsibility. It is my responsibility,' he kept repeating.

Not long after we turned our first corner, the enormous white pig who was fond of the word 'shower' decided to get up and go to the toilet. She was in the front row of the bus, reserved for the handicapped and the seriously fat, of which there are many on Greyhound. She slowly waddled her way back, grabbing onto seat backs for support, and touched me with her huge arse as she went past. The stench was over-powering and I turned to look at her, holding my breath as I did. Actually, I just continued to hold my breath as I had been doing intermittently for ten minutes in the hope of averting the contraction of a case of the plague—the baby across from me was coughing and wheezing, and, of course, wailing loudly.

I focussed on the fat woman. God, she was hideous. As I turned, I noticed that Ash's sugar daddy was actually a grossly overweight woman. She was built like a double-lined shithouse door and looked like she could have been a contestant in the World's Strongest Man competition. She was one of those big-boned women with a big skull. She stunk too. Things couldn't get much worse.

It wasn't until ten minutes later, as we reached the outskirts of St. Louis, that the driver decided to set out the rules of the Dog. There were always the set company rules for each Dog, but the driver usually listed a few additional, idiosyncratic ones as well.

'Hello and welcome to the 9.25am Greyhound service to Nashville.' It turned out that the driver was the woman wearing the fluorescent yellow vest. She went on, well-rehearsed.

'It is not permitted to smoke on this service, including in the bathroom that is located in the rear of the bus for your convenience. No alcohol or illegal drugs are permitted. If you use electronic devices such as music or DVD players, you must use headphones so you, and only you, can hear them. Turn the ringers on your cell phones down and only talk on the phone in quiet tones. If you have a conversation with someone next to you, do so in a quiet manner so as to not disturb the other passengers. Many people have been travelling all night and want some rest. Let them have that rest. If you choose to contravene any of these rules, your journey will be terminated early. I am the driver of this bus and it is my job to drive. Do not attempt to speak to me while I am driving. I will not respond to any such attempts. Thank you for choosing Greyhound and I hope you enjoy the journey. My job is to drive. Your job is to relax. Now, let's ride. Ruff, ruff.'

'What was that last bit?' Lucy asked, pulling her head-phones out of her ears.

'She barked. You know, like a dog.' I laughed loudly then checked myself so as to not draw attention.

'And finally,' the driver ended after a pause. 'I pray to my one true love and almighty saviour our lord Jesus Christ to deliver to us today a safe trip.'

Still laughing, I turned my head. Mustang Man was glaring at me from across the aisle through those cold and beady eyes.

'Amen,' I thought. 'A-fucking-men'.

3

REDEMPTION

'It's a death trap, it's a suicide rap. We gotta get out while we're young, 'cause tramps like us, baby we were born to run.'

— **'Born to Run', Bruce Springsteen**

'I need a bit of Bruce to get me through this,' I said to Lucy, as I put my headphones on and pressed play. My iPod was almost at full tilt and at least it drowned out the sound of the blood bath of a bus trip.

I got my rucksack down from the racks above and extracted my netbook computer. I opened the lid. People stared. I started typing, describing the scene and the people around me. I typed in size seven font, too small for anyone nearby to read. I figured that most of them would be illiterate anyway, but I couldn't take that chance. Not in this crowd.

Typing was difficult. The baby across the aisle screamed constantly and was intermittently throwing its shoe at me. The shoe would hit me in the leg, the mother would pick it up, hand it back to the baby without saying anything to me or it, and the process would be repeated. I turned up my iPod.

The bus drove on through the Missouri sunshine and passed into the fields of Kentucky. There is no such thing as relaxing and enjoying the ride, but I sat back, listened to the Boss, and did the best I could. Lucy slept.

A few hours into the trip, we stopped for a food and rest stop. The Greyhound website trip schedule had this stop in the route down as a thirty minute break. As the bus slowed down, the announcement began.

'I am about to stop the bus. We will be stopped here for five minutes and five minutes only. This is a rule. Do not break this rule under any condition. I will be leaving in five minutes. I repeat, I will be leaving in five minutes. You have five minutes at this stop. This is a condition. Do not break it. I will leave without you. See you soon. Enjoy the break.'

It was a six hour trip to Nashville and this was the one stop. And there was no food there. It was a Greyhound station that had one vending machine in it. The machine contained only crisps and chocolate, but the queue to it wound out the door of the building. Americans will buy food at every possible opportunity. There was no point. Lucy and I remained in our seats. Mustang Man spent the five minute break staring out the window and into the distance. He had done that all trip.

A family of Amish got on the bus just before take off, the men with their bushy beards with no moustaches, long pants and polished leather shoes, long-sleeved shirts and braces and straw hats with stiff brims that flattened out their clean hair. The young boys were the same, just smaller. The women wore home-made dull looking dresses and had bonnets on their heads. They carried old-fashioned cardboard-like suitcases. They all looked so very innocent, and somewhat surreal when juxtaposed with the Greyhound filth. The teenage boys stared at me and Lucy with our colourful clothes and technology.

'They look sweet,' Lucy said.

'Yeah, they do,' I said. 'I feel sorry for them for some reason. I don't know why. They look so out of place.'

By the time we crossed the Tennessee state line, Fit Black Man and Ash were starting to hit it off. He kept on with his monologue about 'serving my country and fellow man' and she nodded along, smiling her drug-fucked smile.

I'm not sure who instigated it, but I put my head down to type and when I looked up, Ash's head was resting on Fit Black Man's shoulder and his left leg was well over the half-way line. I couldn't see where his hands were, but I had a fair idea. He was playing it cool, though, moving away from her head from time to time then back again.

'Check it out,' I said to Lucy, looking at the amorous couple.

'I know,' she said. 'How did it start?'

'I'm not sure. But he's on.'

'Do you think so?'

'No doubt about it,' I said. 'She looks like a first-dater.'

The bus kept driving. A few hours later and the small city of Nashville was finally upon us. The Dog found its way to the grotty bus station on the outskirts. We had made it.

As was customary with every Greyhound journey, the driver made some final comments.

'Hello and welcome to Nashville,' she said over the speaker system. Then came the rules. 'Remain seated until the bus has come to a complete stop. Do not stand up until it has stopped. Remain in your seats. Once we have stopped, ensure you have all of your belongings. Check on the seat and under your seat and the seat in front of you. Greyhound has no liability for any lost luggage or anything else.'

After repeating the rules a number of times, it was time for her summing up.

'My name is Berta. Thank you for choosing Greyhound and we look forward to having you back on the Dawg shortly. Ruff.'

The bus stopped and we got off. Fit Black Man walked down the aisle in front of me. Ash was in front of him and he tapped her on the arse as he walked. She giggled, looking back at him and smiling. She wasn't completely hideous, although she did have one key tooth missing. It wasn't an uncommon trait amongst passengers on the Dog. As we climbed down the bus steps, the fit guy looked back at me and smiled. He had a pretty cool way about him.

'Kudos, hombre,' I said, smiling. 'Kudos.'

He smiled at me and walked off after Ash. He knew what I meant.

Berta was standing next to the bus, monitoring the unloading of the baggage.

'Good driving, Berta,' I said to her as I grabbed our suitcases.

'Whaaaat?' she yelled.

'Good driving, Berta,' I repeated. 'And I loved that bark.'

'Weeell,' she said. 'We're on the Dawg, we might as well bark like one.'

'Amen,' I said.

I wheeled the suitcases over to Lucy and we walked through the Nashville bus station. It was packed with drunk and hung over people sitting on the ground in queues and slouching around dejected in the heat. We walked out into the sun of the street. A policeman was standing just outside the door.

'Can I help you folks?' he said.

'We're after a cab,' I said.

'Where you staying?'

'The Days Inn.'

'Well, you could walk there. It's eight blocks thata way and two blocks the other way.'

'Do taxis come here?' I asked.

'Or you could get a taxi. They stop over there.' He pointed across the road where three men were hunched down sitting on the curb, their heads in their hands.

'Are they waiting for cabs?' I said, referring to the men.

'No, I don't think they'd be waiting for a cab,' he said.

'Thank you, sir,' I said as a cab pulled up and we got in. Mustang Man was walking out of the bus station and down the main street. He was alone and carried no bags.

'What were you talking to the bus driver about?' Lucy asked as the cab drove away.

I recounted my discussion to Lucy.

'Why'd you call her Berta?' she asked.

'That's her name,' I said. 'She said it at the end of the trip.'

'She said her name was Michelle,' Lucy said.

'Well, that's strange.'

4

THE TENNESSEE MOON

'In search of a dream underneath the Tennessee
moon, I fell in love to an old Hank Williams'
tune...'

—'Tennessee Moon', Neil Diamond

'What can I get you folks?' The waitress was wearing a tight
vest, very short demin skirt and leather cowgirl boots that
came up to just below her knees. She had bleached-blonde
hair and was heavily made up. Probably early forties.

We were sitting in the Bourbon Street Blues and Boogie
Bar in Nashville, trying to wash away the Dog trip. It was
lowly lit with friendly shadows. Neon beer signs on the
walls.

'Do you have a cocktail list?' Lucy asked.

'No, we don't sweetheart, but we do nearly well anything.'

'Can I have a daiquiri, please?' Lucy said.

'Oh, we don't do them.'

'Okay. A mojito?'

'No, don't do them neither, sorry.'

There was a pause.

'How about a bloody mary?'

'Sorry.'

'I'll have a Budweiser. A bottle,' I said, hoping to put an end to the pain.

'Can I have a glass of red wine, then?' Lucy said, not giving up.

'I'll check if we have any,' said the waitress and she walked off.

She didn't come back for fifteen minutes. She had my beer and a large glass of wine.

'Found some,' she said, looking pleased with herself, as she put the wine glass on the table.

She had found the wine, but Tennessee is definitely more a beer and bourbon type of town.

We drank down those drinks and ordered two more. The grime of the Dog was slowly fading away. There was a small stage a few tables over and a band was preparing to play, doing all that 'check, check, one, two, two' bullshit. Thirty minutes of instrument tuning and superfluous sound checks later and they started up. There were only a handful of people in the place. The band played a mixture of blues and country and weren't bad. But they only played for twenty minutes and then had a 'short break' of twenty minutes. Playing music in bars must be a lot more tiring than in proper concerts.

All the bars in Nashville had live music. We were there during the Country Music Awards and the live music went all day and all night. Most of it was good, although a lot of the modern country, all just subtly adapting Hank Williams and his trademark twang, gets hard to distinguish. And the only thing the modern country singers sing about is women. The good old boys like Johnny Cash, Willie Nelson, Kris Kristofferson and Waylon Jennings varied it up. They sang about trains and hard drinking and killing men. Better topics. There are only so many variations to how a woman can break your heart.

All the bars had live music and there were a lot of bars condensed in a small area of a few streets. A lot had neon signs and the outline of guitars in neon out on the street. Most of the bars were dark and inviting and it's hard to tell what time of the day or night it is once inside.

There is a lot of neon in Nashville. And there are a lot of women dressed as cowgirls. It's like they have a uniform that doesn't vary. It comprises leather boots to just below the knee, a tight-fitting short skirt that just covers an overweight arse, a tight vest top, a wide-brimmed western style hat and a lot of make-up, inexpertly applied with a trowel. Every girl and woman in Nashville is dressed that way. All the bartenders, all the kids, all the teenagers and all the groups of middle-aged women, of which there are many. Most of them look rather ordinary as well. All the men wear cowboy hats. Big ones. And there are a lot of Mustang Men.

There are a lot of bars in Nashville, but there are just as many boot shops. RCC Western Stores, Trail West, Boots 'N More, Nashville Boot Co, Big Time Boots. Hundreds of them. Every second establishment is a bar and every third is a boot shop. And do they sell boots. Thousands of pairs in all sizes, some with swirling patterns carved into the leather and others in bright colours with tassels. Men's on one side of the store, women's on the other. But no matter what the colour or pattern, all the boots are in the similar style, coming up to just below the knee. The shops smell of leather and linseed oil and photographs are not allowed. The reason for this is never explained, so I asked a lady in one of the shops.

'So it don't fade the boots,' she said. 'If y'all come in here takin' photographs, the boots will fade.'

After each boot shop is a T-shirt and souvenir store. Most of the T-shirts have country music bands on them and the shops are crowded with tourists who look and touch, but seldom buy.

On our second day in Nashville, we were leaving the hotel for the day and met a group of women in the elevator. There were four of them, all about fifty, and all dressed in the uniform. They were wearing a lot of bright make up.

'Y'all here for the fanfare?' the leader of the pack said to us.

'Sure are,' I said.

'How y'all enjoying Nashville?'

'Really good,' I said. 'It's a great city. Lots of action.'

'There sure is darlin'. We love it here. We're out on the town now.'

'Us too. Might see you out there. Good luck.'

'Bye darlin',' she said. 'Good talkin' to ya. Have fun y'all.'

We walked into town. It was hot and sunny and humid and the sky was blue. We went to the Farmers' Market. The guide book we had said it was 'well worth making the trip to this colourful outdoor market'. It was a market of just fruit and nothing else. It was time we stopped listening to the crap guide book recommendations. We bought a few bananas and some peaches. They were fresh and juicy, but it was just fruit.

'Is everything shut today?' I said to the girl serving us. She was about twenty. 'Because of the Music Awards?'

She just looked at me. I tried again.

'Has the town shut down for the Music Awards? We just walked past the court house. It seems closed. Everything does.'

'On Saturdays we have so many people in here that there's a line goin' all the way out the door. All the way up there and out the door. It's truly amazing. Truly amazing.'

I wondered if we were speaking the same language.

'Is that right?' I said, deciding to abandon my line of questioning.

'Yep,' she said.

'Amazing.'

We walked back out on the street and into the busy part of town. It was only noon, but the main bar area was full of people and the sounds of country music. It was oozing out of every door. It was a change from St. Louis where we'd been the night before. There's not much in St. Louis, apart from that big arch, and what is there wasn't open. It seemed a nice enough place, if you like nothing to do, or eat or drink. It's like we went to St. Louis and it was closed. But Nashville was all action. We went into one of the biggest bars. It was three storeys with balconies on the upper levels and every floor had a different band on and every floor was packed. We took a table on the ground floor. A four-piece band was playing loudly as the singer wailed away whilst wearing a big cowboy hat. All the singers wear big cowboy hats. Their hat is their signature. He did a few songs then got his daughter up to sing, while he had a twenty minute break. His daughter must have only been about eleven and was dressed in the customary cowgirl garb. They start 'em young in Nashville. She was quite a showgirl, gesticulating during the songs and commenting to the crowd, with the occasional 'holler y'all' thrown in. She was reading the lyrics to the songs off her iPhone. Most of the crowd thought it was all very cute, 'oohing' and 'aahing', but in reality, she was an overweight and ugly little child who was inappropriately dressed and couldn't sing for shit.

We left and had a few more beers in a few more bars, crawling along the main street, before settling on a quiet little joint on a side street, a bit away from the congestion. It was called Benchmark. It was dark, but clean, with a wooden floor, wooden tables, chairs and bar stools. The typical neon signs were inside and out and the bartender girls were in the uniform, but with tighter skirts on than usual. A sign read that they worked 'only for tips'. We sat at the bar and watched a Yankees game on the television. Lucy drank red wine. There was no point asking about cocktails. I drank quite a lot of beer. A lone guitarist was sitting on the stage in the window singing tunes by the Eagles and Johnny Cash. He was good and not too loud. A lot of the live music in Nashville is too loud.

Venus crossed the Sun that evening for the last time until 2117. We missed that celestial milestone. We were sitting in the Benchmark in Nashville, underneath the Tennessee moon, drinking beer and wine and listening to country music.

5

MEMPHIS CABBIES

'But I've reason to believe, we both will be received in Graceland...'

—'Graceland', Paul Simon

There are not many taxi drivers in Memphis. We arrived in the centre of Memphis in the mid-afternoon and stood on the corner of the main street. No cabs came. We walked to the Marriott Hotel and there were no cabs. We finally got one, an hour later, by me yelling at a lone cabbie in the distance, who just happened to see or hear.

There are not many taxi drivers in Memphis, but the ones that are there have a lot to say. And a lot of them are in vans. The cabbie that we eventually managed to hail was in a van. He said 'y'all' a lot and then, unsolicited and in monologue fashion, proceeded to explain his use of the contraction.

'We say 'y'all' a lot in these parts. Have you noticed how we all say 'y'all'?' he said.

Before I could respond, he kept talking.

'It's a very country word 'y'all',' he said. 'It means 'you all'. You know what I mean by 'country'?'

Still I was unable to respond.

'It's very country. Hell, even as a black man I feel country saying 'y'all'.' He was a black man.

'Do you like music?' he continued to himself. 'Lot of music in Memphis. I love music. Y'all want some music on?'

'Yeah, that'd be good,' I said, finally getting a word in.

He pulled a cassette out of the glove box and put it in the stereo, pressed rewind and then play. Was it still 1980 in Memphis? Some fast-paced blues crackled out of the speakers.

'This is good music,' he said. 'You'll love it. We're heading towards mid-town. Your hotel is in mid-town. We're nearly there. It's not far.'

A few minutes later and we were there.

'Here we are y'all. We're in mid-town. It's the medical area. That's a hospital there,' he said, pointing at a large grey concrete building that was unmistakably a hospital. 'School of dentistry there, pharmacy there. It's the medical area. A good place to be.'

'Nice one,' I said, as we pulled into the hotel drive-way. 'Thanks very much.' The fare was $11. I gave him twelve.

'Thank you very much, sir,' he said. 'Enjoy mid-town y'all. And have a nice evening. Welcome to Memphis.'

I liked the feel of Memphis. It was difficult to pinpoint, but there was something about the place. After checking into our hotel, we walked into town and past Sun Record Studios where producer Sam Phillips had signed the Million Dollar Quartet in the 1950s—Elvis Presley, Johnny Cash, Jerry Lee Lewis and that fourth guy, Carl Perkins. A lot of people outside of Memphis haven't heard of Carl Perkins, but in Memphis Carl is very famous. We got into town and walked down Beale Street. Beale Street is also very famous, although I'd never heard of it. Beale Street was just like Nashville. The street was jammed full of people pouring out of bars that were advertised with neon signs.

We walked the length of the street to the far corner, where a queue of people trailed from a doorway. It was the Blues City Bar. We waited fifteen minutes for a table, before being taken into the depths of the joint, where a band had, thankfully, just finished setting up and were about to play.

'We're the Stunning Cunning Band,' the lead singer announced. 'Y'all wanna hear some rock 'n' roll tonight? Wehell, since my baby left me…' He started off with Elvis, then did covers from the rest of the Million Dollar Quartet. The band was excellent and well-polished and the lead singer had genuine stage presence. He was not a good looking man and his face had not ignored the passage of time, but he was a prime example of an ugly guy who'd get women based on confidence and talent. Women love talent, especially musical talent.

The band played fast rock for half an hour, before slowing down.

'This song's so slow y'all,' the singer said. 'That you'll need to put your sunglasses on. It's that slow.'

Throughout Tennessee, 'y'all' is used indiscriminately and often out of context. It's a bit like 'innit', that many odious creatures from Essex in England use in a nonsensical manner as a contraction of 'isn't it', but 'y'all' has far more charm, as do the people who say it.

We stayed in the Blues City Bar for a few hours drinking beer and listening to the band. We ordered some food. I got gumbo, a seafood chowder common to the south of America, and Lucy ordered a steak. The steaks were $16 per pound and the smallest was two and a half pounds. The gumbo was incredible and the steak was massive and the best we'd had. I ended up eating most of it. We liked the Blues City Bar.

We caught another taxi van back to the hotel around midnight. The first three cabs we saw wouldn't take us, for reasons unexplained. Then a fat, ebony-skinned man approached us.

'Hell, I'll take y'all,' he said. 'My van is just up here.'

We walked to his van and clambered in, struggling to shut the chunky sliding door.

'Are we on the meter?' I asked, noticing that it wasn't on. Cabbies rarely forget to put the meter on.

'Hell, man,' he said. 'I ain't gunna rip y'all off. It's seven dollars. Flat fare.' It was the first flat fare in America that was actually a bargain.

Then the catch.

'Besides,' he said. 'I just have to make a quick stop to pick up a lady.'

We drove up to a five-star hotel lobby. I didn't see the name. A doorman came out.

'Has Heather come down yet?' our cabbie asked.

'I've not seen her, sir,' the doorman said.

I could see the name 'Heather' typed on the monitor in the front of the cab. 'Heather Midnight' it read.

We sat there for five minutes.

'Well, I tried,' said the cabbie, slowly driving away. 'At least I did that.'

'Where do you think she is?' I asked.

'Hard to say,' he replied. 'Heather works some strange hours and often works over time if the need arises. I've been drivin' her for years.'

The next morning the local news headlines reported a huge brawl on Beale Street, where four cops were badly injured trying to calm a mob of people who were being ejected from a club because of the dress code. An unrelated elderly guy who was interviewed on the street commented on the police behaviour.

'It's not on,' he said. 'They got way too much power. Way too much.'

Knowing it would be shithouse, we didn't even bother with the hotel breakfast, and I asked the receptionist to call a cab to take us to Graceland. We'd waited an hour and the cab still hadn't turned up. I got the receptionist to call again.

'It'll be here in five minutes,' she told me.

Ten minutes later, the cab arrived. The driver was an overweight lady. The smell of freshly eaten McDonalds explained the delay, as did the empty drink container and fries packet—both supersize, of course.

'That took a long time,' I said.

'Had to make a quick stop,' she said. 'Now, where y'all goin'?'

I told her that we wanted to drive across the Mississippi River and into Arkansas, turn around, come back across the same bridge and then head to Graceland. That was not easy to explain. I even gave her the road numbers, but she couldn't seem to follow it.

'You wanna do what?' she kept saying.

I told her we'd never been to Arkansas where Johnny Cash was born, so just wanted to see it briefly.

'Alright,' she said. 'But that'll cost you around $45.'

'What do you think?' I asked Lucy in the back seat.

'It's a bit much,' Lucy said.

'No, let's just go to Graceland please,' I said to the cabbie.

I could see her thinking, panicking.

'Why don't we give it a try?' she said, not wanting to lose the big fare. 'It should only be thirty-something anyways.'

'Okay, then,' I said. 'Let's go.'

She set off and we drove past the place where Martin Luther King was shot.

'That's where Doctor Martin Luther King was shot and killed. Shot and killed right there.' She was commentating on things as we drove.

'That'll be crowded tonight,' she said as we passed Beale Street. 'Real crowded.'

'Tonight as well?' I said.

'Oh, baby,' she squealed. 'It'll be the most crowded thang y'all ever saw. Ya won't be able to move in there tonight, baby.'

'Crowded tonight too?' I said again.

She paused. 'What day is it?'

'Sunday.'

'No, it ain't gunna be crowded in there tonight,' she said. 'But last night, hell baby, you should have seen it last night. It was crowded. Last night you couldn't move in there.'

We drove on the bridge across the mighty Mississippi and past the Arkansas state line. There was a sign which read 'Welcome to Arkansas' half way across—the state line is actually in the middle of the river and West Memphis is in Arkansas, not Tennessee. After a few minutes in Arkansas, we turned around and she took us to Graceland.

'Graceland,' she said. 'Here we are. You gunna go up in them planes?' Elvis's two private jets, the Lisa Marie and Hound Dog II, were next to the drop off point.

'Yeah. Can you go up in them?'

29

'Hell yeah. No, not up, but them's planes are amazing. Them's like a whole house by themselves. Real amazing. That'll be $43,' she said.

'Forty-three. Okay.'

'There,' she said. 'I told ya I wouldn't charge ya much.'

I only had three twenties and handed them over.

'Hell baby, I don't have change for this.' Cabbies never have change. They always looked perplexed by the size of the notes furnished, no matter how small they are.

'I tell you what,' she said. 'Here is my card. I'm Veronica. You call me when you get out and I'll come to right here to get you. Right to this spot. Forty will do me.' She handed me back $20.

'Thanks Veronica,' I said and we walked off.

The card was handwritten in pencil on a Greyhound bus baggage tag. We never saw Veronica again.

The main area of Graceland where you buy tickets and get food is very tacky and full of glitz. Music by the King is played constantly in all places. We looked at Elvis's private planes and at his impressive array of sports cars. There must have been twenty of them. Then we stood in the queue to get a shuttle to the Graceland mansion. There was a man next to us in the queue who was on the phone. He had a shaved head and a goatee beard and rings on his fingers, as well as various tattoos. He was a Mustang Man.

'I want the name of the kid who done this,' said the Mustang Man loudly. 'I want fucking names, addresses and fucking heads. Fucking heads, you hear me, man? Find out who fucking did this.' He was agitated.

'Fucking find him,' he yelled again, then thrust the

phone at his wife.

'Fucking find him, Blake,' she said. She was fat and hideous and had one of those female mullet hairstyles that frizzes up at the front. She looked like she could haunt houses and seemed even tougher than Mustang. She was shaking with anger. Mustang took the phone back.

'Find him, Blake. Name, address. Call me back. Got it? Good.' He hung up the phone.

The shuttle bus arrived and we got on. Mustang and Mullet got on as well to explore the mansion with the rest of the happy tourists.

The Graceland mansion is a superb house and well worth seeing. Large white pillars at the front guard a multitude of rooms decorated in the style of the Seventies and as Elvis left them. It's opulent, but not gaudy. There's a games room, a huge room with hundreds of gold records framed on the wall, a shooting gallery and horse stables. There's a television room decorated in bright yellow and blue that contains three TVs. When Elvis heard that President Johnson watched three network newscasts at once, he wanted to as well. Then there's the Jungle Room. The Jungle Room is on the ground floor of the house and contains carvings of animals. The furniture is predominantly wood, also carved into the shapes of animals. It's quite surreal to think of Elvis sitting in there playing his guitar. There's also a recording studio and grand piano in the house. Although tourists are not allowed to the upper floor of the mansion where Elvis died, outside by the pool is a fountain in what's called the Meditation Garden. The Garden contains the graves of Elvis, his two parents and his grandmother.

We walked around the mansion for an hour, before catching the shuttle back across the road to the Graceland complex. You have to wait thirty minutes for the shuttle and then it takes you about 100 metres in a ride that lasts two minutes. That's the Yanks for you.

There are a number of cafés in the complex and we looked at them all, searching for something to eat. As is the case throughout America, pretty well all that was available was burgers. As we stood reading the menu of the final café, Lucy broke into tears. Uncontrollable tears. A lot of people were walking past looking at her. I put my arm around her to conceal and comfort her.

'What's wrong?'

'I just want some eggs and a plate of vegetables,' she said, barely able to speak amidst the sobbing.

'It'll be alright.'

'I just want some eggs.'

She cried for five minutes and then we got a cab back to the hotel.

The driver was a morbidly obese man who made his van seem small. He was the fattest cabbie yet, and we'd had some fat ones. His name was Carl. That was the name on his ID. Carl was so fat that his right leg rested on the front passenger seat, despite the large central console. The steering wheel was wedged deep into his stomach so that it was no longer visible. When rounding hard corners, Carl used his hands, but for subtle steering, he simply moved his gut. He really was fat.

Back at the hotel, Lucy went to the room and I went in search of food. I asked at reception where a grocery store was.

'It's a fair way from here,' the woman at reception said.

'You could try the Walgreens chemist across the road. It has some food.'

'I've been there, thanks,' I said. 'There's not much in there. It's a waste of time. About how far is the grocery store?'

'The grocery store?' said a patron next to me who had been listening in. 'Man, that's a walk. It's a ways off. Hell of a walk.' He was a skinny, drug-fucked man in his thirties.

'A mile?' I said.

'More than that,' the woman said.

'More than that,' he echoed. He looked outside then back at me, smiling a vulpine smile.

'You'll never get a cab out here,' he said. 'Not in mid-town. But I tell you what. My wife could drive you.'

I looked out the door of the hotel and saw a decrepit car with a fat woman who looked drug-fucked too and three snotty-nosed kids.

'I appreciate that,' I said. 'But I'd have to come back too.'

'Hell, she can drive you back.'

I paused, thinking.

'No,' I said. 'Thanks, though. I think I'll check out the Walgreens.'

He looked disappointed. I went back to the room.

Lucy's bags were packed. Then Lucy left.

6

GENESIS

'She'll let you in her heart, if you got a hammer and a vice, but into her secret garden, don't think twice.'

—'Secret Garden', Bruce Springsteen

I met Lucy on the salt plains of Bolivia. Actually, it was in Uyuni, a terrible little backwater town that is the gateway to the salt plains. Uyuni is the arsehole of the Earth, but a lot of people go there to get to the plains, which are Bolivia's biggest tourist attraction.

When we met, it was as close to love at first sight as you can get—for me anyway. I guess I have some pushy middle-aged Canadians to thank for it. I stayed the night before in a hotel in town and arranged a three-day tour to the salt plains. The next morning, a rep from the tour company met me in the hotel foyer and we waited outside for the 4WD to turn up. A Canadian couple had also booked. A 4WD arrived and the tour guide said it was for me. But the Canadian couple, who had come outside as well, led by the woman (middle-aged women are always the worst), pushed in front and got in the car.

'It doesn't matter,' said the tour rep. 'You can get in the next one.'

I wasn't too unhappy, because as the first car drove away, I could see that all the passengers were middle-aged couples.

The next car arrived a few minutes later. It was empty, apart from Waldo, the driver. Waldo was a five feet high Bolivian with dark hair and a ready smile. He wore leather driving gloves with the fingers cut off.

'Que es el mejor asiento?' I asked him, wanting the best seat.

'Este,' he said, pointing to the front seat next to him. I got in and introduced myself and then we drove to pick up the rest of the tour group. It was a nerve-racking time, wondering who I'd be in the car with for the next three days.

We pulled up at a nearby hotel and there was a group of young people waiting on the windy corner of a dirty street. That was a good start. There were five of them, two guys and three girls. One of the girls was Lucy. She looked beautiful and I hoped that was the group for the car. It was. I introduced myself, fixated on Lucy, but trying to appear aloof. I helped them load their bags onto the roof rack of the car in an act of chivalry, then we all boarded and Waldo drove away.

'Do you speak Spanish?' one of the guys asked me. 'We want to go to the train cemetery first.'

'Yeah, a bit,' I said. 'I'll have a go.' I did my best Spanish to Waldo, who didn't speak any English at all. He got the message and took us to the train cemetery, a desert area near town that had rusted old train engines on it. The rest of the group raced out to see the defunct trains. I hung back a bit, but then decided to join them so as to seem friendly and to try to figure out who was with who. And to get a better look at Lucy.

The group was a young Australian girl, a young Dutch girl, Lucy, eleven years my junior at twenty-six and from England, and two guys in their mid-thirties, one from the US and one from Canada. I couldn't tell if any of the guys were with the girls or not. They all seemed to know each other well as they'd been on an arranged truck tour through Peru and Bolivia. I was hoping that none of the guys were with Lucy. I did manage to get a better look at Lucy and, if anything, she improved. I was happy with the group.

We set off again with Waldo and I started pummelling them with questions, trying to ascertain the dynamic. It wasn't easy and they weren't giving much away (I later found out this was a ploy of theirs and a big in-joke). We stopped an hour later at a little town near the salt plains. The others went souvenir shopping and I went looking for beer. I figured beer might loosen a few tongues. Driving again, I offered the beers around. Lucy and the Dutch girl took one, as did the American.

'What about you, mate?' I said to the Canadian in the far back.

'No, I'm fine, thanks,' he said. 'They're your beers.'

'I got them for all of us.'

'That's very kind,' he said. 'But we'll just share one.'

With that, he reached forward and grabbed the beer from the American guy and had a sip. I found that very strange and it was my first clue that they were a gay couple, a fact that wasn't confirmed to me until the next day.

That night I slept in a room with the three girls, all in separate beds. Everything in the hotel was made of salt—the walls, roof, floor and even the beds. It wasn't comfortable. Lucy was close by, but seemed a mile away. In the morning we left early. The front seat next to Waldo was far and away the most superior and commodious position in the car and the far back was easily the worst. Nobody wanted the cramped back seat, but two had to go there.

'Okay, then,' Lucy said in discussions about the seating arrangements. 'I'll take the back seat.'

I knew I had to move quickly.

'I will too,' I said. 'I had the best seat yesterday, so it's only fair I take the back today.'

The back seat was very cramped and Lucy and my knees were close to touching. We chatted generally and she seemed friendly enough, but I'd yet to lob onto a common topic of genuine interest. Then she mentioned that she'd gone for some advertising jobs. I saw my opening.

'Do you watch the show *Mad Men*?' I asked.

Well, she was away. She was obsessed with the show and rabbited on about it, me asking a few prompting questions. It was enough to form a bond and we got on well for the rest of the day. When Waldo would stop at a place of interest— usually some rocks or something as there isn't much of interest in a desert of salt—Lucy and I would return to the car before the others to talk alone. She was very smart and worldly, yet innocent.

That night everyone had altitude sickness so it wasn't very lively. I went to bed trying to think of an opening to ask for Lucy's contact details. The next was the final day of the tour.

The following morning Waldo dropped me off at an artic outpost in Bolivia, close to the Chilean border. I was getting picked up there by another car to go into Chile. The rest of the group were heading back to La Paz in Bolivia. I'd been waiting all morning to get Lucy alone so that I could ask her for an email address. I'd formulated a plan the night before.

Ten minutes before I left, the others went to look at a geyser. It was freezing cold so Lucy decided to stay in the car. So did I.

'I was thinking,' I said. 'I've got a really good Spanish verb table I can send you.' I knew she was heading to Buenos Aires to do a five week Spanish course. I knew I'd be there in that time too.

'Okay,' she said, giving little away.

'Give me your email address and I'll send it to you.' I handed her a piece of paper and a pen.

'Just write it here?' she asked.

'Yeah,' I said. 'Anywhere there.'

She wrote it down, but seemed reluctant.

I parted from the group and went into Chile, unsure about the Lucy situation. But I figured it was worth a try.

I emailed her the next day, sending her the Spanish table and asking if she wanted to meet for a drink in BA. She said she did, and for the next few weeks we emailed each day, just updating each other about our travels. She was very witty and a little flirtatious on email and it felt good, but three weeks later as I sat in a bar in Palermo in Buenos Aires waiting for her, I was still unsure what her intentions were.

She arrived fifteen minutes late and she looked great. She was well-dressed with make up on and I remember thinking that the effort she had gone to was a good sign. We got on well and had a lot of drinks and a huge steak, as only the Argentineans can produce. Towards the end of the night we were drunk. We kissed.

The two of us were inseparable for the next five days in BA, but then I had to leave for Rio de Janeiro. She was going to be there a few weeks later too, so we arranged to meet in

Rio, which we did. We stayed together for a week in Rio and then in a quaint little beach town nearby called Arraial de Cabo. From there I asked her to join me in Salvador, a plane flight to half way up the Brazilian coast. She did. We'd been together for two weeks in Brazil. The night before she was due to fly back to England was her birthday. It was a bitter sweet day. We'd had an amazing few weeks together, but it was over. I was scheduled to keep travelling for the next two years and we would potentially never see each other again.

'This is just unacceptable,' I said to her at the end of the night. 'It's unacceptable that we might never see each other again.'

She was crying. We'd only been together a few weeks, but I felt I really knew her.

'Come to Spain with me,' I said.

'I can't.'

'You can. Six months in Spain, then we'll see what happens.'

She cried some more, but an hour later it was agreed. I'd keep travelling through South and Central America for the next two months, before we'd meet in Spain in the new year.

The two months that followed were enjoyable, but it always felt that I was just biding time, waiting to see Lucy again. In emails we decided to bring our meeting forward and to Mexico. We met in Mexico City and travelled around the country for ten weeks. We fell in love in Mexico. Two years after a marriage break up and actively not looking for another relationship, I'd fallen hard for Lucy. After Mexico, we flew to England and then to Spain. Six months of following the bullfight season around Spain and we flew to China and travelled from there through South-East Asia for a few months. I then went to Australia for Christmas and Lucy went back to England. She met me in Australia two months later and we spent seven weeks there together, before flying back to England.

We'd been together a little over a year, but our time with each other probably amounted to the equivalent of three years. At one point we had gone four months without being out of each other's presence for more than an hour at a time. We stayed in 120 hotel rooms together in seventeen countries.

But it was time for Lucy to start work. We'd discussed that fact a lot, but I really wanted to travel around North America for a few months. After a lot more discussions, we agreed that we would do a ten week trip around the United States and Canada. It was the perfect time for it before she got bogged down with a new job. We started the preparations.

'I can't wait for this trip,' I said to Lucy at her parents' house in England, once all the planning was over.

'I know,' she said. 'We've been to some great places in the last two years, but I've always wanted to see the US properly.'

'Me too.'

'It'll be the trip of a lifetime.'

'Yeah,' I said. 'It will.'

I should have knocked on wood at that point, but I didn't. There was a lot of wood in that room, too.

7

MUSTANG MEN

'I got a 1966 cherry red Mustang Ford. It's got a 385 horse-power overload. You know it's way too fast to be crawlin' on these interstate roads.'

—'My Mustang Ford', Chuck Berry

A Mustang Man is a man who owns a Ford Mustang car, or would if he had the money. He knows a lot about cars and how to fix them, and what's worse, he enjoys fixing them. He's one of those absolute fuckwits who stands around with other fuckwits looking under the hood of the car, tweaking things in the engine, mumbling and sighing, hands on hips, a concerned expression on his face. He always looks angry and tough, tries to walk slowly and deliberately, like he is in some Western movie, and is willing to fight for his cause or any cause, or any reason at all. Nobody who is stupid enough to tussle with a Mustang Man emerges unscathed, most don't even emerge alive. America is full of Mustang Men.

America is full of Ford Mustangs as well. On the four hour bus ride from Miami to Key West, I counted fifty-six coming the other way. They were in varying colours, black being the most common, but there was also a preponderance of neon models—bright greens, blues and oranges, the drivers aware of their own desperate inadequacy and trying in vain to compensate with ostentation.

The car itself looks like it is alive. There are often thick white stripes on the roof and down the bonnet and the curve of the headlights makes them look like the eyes of a snake, almost giving the car a personality, as insidious as its driver's. They tend to have two large exhaust pipes and make the noise of a revving motorbike as they pass.

The real mustang is, of course, a horse. It is a free-roaming horse of the American West. In 1971, the US Congress enacted The Wild Free-Roaming Horse and Burro Act, which stated 'that Congress finds and declares that wild free-roaming horses and burros are living symbols of the historic and pioneer spirit of the West; that they contribute to the diversity of life forms within the Nation and enrich the lives of the American people...as an integral part of the natural system of the public lands.'

The owners of Ford Mustangs buy into this wild freedom, similar to the riders of Harley Davidson motorbikes. They are freedom riders escaping repression, searchers of the American dream, complete losers and the epitome of the lower class.

Mustang Men drive with the attitude of the wild horse. Every near miss we had on the roads of America was because of a Mustang driver. They show no quarter and are proud of the fact. A number of times I nearly crashed into a Mustang, as when I was passing a car, if there is a Mustang coming the other way, the driver will always speed up to make it more difficult.

One day whilst driving in Tennessee, I was following a Mustang, or trying to—they always go as fast as they can. It was a peaceful and sunny day and the road was lined with deep green pine trees. I was suddenly forced to swerve as a full bag of McDonalds fast food came flying out of the Mustang driver's window. The bag spewed open as it hit the bitumen, releasing a part-eaten burger and some fries, as well as a drink container of ice, its lid careering across the road.

I sped up, taking my economy-sized hire car to its limit, as I wanted to get a better look at the driver. He was pure filth. A complete dirt tracker, with a missing tooth and cigarette-stained skin. He was smoking and talking to his skank of equivalence in the seat next to him. A low-life identikit couldn't have created two more quintessential beings.

'My God, look at that little battler,' I said.

'Shocking,' Lucy said. 'He's just chipping away at the edges of life.'

By the look of the driver, in his torn sleeveless shirt (the sleeves had been ripped off), he was clearly a highly unintelligent member of society, and I couldn't help but wonder what sort of things he might be thinking about, if anything at all. What was going through his mind? Was it like a dog's thoughts, or no thoughts at all, or just static white noise?

I would never know, but I did know this—if you experience anything bad or dangerous on the roads of America, the culprit is bound to be at the wheel of a Ford Mustang. And if you experience anything bad or dangerous in America generally, the culprit is bound to have a Ford Mustang parked out the back. Mustang Men are the dregs of society, a terrible breed.

8

THE STARTING DOG

*'You ain't nothin' but a hound dog… And you
ain't no friend of mine.'*

— 'Hound Dog', Elvis Presley

Our first encounter with the Dog and all its charms was in
Miami.

We'd flown from London to Miami and spent three days
there, fairly bored, as there is very little to do in Miami. Sure,
the art deco buildings and their pastel-coloured exteriors are
good to look at for a minute, and it feels like you're in the
1950s, but that novelty quickly wears off and there is only a
string of restaurants and not much else at Miami Beach. I'd
been told all the action was there, but it wasn't. The beach
was fairly unimpressive as well, nothing but a deserted sandy
stretch with no waves.

The first language in Miami is Spanish. The announcements
at the airport are in Spanish, all the workers in the city are
Cuban and all the street and shop signs are in Spanish. I

even saw Plaza Sesame on TV there, the Spanish name for Sesame Street.

It was in Miami that I got my first taste of what morons the Americans can be. Going to the States, I was a little apprehensive about the beer. I knew that a lot of the beers were 'light', but that meant low in carbs. I was concerned that it also meant low alcohol as well. In the first joint we went to, the News Café, I spoke to the barman. He was in his forties, had a 'longer than it should have been' hairdo, and looked as if he'd worked in bars his whole life.

'How can I help you folks?' he asked. Behind him were fridges full of beer—Budweiser, Coors, Michelob, Miller, Corona and their various incarnations of 'lights' and 'ultras', which is just another way of saying 'light'.

'What percentage alcohol are the beers?' I said.

'3.5,' he said, without hesitation.

'All of them?' I questioned.

'Yep, all 3.5.' He started wiping down the bar.

'What about those?' I pointed at the Coronas.

'3.5.'

'And the Budweiser too?'

'All 3.5.'

'The normal Budweiser, not the light.'

'They are all 3.5,' he said, starting to get annoyed.

'Okay, then,' I said, frustrated. 'Give me a Budweiser. A normal one.'

It was not good news. I despise low-alcohol beer. It tastes like shit and there's little point in drinking it. It doesn't get you anywhere.

He opened a Budweiser, handed it to me and walked to the other end of the bar to serve someone else. I examined the bottle.

'It's 5%,' I said to Lucy. 'Look.' I pointed to the words on the back of the label.

The barman made his way back to our end of the bar. I called him over.

'This beer is 5%,' I said.

'No, 3.5.'

'No, it's five,' I said. 'Look.' I pointed at the label. He had a look and laughed.

'That's the return deposit,' he said. 'Five cents.' The label did refer to the deposit.

'Yeah, it says that too,' I said. 'But look at my finger.'

I held my index finger out in front of his face and he stared at it, following it with his eyes as I moved it towards the '5%'.

He took the beer off me and held it close to his face, squinting at it for a few seconds, before putting it down on the bar.

'Well, god damn,' he said, shaking his head in disbelief.

I quickly came to terms with all the American beers. They were all shit, but the light ones were undrinkable. They were low in carbs, but they were a little lighter in alcohol too, generally 4.2%. Despite this, they tasted like chemicals and you could feel the impending headache as you were drinking them. It's like injecting the antithesis of paracetamol directly into your brain. You might as well hit yourself over the head with the bottle instead. But if there are ten beers on the menu in any American bar, seven or eight of them are 'light'. A lot of the beers don't even state their alcohol volume on the bottle, despite many Americans telling me it was mandatory by law. Normal Budweiser is just bearable, but that's only because it's served so cold, to disguise the taste. This is all a very difficult concept to grapple with at the start of a ten week trip when all you drink is beer. Fortunately, a lot of American towns have microbreweries that serve superb beers. The pilsners and pale ales at them are excellent and the disparity between the microbrewery and the commercial beers is immense.

Leaving Miami to head down the Florida Keys to Key West, was our first Dog experience. The bus station was thirty minutes drive from Miami Beach in a grotty part of town near the airport. The Greyhound bus stations are nearly always in the worst part of town. After buying our Discovery Pass tickets, Lucy and I sat down in the waiting room. The Discovery Pass ticket cost $564 and lasted sixty days. We wanted to get the Pass as we needed the full sixty days and it is far cheaper than paying for single journeys. Ten minutes after buying the Pass, I realised that the date had been written on incorrectly, meaning it expired three days too early. And we needed it for those three days. I went back up to the counter. I was met there by a fat, angry, middle-aged woman wearing a wig. I think they all wear wigs, but it's hard to tell.

'Hmmm, hmmm,' she said.

'Yes, hello,' I said. 'I was here a few minutes ago and bought this Discovery Pass.' I held it out.

She remained silent, glaring at me.

'Anyway, it's been dated wrongly so it expires three days too soon,' I said.

'Nothin' I can do 'bout it.'

'But I just bought it ten minutes ago,' I said.

'Who'd you buy it from? 'Cause it weren't me.'

'A man, a young guy. About ten minutes ago.'

'Well, he ain't here now, so I can't check.'

'Can't check what?'

'Whether he did it?'

'Of course he did it. Who else could have done it?' I said.

'I don't know,' she said. 'But he's not here so I can't change it.'

'Well, that's absurd,' I said. 'The date's wrong.'

'Nothin' I can do 'bout it. Next?' she said, looking past me at the person behind.

I sat back down. There's no point arguing with them. The waiting room started filling up. It was not a glamorous crowd. Most people were black and poorly dressed. Anyone white was covered with tattoos. But there was an electric fan on, providing a modicum of respite from the humidity, so we had to suffer the clientele. The heat was standing at the door like an enemy.

Ten minutes before the scheduled departure time a bus arrived, jerking its way into the car park. It was covered with rust and its paint was faded. I could only just make out the word 'Greyhound' and the picture of the blue dog on the side. The tyres were completely bare. It was almost like a scene from a comedy sketch, where the ailing vehicle spits and splutters and smoke billows from all parts.

'That can't be our bus,' Lucy said.

'Not a chance,' I said. 'That's a 1970s model at best.'

'I wonder why it's here.'

'Who knows, but it won't be for us, that's for sure.'

We sat in the waiting room, while the other people started leaving, walking out to the bus.

'I think it might be for us,' Lucy said after a few minutes.

People started getting on the bus and the driver turned a revolving sign at the top corner of the windscreen until it read 'Key West'.

'Christ,' I said. 'It is for us. Good Lord.'

We walked out into the car park and climbed on board. The bus was filled with low-lifes who had no concept of personal space. Then the bus chugged away through the heat, labouring from gear to gear, slowly building up pace. There was no air-conditioning, only sliding glass windows that were virtually impossible to prise open.

Once we'd cleared the grime of Miami, we made our way down the almost innumerable Florida Keys, the road bridging the various atolls. A disused railroad track shadowed the bitumen for part of the way, its iron ribbons often stranded in mid-air above the water. Billed as around two and a half hours by car, the trip took us four hours. Naming the company Greyhound was clearly done for the purposes of irony.

By the time we made it to our hotel in Key West, we were ready to go straight out for a drink. I don't know what I was expecting from the town, but I didn't get it. Maybe I thought it was going to be run down, dirty and cheap—a neglected port town. But it was the most expensive place we visited in all of America. Our hotel was nearly twice the price of anywhere else. And the town was done out very nicely. Most of the colonial-styled houses were two-storey and immaculately painted in creams and off-blues and pale yellows. The shops in the main part of town were similarly presented. The town was clean and quaint and had a vibrant feel. There were many bars, most bulging with drunken people. In fact, every bar was heaving and everyone in them was drunk. A lot of the bars and stores hung the multi-coloured gay flag from their door. There are a lot of gays in

49

Key West. We had a drink at Sloppy Joe's, a well-known watering hole and a one-time favourite of Ernest Hemingway's.

The next morning we visited Hemingway's house from the 1930s—there are still many six-toed cats residing there, descendants of the ones the writer owned—before going to the most southerly point in the United States. There was a queue of tourists getting photos at the condom-like monument to mark the spot and we joined it.

At sunset, armed with key lime pie, the thing to eat in Key West, we made our way to Mallory Square. The large plaza by the water was filled with singers and street performers, including men who had painted themselves silver and stood motionless as if they were statues (surely that's had its day). The sun sunk into the water with everybody watching intently. Once it had disappeared, everybody disappeared as well, turning and walking back into the main part of town to keep drinking.

Two days later it was time to get the Dog back to Miami to head up the east coast. We needed a bus to Savannah, Georgia, changing in Miami. I was concerned that we'd get to Miami and the bus there to Savannah would already be full—the Miami station was a major terminal. We walked into the ticket office in Key West. I was anticipating problems. But as only luck would have it, behind the ticket counter was a mild-mannered, slender, well-turned-out man. It was one of the only men we ever saw at a ticket counter and one of the few non-overweight ticket staff. And, as it turned out, the only helpful person. Completely contrary to the array of stringent Greyhound rules and protocols, he arranged for tickets from both Key West and Miami, even though we had a Discovery Pass. He had to make three phone calls to do it, but it guaranteed us a seat in Miami, a seat we would not have otherwise got, as the station there was packed when we arrived.

Our driver for the leg back to Miami was strict. He began the journey with the usual set of rules and reiterated that nobody was to talk at a loud volume.

'Lower your voices,' he said at the slightest breach of this dictate.

'I said lower your voices,' he repeated if the perpetrator continued. 'I will not tolerate raised voices. Lower your voices.' The loud speaker nearly made the rickety old bus shake.

It was drizzling rain as we island-hopped up to the mainland, but the water was still turquoise and clear. I saw a couple of pairs of large sharks cruising the bay, looking for an easy meal, their fins cutting the surface of the water.

As I was gazing out over the horizon, wondering where this American journey would take us, I felt a sharp jab in my ribs. I spun to my right and there was a young man staring at me, his finger poised for a second shot. He had yellow puss coming out of one of his eyes.

'Gotta phone?' he said. 'Can I use your phone?'

Before I could reply, another hard jab.

'Phone? Gotta phone?'

'I haven't got a phone,' I said and turned back to the window, covering Lucy.

Another jab.

'Can I use your phone?' he said, ready to hit me again.

'Don't fucking touch me,' I spat, squaring up to him. 'Do not touch me again. You hear me? I don't have a phone. Don't touch me again.'

I stared at him hard. He looked back, but lowered his hand and eased back into his seat.

A minute passed and nothing. But he was still looking. I could feel it.

'Oh my God,' Lucy whispered to me. 'I'm petrified. He's staring at us.'

'We'll be alright,' I said. 'Don't worry. Just stay calm. Don't worry.'

The truth was we would have been safer in the water.

9

AN INHERENT DISLIKE

'I didn't mean to be mean, oh no, no no no.'

—'I Didn't Mean to be Mean', Mental As
Anything

Black women usually hate me. It's as if they have an instant and inherent dislike for me, like they sense it as a dog might. Virtually every person that Greyhound employs to work behind their ticketing counters is a black woman. The prerequisites for the job are simple: black, fat and angry. Most of them are middle-aged as well, and they're the ones that hate me the most.

A typical conversation at a ticket counter might go like this.

'Excuse me, ma'am, what time does the next bus go to Washington?' There are no greetings or pleasantries. You have to get straight into it. No smiling either.

'What sorta ticket you got?'

'Discovery Pass.'

'Come back in an hour. No point in talkin' to me now. Nothin' I can do.'

'Yes, but what time is the next bus?'

'3pm. Come back in an hour.' She said this final sentence under sufferance, without looking at me as she walked away.

'Good talking to you,' I said.

Everything the women do at the ticket counter is under sufferance. It's as if they're doing you a favour by even answering a question. And every answer is made in a dismissive fashion, with an air of superiority. A 'yes' is rarely given. It's usually a 'hmmm, hmmm' as they turn their heads away, disgusted. It doesn't matter how polite you are, it makes no difference. Any question is an imposition.

And there's no way to beat them. If you seek clarification of an answer, they'll just repeat what they originally said. Or they won't answer at all. More often than not, they just walk away. The only time I came close to a victory was in Washington. I walked up to the ticketing counter and was met with the usual suspect. She was about fifty, very fat—especially in the arse region—and wore heavy make-up, slicked down dark hair and an ill-fitting Greyhound uniform.

'Yeeesss?' she moaned at me as I approached the counter.

'I need two tickets on the next bus to New York please.'

'Next bus is an express. There's no tickets.'

'Why's that?'

'Next bus is an express. There's no tickets,' she repeated. 'Wait around the corner.'

'What about our bags?'

'Take your bags with you and wait around the corner.'

'Don't we need tickets on our bags?' I asked.

'No. Take your bags with you. When the bus comes, get in the line and get on.'

'Can you guarantee us a seat?'

'No,' she said. 'Line up when the bus comes.' Then she walked off.

Lucy and I went around the corner, sat down and waited for the bus. A few minutes later, another middle-aged woman in a Greyhound uniform walked past. She glared at us as she passed, then stopped and came back.

'Those bags been checked?' she barked without introduction.

I was strangling a yawn.

'Those bags been checked?' she yelled again.

'What do you mean?' I said.

'Have they been checked at the counter?'

'No, the lady there told us we didn't have to.'

'Did she see them?'

'Yes.'

'Well, they need to be checked,' she said.

'No, she told us to take them here and not to check them.' I was gaining in confidence.

'I'm telling you they need to be checked.' She was gaining in anger.

'I'm telling you that you need to talk to your colleague as she has other views.'

She stared at me for a second, her hands on her hips and her feet spread.

'What did she look like?' she spat.

'Like you,' I said.

'How?'

'You know,' I said. 'Big and angry.'

'Hmmm,' she huffed and then strode off towards the ticketing counter. We didn't meet again.

I imagine that Greyhound has a military-style boot camp to recruit and train these women, as they all look and act exactly the same. Mantras like 'the customer is always wrong' and 'never smile, never make eye contact' must be drilled into them and put on signs in the kitchen room to motivate staff. The company's goal is to produce fat, angry women who hate men and breathe disdain and venom. They achieve it.

10

THE DOG MARATHON

'Get back Gruffy, back Scruffy. Get back you flea infested mongrel.'

—'Who Let The Dogs Out', Baha Men

It was a simple enough equation. Thirty-eight hours in four days. Sixteen hours from Miami to the Georgian town of Savannah, sixteen from Savannah to Washington D.C., then another six up to New York City. Simple enough on paper. But it was thirty-eight hours in the world of the Greyhound bus. In Dog years, that's 266 hours. A Dog marathon.

The journey didn't start well. As we were queuing up for the bus in Miami, a police car pulled up. A cop got out of the front then helped a woman from the back seat. She was covered in tattoos, had unkempt hair and was wearing a one-toned bile-green prison jumpsuit, as well as handcuffs. The policeman spoke to the woman behind the Greyhound desk then uncuffed his prisoner, who joined the back of the queue.

'My God,' Lucy said. 'She's getting on our bus.'

'Well, that is a bizarre turn of events,' I said. 'At least she'll be used to all the rules.'

I'd been told by a cab driver that prisoners who are released from jail get one free trip paid by the State, so quite often there are jailbirds on the buses. And anyone is permitted to ride the Dog if they have the money for the fare.

The bus set off and stopped at Jacksonville in the middle of the night for over an hour. The timing or length of the Greyhound stops is never explained, nor do they make any sense. Another group of inbreeds boarded and we set off for Savannah, arriving at 1am, eighteen hours after we'd left Miami.

The Savannah Greyhound station was not a pretty sight at that time of the night. It was full of plebs and low-lifes sleeping on the seats and lying against their bags. I asked the big woman behind the counter how to get to our hotel.

'You'll need to get a taxi,' she said. 'There's a phone over there.'

'I don't have the number,' I said. 'Would you mind calling one for us?'

'Well, I suppose so,' she said, quite put out.

She called the cab, describing me in detail on the phone.

'Alright,' she said to me when she'd finished. 'It'll be here shortly. But you wait inside now, ya hear me? Do not go outside under any circumstances.'

The taxi arrived twenty minutes later and waited at the curb. I went to go outside, but the door was locked. I walked over to the counter and told the woman.

'Didn't I tell you not to go outside?' she said. 'I'll open it.

You wait here.'

She unlocked the door, looked left and right, then walked over to the cabbie. They had a discussion and she came back.

'I've told him you're the passenger, but he won't get out of the cab. Too dangerous, he says. Walk over there quickly and get in.'

I thanked her and we got in the cab. The driver was locked in with the windows up and I had to put our bags in the boot.

'Is it dangerous around here?' I asked him.

'You bet,' he said. He had a skin head and tattoos on his neck and looked dangerous enough himself. A *US Army Retired* sticker was on his side window. 'I don't get out at the Greyhound station at night. Too many undesirables ride that thing.'

He lit a cigarette.

'Do you mind if I smoke?' he said.

He didn't wait for a response, just started speaking at us in an aggressive manner.

We arrived at the hotel and got out of the cab.

'Hold on a second,' he said to me as we were walking away. 'Can I offer you a piece of advice?'

'Yeah, sure,' I said. It was more of a statement. We were going to get it anyway.

'The cops here are assholes. I hate them. They'll come up and question you in the street. Make sure you carry your passport with you at all times. At all times.'

We went into the hotel and checked in. By now it was 2am and the woman at reception would not shut up.

'Where ya come from?' she asked.

'Miami.'

'Where?'

'Miami.'

'Wow. But where ya come from before that?'

'England.'

'Where did ya say?'

'England.'

'Oh, wow,' she said, gazing at us like we were from a superior planet. 'I had a cousin in England once. In the United Kingdom. England.'

'Really? Anyway,' I said. 'We'd better be heading off to bed.'

'England, wow. Whereabouts in England?'

'Good night,' I said and we walked off to our room.

The following morning we woke up late and got another cab into town. It didn't go well either. When we climbed out, I looked at the change he'd given me. It was $10 short. The cabbie had sped off, but the street was one way and he'd dropped us on a square. He had no choice but to drive around the square. I ran across the grass and caught him at the far set of traffic lights. I hit hard on his window. He hadn't seen me coming and looked up in surprise.

'Yes,' he said, after winding down his window. He was a young Hispanic man.

'You didn't give me enough change,' I said. 'You owe me $10.'

'$10?' he said. 'Okay.'

He handed me $10, didn't say another word, and drove off.

We walked the charming streets of Savannah, with its palm trees and colonial houses, and hopped on a tourist bus that took us to the main sights in town. As we got off, I saw a sign next to the driver that read 'Adults $25', but we had not paid and the driver didn't say anything. Perhaps it was an honour system; they rarely work. We had a seafood lunch overlooking the Savannah River and its many paddle steamers. Then we walked in the sunshine to the main square. A two-man band was playing there and people were sitting on chairs under umbrellas watching.

'Why don't we sit and watch for a while?' I said to Lucy. 'I love this song.'

They were singing *Mainstreet* by Bob Seger.

We sat down and I ordered a beer from an outdoor bar. Georgia is famous for its peaches and Lucy was keen to taste some, but she settled for a peach sorbet instead. She was happy.

It was relaxing to sit in the sun with a beer. The band then sang Don Henley's *The Heart of the Matter*.

'That was brilliant,' I said to Lucy. 'I'm going over.'

I walked between the tables and up to the singers.

'That was the best cover of any song I've ever heard,' I said.

I put $5 in their tip bucket and walked back to Lucy.

'Well, thank you, sir,' one of the singers said. 'Now folks, that must be the best looking guy we've seen all day.'

The crowd cheered and I waved then got another beer.

'After some attention are you?' Lucy said, smiling.

'Just supporting the local talent,' I said. 'They're very good.'

The next day we had to face the Dog and do it all over again. We got up at 3.30am for another sixteen hour journey to Washington.

The Savannah Greyhound station didn't look any less dangerous at that hour. We could see through the window and into the waiting room. The clientele had not improved. It was like we were walking into a prison yard.

'Go straight in there,' said the cab driver who dropped us off. 'And don't come out, no matter what.' A theme seemed to be developing.

There was a burly security guard standing at the entrance and our cabbie called him over. The guard then escorted us into the bus station.

'This is the life,' I said to Lucy.

'I don't know how much more of this I can take,' she said.

'You'll be fine,' I said. 'Just stay close to me.'

'It's not just me I'm worried about.'

The maxim that you can sleep anywhere if you're tired enough does not extend to Greyhound buses. The people in the seats in front leant back as far as they could and a typically fat middle-aged woman across from us was practically yelling into her mobile phone. I turned up the volume on my iPod, pretending I was somewhere else.

Most of the other passengers were asleep, their legs strewn across the aisle preventing access to the toilet. There was no way we were going to risk waking any of those Neanderthals.

As day broke, people started stirring. Two seats over was a man of about thirty. He was tall and muscular and looked strong. He was wearing an old T-shirt covered with a sports jacket, torn denim jeans and pointy metal-capped crocodile skin boots. He'd been sleeping with a ten-gallon hat over his face, but as he woke he put it back on his head. He had a steely look in his eyes and he looked angry. A Mustang Man in his prime, if ever I saw one.

Greyhound has a strict no alcohol policy whilst travelling. But that does not prevent a passenger boarding while drunk. And Mustang was blind.

There was a spare seat next to him and he sat alone, just staring at the back of the seat in front of him. After an hour of that, he started turning his head, looking around the bus for action. I watched him scour the bus, assessing every seat. Those eyes could look a hole through you. The bus stopped for a short break, and as we were reboarding, he sat down next to a young girl who was sitting just behind us.

'You sit over there,' he said to the man who had originally been in the seat.

And then he started on this girl. Flirting, but in a forceful way.

'Where you from, darlin'?' he said.

She was trying to be polite, probably to avert a disaster. She asked him a few questions, but most of what he said was unsolicited.

'Hell, I'm from St. Louis,' he said. 'But I thought I'd try my luck in the Big Apple. You know, take a bit of a bite and see how it tastes?'

A little while later the bus stopped and the girl stood up to get off.

'I am letting some passengers off at this stop,' said the driver. 'If you are not getting off, you must stay seated.'

The girl walked down the aisle and Mustang followed her.

'Are you getting off as well?' the driver said to Mustang.

'No, sir, just helping her with her bags.'

'Well, you must sit down. Do not get off the bus.'

Mustang hit the back of the driver's seat with his fist.

'Fuck you,' Mustang yelled. 'Why can't I help the poor girl with her bags?'

'Be seated,' the driver said. 'Or I'll have the station police remove you.'

Mustang hit the seat again and stood staring at the driver. With some reluctance, he slowly swaggered back down the aisle, hitting seats and using swear words as punctuation rather than vocabulary.

'Fuckin' Greyhound can go fuck themselves,' he said. 'It's a fuckin' joke, fuckin' assholes.'

'He doesn't really speak does he?' I said to Lucy under my breath. 'His normal words are just there to pad out his swearing.'

'Be quiet,' Lucy said. 'He'll hear you.'

'He's a coward. I'm not worried about him,' I said. 'A few drinks will work wonders in a cowardly man.'

'Fuck,' he screamed as he passed our seats. I sat in silence.

The bus stopped in Richmond, Virginia for a couple of hours and we had to change buses. That meant queuing again and hoping to get good seats. The problem was, that by the time we got there, a lot of people starting their journey in Richmond were already waiting for the bus and we were the last to get on. By the time we did board, there were only two single seats remaining. One was next to Mustang.

'Oh my God,' said Lucy as we got on the bus. 'There are only single seats. I can't sit next to him. He'll eat me alive.'

'I'll sort something out,' I said.

'How?' She looked very scared.

'I'll pay someone if I have to.'

There was a young man with a pointy jawline sitting by himself in front of Mustang.

'Excuse me, sir,' I said. 'My wife is very sick. Would you mind if we took these seats and you move to that one?' Mustang was observing all this with interest, no doubt hoping for Lucy to be next to him.

The pointy-jawed man had his phone plugged into a power socket on the wall at his seat.

'Sorry,' he said. 'I need the power.'

I took my chances and looked across Mustang to the wall.

'There's a power socket there too,' I said to the man. 'Maybe that gentleman will let you use it.' Mustang just stared.

'I'm sorry, I can't.'

'Will this help?' I said, holding out a $10 bill.

He took the money and without saying anything, stood up and sat next to Mustang.

'Thank you,' I said.

'You know,' he said, looking up at me. 'I would have moved for five.'

I looked down at him and smiled. 'I would have paid twenty.'

We sat down and there were tears of joy in Lucy's eyes.

'Thank you so much,' she said. 'I think I owe you $10.'

'That's alright,' I said. 'But I think you owe me your life.'

The bus stopped an hour later. The young man disembarked and a girl of about twenty boarded and was forced to sit next to Mustang, who still appeared quite drunk.

'How do you like my jacket?' he said to the girl after he'd introduced himself.

'It's nice,' she said. There was fear in her voice.

'Not bad for a redneck like me, hey?'

He spoke non-stop for the rest of the trip, the girl being friendly to appease him. But when the bus pulled up at the Washington station, she almost ran off.

It was late and we were exhausted. We got a cab to our hotel and went straight to sleep. The gruelling Dog schedule was starting to take its toll on Lucy.

The next day we walked the streets of Washington, seeing the famous sights—the White House, Capitol Hill, the Lincoln Memorial and various museums, the names of which I cannot recall. The highlight of the day was the Arlington Cemetery, which is actually across the Potomac River in Virginia (Washington itself is not in a state at all, but the District of Columbia). There were a lot of people at the cemetery and they all made a beeline for JFK's grave, as did we. There were a number of Kennedys buried there. We then went to the tomb of the Unknown Soldier. It is guarded around the clock by an armed soldier and we watched the very formal and impressive changing of the guard ceremony.

Washington is a good clean city that is very accessible. That said, we walked around it for twelve miles.

The next day it was time to take the final leg of the Dog Marathon, a meagre six hour trip to New York City. The bus station in Washington was fairly central, but when we arrived it was packed and there was a long queue for the ticket counter. We finally made it to the front.

'You are very lucky,' said the woman, engaging in some rare partially-polite conversation.

'Why's that?' I asked.

'You got the last pair of seats. There's only one seat left and the next bus doesn't leave until tomorrow.'

'That is lucky,' I said.

'Next,' she yelled.

The trip was uneventful and almost bearable and we made it into New York on time. The marathon was over. We had rolled up the better part of the east coast. And, Lord, how the money rolled out as we did, along with our sanity.

11

THE YANKEES

'But I'm taking a Greyhound, on the Hudson River line. I'm in a New York state of mind.'

—'New York State of Mind', Billy Joel

The ball flew high and wide and landed fifteen rows back in the furthest part of the stadium, bouncing off a seat while people grappled to handle it. The entire crowd jumped to its feet as A-Rod swaggered around the bases and into the dugout where his team mates high-fived and hugged him.

Two men sitting in front of us leapt up and embraced, slapping each other on the back and spilling their beers as they did.

'Oh yeah,' one of them yelled.

They turned to us.

'High-fives for A-Rod,' the other said.

Both men had their hands in the air and were looking at Lucy and me. There was little choice.

After we high-fived each of them, taking turns with pauses, then hesitation, like clinking glasses in a group of people, we all sat back down.

We were at Yankee Stadium in the Bronx, New York and Alex Rodriguez had just hit his second home run for the night against the Kansas City Royals.

Every seat was full and the atmosphere was electric. During a break between innings the big screen displayed bloopers from past games—almost always players from the away team crashing into each other. The crowd watched and cheered every time. The screen swapped to 'Crowd Cam'. Each person who was filmed jumped and screamed when they saw themselves live on the screen.

Vendors were walking the stands selling hot dogs as well as beer. The beers were $15 a piece, but we bought two anyway. They came in blue plastic souvenir cups. I got a large spicy Italian hot dog too.

The Yankees were still on top at the end of the next innings. During the change over, the two high-fivers in front of us turned around. They were in their twenties and both had goatee beards. Like everyone else in the 50,000-strong crowd, they wore Yankees caps.

'Hi, I'm Hank and this is Chip,' one of them said to us, putting out his hand.

I did the introductions and we all shook hands.

'What's Chip short for?' I asked.

'Nothing,' he said.

'You're Yankees fans I take it?' Hank said.

Lucy was wearing a Yankees T-shirt with 'A-Rod' and the number '13' on the back. I had a New York Yankees cap on. We'd bought them in the gigantic merchandise store under the stadium just before the game.

'I am now,' I said.

'Greatest team on Earth,' said Chip. 'You won't regret it.'

'Who's the best player—A-Rod or Jeter?' I asked. I'd read

a lot of press discussion on the topic.

'That's a tough one,' said Chip. 'A-Rod's considered by many to be the best all round ball player ever.'

'He was the youngest man to hit 500 homers and then the youngest to hit 600. He beat Babe Ruth by over a year,' said Hank, keen to interject.

'And he's the richest,' said Chip. 'His ten-year contract is $275 million and is the biggest ever. He beat his own record of $252 million.'

These boys knew their baseball stats.

'What about David Jeter?' I said.

'Jeter's amazing as well,' said Chip. 'He's played eighteen seasons for the Yankees, winning five World Series.'

'And he gets paid almost as much as A-Rod, but has a higher batting average,' said Hank.

'So who's the best?' I said.

'Who knows,' said Hank. 'They're both fucking good.'

We all laughed.

'Why is it called the World Series when only American teams play?' Lucy asked.

Hank and Chip looked at each other, as if they'd never considered the question.

'Well, it just is,' said Chip. 'It's the World Series.'

'Yeah, but why?' said Lucy.

'It just is, that's why.'

There was a short silence while we all looked at each other.

'Here comes the beer lady,' I said. 'Do you boys want another?'

We all had another beer and the game came to an end. After another comfortable triumph by the Yankees, extending their winning streak to ten straight games, we caught the subway back to Manhattan. It had been a superb night of Americana.

The next day we awoke to torrential rain. We only had a few days in New York, so we decided to leave the hotel for the morning and face it. We went for lunch at the Carnegie Deli, with its walls of famous signed photographs, most of whom I'd never heard of. We ordered a pastrami sandwich, one of their specials. It was just a huge pile of pastrami, about four inches high, covered in melted cheese. It cost $34, with an extra $8 because we shared it. The place was a rip off.

We walked to the Empire State Building as we wanted to go up to the viewing tower. But a thick fog shrouded the top third so there was little point.

Still the rain kept falling. We looked around a few fashion stores, but we couldn't keep dry. Lucy wasn't feeling well. She was starting to get irritable so we went back to the hotel in the afternoon for a rest.

Lucy started crying as soon as we got in the door of our room.

'I don't think I can take this,' she said. 'I'm too tired.'

'You'll be alright,' I said. 'The big bus days are done and now it'll be a bit more relaxed.'

'I think I want to go home.'

'You can't go home,' I said. 'The trip's only just started really and we've got a lot of things booked.'

'I don't care about the bookings. I want to go home.'

'Well, I do,' I said. 'I've paid a lot for them. It'll cost me a few thousand if we leave now.'

'I'm tired. I just want to go home. That's all I want.'

Lucy put her head into the pillow and sobbed. After a while she fell asleep. I watched her sleeping, wondering what to do. I wanted to continue with the trip and I wanted her to as well. And I didn't want to lose the money I'd spent on bookings.

A few hours later Lucy woke up. She felt a little better.

'Why don't we go down to Battery Park?' I said. 'Catch the Staten Island ferry?'

It was still raining quite heavily, so we huddled together and made it to the subway station dry enough. We got down to the ferry landing, but could only just see the Statue of Liberty because of the cloud.

I spoke to one of the security guards at the dock.

'If you want to see the city,' he said. 'Don't bother going on the ferry. You won't see a thing at the moment. Not in these conditions.'

'Are there any good bars around here?' I asked.

'Sure are, sir,' he said. 'Head up Wall Street, go past the big bronze bull and just near there are a few streets of bars. Some good ones, too.'

'Thank you, sir,' I said. 'That's very helpful.'

We walked as directed through the drizzling rain, but couldn't find any bars. Just as we were about to give up and go back to the hotel, I saw a window lined with bottles just below the level of the street. We climbed down the stairs and into the bar, through the eight feet high vault-style door. The room was lowly lit, but the bar was illuminated by fridge lights and neon. It had just gone dark and the place was full of young professional types in suits. Lucy sat at a table and I went to the bar and ordered. As the drinks were handed to me, a waitress on my side of the bar hurried over.

'You can't order here,' she said. 'You have to order from me at the table.' She was agitated.

'But I just have.'

'No, you can't. Please sit back down and I will take your order.'

I picked up the drinks.

'I have just ordered these off this lady,' I said, pointing at one of the barmaids. 'Paid her and she's given them to me.'

'Okay, I'm sorry,' she said, looking a little embarrassed. 'If you need any more drinks, please get them from me. I'll be happy to help.'

'What was that all about?' Lucy asked when I sat down.

'The waitress trying to make sure she got our table so she gets a tip.'

'She seemed quite worked up about it.'

'She was,' I said. 'And I wish her good luck with the tip after that performance.'

It'd been a long few days. I had a thirst you could photograph, a murderous thirst. I poured a good tall glass of beer, belted that and poured another. Then I ordered some more, this time from the waitress. I was really enjoying the beer, not just drinking to make something happen. Lucy drank red wine, a Malbec from Argentina, and her mood was inexplicably ebullient, despite the scene from earlier. We went on drinking, celebrating something or other. Indeed, the night began to pick up steam.

We were getting along very well, laughing and joking with each other. I was talking a lot and at one point lost my train of thought.

'What was I saying?' I said.

'I don't know,' Lucy said. 'Just drink the beer. Then you won't seem so stupid to yourself.'

She laughed.

'Where's that from? Is that a line of mine?

'No, it's not yours,' she said. 'Definitely not yours.'

'I'm not so sure. It sounds like one of mine.'

A few hours later we left the bar. Despite her early mishap, I tipped the waitress well. It had been a good night.

We wandered the streets of New York, ambling back to our hotel. The rain had cleared and the air was fresh and cool. We could see the lights at the top of the Empire State Building.

'Do you think you'll be hung over tomorrow?' Lucy asked.

'Oh yes. Like the Gardens of Babylon,' I said. 'But it'll be alright. I take my hangovers as a consequence, not as a punishment.'

'Good one,' she said and smiled. 'I think I will be.'

A beggar approached us from the darkness. He was having difficulty walking.

'Any mo-money?' he slurred. 'Can I have some money?'

We kept walking and he mumbled away.

'Oh, you'll be hung over for sure,' I said. 'Probably not as much as him, though. He'll be able to sell his to science.'

'I'm sorry about this afternoon,' Lucy said. 'I don't want to go home.'

'Fitzgerald,' I said. 'Scott Fitzgerald. Your line before was from The Great Gatsby.'

'I don't want to go home,' Lucy repeated.

'I don't want you to go home, either.'

We stopped at a café. It was about to close and a man was sweeping the floor. We went inside and shared two large slices of pepperoni pizza.

I didn't remember going to bed, but in the morning I was there. And so was Lucy.

12

A COUNTY OF IRELAND

'We have come to answer our country's call, from the four proud provinces of Ireland.'

—'Ireland's Call', Phil Coulter

'What do you think you're doing? Where are you going?' He was looking at me strangely, as if in disbelief.

'To Boston,' I said.

'Not on this bus. You don't want to go on this bus.'

We were tenth in line and other people were walking up the bus steps. We'd got up early and had waited an hour. But the driver had singled Lucy and me out and seemed intent on stopping us.

'Why not?' I said.

'It's a gruelling journey to Boston. Very gruelling. At least seven hours and the passengers aren't, how should I put it, the best types.'

'Mate, we did a couple of sixteen and fourteen hour rides up the coast,' I said. 'We'll be fine.'

'I really don't think you should be on this bus.' He was almost pleading.

'We have to get to Boston today,' I said. 'The later bus is sold out.' I handed him our tickets.

'Okay,' he said, taking them. 'But don't say I didn't warn you.'

'Excuse me, excuse me.' It was a Mustang Man ushering an old woman to the front of the line. 'This lady needs to get on first.'

It was obvious that Mustang didn't know her, but he was being a hero and helping her to the front of the line like it was life and death. People have a liberal interpretation of special needs and use the slightest hindrance as a ruse to jump the queue that others have been waiting in forever.

The lady walked up the stairs of the bus. She was only about sixty anyway.

'We're in front of you, mate,' I said to Mustang, who was edging forward himself.

'I know,' he replied. 'I'm just helping this lady on.'

Lucy and I climbed onto the bus.

'There's always a good Samaritan martyr making a scene,' I said to Lucy.

'He was just trying to get on before the queue as well,' Lucy said.

'Yeah, probably.'

The queue was long and competition for good seats was fierce.

We sat near the front of the bus. The loud talkers usually congregated near the back.

A woman carrying an oxygen tank got on.

'This seat is for me,' she said to nobody in particular. 'I need it because I'm handicapped.' She sat in the front row.

'I was on a Dog from New York the other day,' she said to a man sitting across the aisle who had made eye contact. It is not a good idea to make eye contact with a fellow passenger. 'And the driver wouldn't let me bring my oxygen onto the bus. He said it wasn't hand luggage and it had to go under the bus. Well, I told him I need it and we argued and then he let me. But I'm having my lawyer put in a formal complaint at 9am this morning. Well, I sent an email so they probably already have it, but it's a formal complaint.'

The man just looked at her and didn't respond.

The bus filled up and the driver took his position. Then came the announcement with the usual Greyhound rules.

'My name's Pete,' the driver said at the end of his speech. 'And I will not tolerate noise of any kind. Please do not make any noise and do not attempt to speak to me while I'm driving.'

The bus started up and we drove out onto the streets of New York and headed north. People were talking quite loudly and coughing and snorting. People cough and snort a lot on buses.

'Please refrain from talking,' Pete said over the loud speaker. 'I can't have any noise today.'

There was a momentary silence and then the talking started up again.

'No talking. I'm warning you.'

Pete started off strongly, but he soon lost control of the bus. The talking went on and Pete ended up just accepting it.

After a few hours we stopped for a short break in Providence, Rhode Island. Pete designated it as a five minute break.

'I will go without any passenger who is not back in five minutes,' he said. 'This is a five minute stop. No more.'

The woman with the oxygen tank painstakingly hobbled off the bus and lit up a cigarette, and then another. Twenty minutes later the final passenger ambled up to the bus. Pete didn't say anything. He just shook his head and drove on.

After eight hours, we arrived into Boston. It hadn't been a bad journey.

Pete was standing at the bottom of the steps as the passengers left.

'Thanks very much, Pete,' I said as we got off. 'It was a walk in the park. Nothing to it.'

'Thank you,' was all he said in reply. He looked defeated.

After an early night in—the long Dog trips really wore us out—we spent the next day looking around Boston. It was warm and sunny, with a vernal freshness in the air. A perfect day to explore a city.

We walked in the sun, poking in and out of shops and stores and bought a Red Sox cap each. We went to the famous bar from the sitcom Cheers and followed the Freedom Trail, which linked the key landmarks of the city. It led us to the Faneuil Hall Marketplace and its string of food vendors, where we sampled a couple of free clam chowder tasters.

The city was very liveable and apparently very safe.

'There's no trouble at all in Boston,' a cabbie told us. 'Everybody's friendly and ready to help.'

Just after he told us that we saw an old lady lying on the footpath. She had fallen and strangers were rushing to help her. Our cabbie stopped to make sure everything was alright and an ambulance arrived one minute later.

We walked down to the docks and bought tickets for some whale watching. I was sceptical as we motored out into

Boston Harbor, but we saw an array of humpbacks slapping the water and frolicking right next to the boat. It was a worthwhile trip, only marred by the multitude of Indians on board (Sub-continental, not American) who were dominating the decks in groups, yelling and pointing every time a whale breached the surface, which was a lot.

The city of Boston is also very Irish. A lot of people working in shops and bars have Irish accents and most of the pubs are Irish. Apart from the warmth and sunshine and agreeable surroundings, it felt as if we were actually in Ireland.

After the boat trip the night approached and we went to go into a pub near the docks. We were stopped at the door by a bouncer.

'ID please,' he said without smiling. Rarely a smile.

Lucy handed him hers.

'ID,' he said to me.

'I'm thirty-nine,' I said. 'Don't you use any discretion?'

'Well, you don't look thirty-nine.'

'Well, I don't look twenty-one either.'

I handed it over, we walked in, the pub looked shit, so we left.

This ID business happened all over America. Wherever we went, we were both asked for ID. I could understand Lucy being asked, to a degree. She was twenty-eight, but did look young. Perhaps I didn't look my age, but I certainly looked legal.

We got ID'ed at most places. I was even asked by an Iraqi when buying beer in a supermarket in Wyoming. He ID'ed

Lucy too, even though it was me who was buying the beer. Then in a petrol station in Nevada I was asked when buying a six-pack of beer.

'When were you born?' the man said to me.

'Ah, ah, I'm not sure,' I toyed. '1972, I think.'

He laughed and didn't ask for my licence.

Lucy even got asked in Las Vegas because she was sitting at the bar of a Mexican restaurant, even though she was only drinking water. To sit at the bar you needed to be twenty-one.

We tried a couple more Irish bars, they were all Irish, but none of them were any good, with dirty floors and no atmosphere and dirt trackers from wall to wall. Eventually, we stumbled upon one near the main square. It was a little more upmarket and we went inside and sat at the bar.

'What'll it be?' said the barman, a portly man of about fifty who had a beard and spoke with a broad Irish accent.

I ordered us a beer and a mojito.

'What brings you to Boston?' he asked me.

'We wanted to go to Fenway Park, to the Red Sox game tonight, but it was sold out.'

'They always are. Everybody knows that. I don't see much point to it though. Football is the only game that's any good. And it's only good to watch in Ireland, God's country.'

He had an abrasive way about him.

'You're an Irelander are you?' I said.

'Irish. You can't get one passed the Irish.'

'Yeah, that's what I meant.'

'It's the greatest country on Earth, you know,' he said. 'No other place I'd rather be than having the craic in Ireland.'

'I went around it once in a few days,' I said. 'Very small. Like the people.' He had an irritating manner and I couldn't help but have a jibe.

'What do you mean by that?'

'Well,' I said. 'I've never met one who doesn't build his entire personality around being Irish.'

'I don't agree with that.'

'You take yourselves a bit too seriously, don't you think? All the while pretending you love the craic.'

'Some do,' he said. 'But it's a great country.'

'What's great about it?'

'It's just great. God has blessed the emerald isle. And I thank him every day. We don't deserve the troubles we've got.'

He moved away and served someone else.

'Ah, the Irish,' I said to Lucy. 'They have to moan about something or other. No sense of humour.'

I had a long drink of beer and put the bottle down on the bar.

'Ah, there is a God,' I said. 'There's nothing like that first taste of beer.'

The barman heard me.

'You don't strike me as a man of faith,' he said as if he knew best.

'Really,' I said. 'Why's that?'

'You just don't. There's something about you.'

'I gather you're Catholic?' I said to him.

'That's right,' he said. 'I'm a devout Catholic. I find it hard to grasp anyone who's not.'

'Well, I've never desired faith. It's alright not to believe in luck and omens.'

81

'There's nothing lucky about it. God has blessed me and I thank him for my life.'

'You sound like an armchair Catholic to me,' I said.

'Absolutely not,' he said. 'If I transgress, I pay my penances.'

'At confession?' I said. I was starting to warm up.

'That's right. The last civilised bastion.'

'What's the good of confession when you know the result of the crime in the first place? You just do it to make yourself feel better. A Catholic is more capable of evil than anyone.'

'The soul capable of the greatest good is also capable of the greatest evil.'

'I don't even know what that means,' I said. 'You lot have been going on with shit like that since Jesus played left wing for Bethlehem.'

'You should go to church and find out,' he said, now smiling like he'd had a victory.

'I can't foresee stepping into another church in my life. I have no need for it.'

'It is easy to find a virtuous reason for not doing what you don't want to do.'

'I don't have any virtuous reason,' I said. 'It's just a crock and I don't see any point to it.'

'What about death?' he said. 'Aren't you afraid of dying?'

'When I was five I realised that everything dies. I saw a red maple leaf die and turn brown and I knew that would happen to me one day too.'

'And that didn't scare you?'

'Not really,' I said. 'It occurred to me that any fear was based on the erroneous view that there is awareness in death. After death we cease to exist and have no feelings because we are gone.'

'That's very profound,' he said with a sarcastic tone.

'There was a Greek philosopher called Epicurus. He also believed that death was not to be feared. When a man dies, he said, he does not feel the pain of death because he no longer is and he therefore feels nothing. When we exist death is not, and when death exists we are not. The fear of death arises from the false belief that in death there is awareness. That might all sound a bit too scary for you armchair Catholics, but there you go.'

'There's no point us talking about this,' he said, starting to get worked up. 'I know that my God will protect me in life and in death. I don't have time to debate ridiculous philosophy with you.'

'You started it,' I said.

We finished our drinks and stood up to leave.

'Good talking to you,' I said as we walked out. 'Keep the faith, brother.'

The Irishman just mumbled something at me and barely looked up.

'What an idiot,' Lucy said once we were out the door. 'So hypocritical. People don't like it when you tell the truth, do they?'

'No,' I said. 'And a man with a beard is always a little suspect anyway.'

13

THANKS FOR THE TIP

'Go on, take the money and run. Go on, take the money and run.'

—'Take the Money and Run', Steve Miller

America has a tipping culture. Far more than in England or anywhere else that I've been.

It's a nightmare. You are expected to tip pretty much anyone who does anything for you. Taxi drivers, barbers, waiters and bar tenders. They all expect tips. And they expect them no matter what the quality of service.

The rule of thumb is as follows: the usual amount to tip is 15% of the bill (or check, as the Yanks call it). If you receive very bad service, you tip 10%. If you receive very good service, you tip 20%. Most bills even have these three amounts calculated and printed at the bottom to save you working it out. The amounts always struck me as high, and the 10% tip is absurd. Why would you give any extra money if the service was bad? What's more, if you do give a 10% tip for bad service, the waiter is offended and won't thank you. So what's the point? You might as well keep the money.

And all this, 'the tip is part of their wages and they rely on it' business, is bullshit. If it's part of their wages, incorporate it in the price and I'll be happy to pay it. Leave it up to discretion and good luck to them. In one Nashville bar there was a sign which read 'We work for tips only'. I found it hard to believe that the waitresses received no wages at all and only earnt the tips. Mind you, they were scantily-clad and seemed to be doing rather well.

I've always had an issue with tipping generally, especially the percentage concept. If you order a $50 bottle of wine, why should you pay an extra $5 than if you'd ordered a $10 bottle and only paid $1? The waiter has done the same amount of work. It doesn't make sense. If tipping is to exist at all, and I'd only ever tip if the service was good, it should be a flat rate. It's like income tax. The rich are paying more to start with, so why should they be punished and pay an even higher percentage? It's like Sherwood Forest. I know a man who puts down $5 regardless of the size of the bill. The absurdity is, if the bill is $20 the waiter loves him, if it's $100 the waiter hates him.

A lot of restaurants will have a note on the menu which says 'A 20% gratuity will be added to parties of six or more'. That makes even less sense to me. A party of six will have a higher bill, so why should they then pay an even higher percentage? It doesn't work. The system needs to be standardised.

Most places are very keen to tell the customer that the tip will be extra. 'Gratuity not included' notices are everywhere—on menus, on the bill itself and on the wall. Everybody expects a little something. I'm surprised the Yanks aren't lazier, because nobody will do anything unless they think they're going to get a tip.

And it's not as if the service in America is that good anyway. I'd heard a lot about how amazing it is, but it wasn't.

Waitresses tend to introduce themselves at the start of the meal in a bubbly fashion to create a good first impression, but they then take ages to come and take your order. They always seem to be in a hurry to move you on as well, trying to get another table in for another tip. Any finished plates are removed immediately, the waitress often standing over the table, waiting for you to finish. Many times I'd still be wiping my mouth with the napkin when the plate was whisked away. Then the bill will be presented without request and often before you're finished. This happened in a bar in Las Vegas. I'd said nothing, the bill was presented, so I ordered another beer, drank it, paid the original bill, and left.

But it's not just the tips in America, there's the tax as well. Sales tax is added on to every bill and it varies from state to state, ranging from about 7 to 17%. Again, the menu prices don't have this element incorporated. It's added at the end. I gather they do it this way to make their prices appear lower. If something is $10 on a menu, the 17% tax is added to make it $11.70. A 15% tip is then added onto that figure to make a total of nearly $13.50. All these additional amounts should be added in to the menu prices so you know where you stand.

Apart from the extra money it costs, the tax being added on to the menu prices means you get given a lot of coins. If you buy something in a shop that costs $5, you'll pay $6.08 for it and get ninety-two cents in change. Your pockets are full of coins at all times. But the vendors don't like it when you give the coins back to them. I bought a subway ticket in New York with coins that I had counted out, including all the copper coins.

'Come on, man,' said the attendant. 'You gotta be kiddin' me.'

All waiters of every kind expect a tip, but some cities are stricter about it than others. The New York City bartenders expect an extra dollar for every beer they serve. In other areas, such as in the West, the waiters don't seem too put out with small tips.

In our hotel in New Orleans, the breakfast delivery waiter would phone the room to tell us breakfast was on the way. 'Don't forget about me,' he'd say as he hung up the phone. I took that to mean that we should be getting our tip ready. I never tipped him. He'd hand me the breakfast, stand there, glare and then storm off.

'If he expects a dollar for that,' I said to Lucy. 'He's kidding himself. I'll go around and deliver all the breakfasts in ten minutes and make fifty bucks.'

Yes, the waiters expect tips, but it's the taxi drivers who are the worst. And they get quite aggressive about it.

Most taxis have the usual 'The fare does not include any gratuity' style of notice on the window. And they don't like it when you don't give them one.

I gave a New Orleans cabbie $8 for a $7 fare. That's a tip of 14%. He just stood there and looked at me, then said 'Okaaaay,' in a drawn out fashion and trudged off. I handed our shuttle driver to LAX $1 extra. He'd been very friendly on the drive, chatting away, no doubt expecting a large tip. He snatched the dollar out of my hand without saying anything, huffed away, slammed the door of the van and then screeched off. That's the other annoying thing, taxi drivers feel obliged to chat in the hope of a better tip. I'd rather they just shut up and drive.

A taxi took us from the St. Louis bus station to our hotel. He was a black man and he was angry. I found most black men driving taxis to be very friendly, but not this one.

'Excuse me, sir,' I said to him when we got in the cab. 'Do you know the address of this bus station?' We needed it for the return journey.

'How the hell would I know?' he said.

I then asked him something else and he didn't answer.

We got to our hotel and the fare was $13 for only a five minute drive. He hadn't used the meter.

'That seems very high,' I said.

'It is what it is,' he replied.

'Naturally, there's no tip,' I said. 'You're not a very friendly cabbie are you?'

Well, that set him off.

'I've got a lot on my mind, you hear me?' he said. 'I have not disrespected you. I have been polite and now you go and say somethin' like that to me. How dare you.'

'How dare you, sir,' I said.

He slammed the cab door and screeched off as well. It's like their final word.

In my time in America, I developed a number of techniques to counter the tipping phenomenon. You have to be crafty, as the waiters are aware that people are trying to avoid a large tip.

My first rule is not to pay for the drinks as you go. If you pay for drinks as you go, you have to tip each time. There's not really any way around it, because if you don't tip, it's then very awkward for the rest of the time in the place. If you get the bill at the end, you can leave a small tip and then leave, never to see them again. No hassles.

But the waiters have ploys as well. Their standard routine is to wait for ages before bringing the change back in the hope that you'll get sick of waiting and leave, leaving the excess money as well. This even happens when the tip has already been included in the bill and is mandatory. In Chicago I got a bill for $28.57, which included a 15% tip. I gave $30 and waited until my change was brought. I'm sure they expect you to round up so they receive a double tip in those circumstances. Other times when the tip was included I counted out the exact money and still received a glare from the waiter, as if I should have been giving more.

Waiters will also give back heaps of $1 bills in the change so it makes it easier to leave a few, rather than giving a $10 note and running the risk of getting nothing because a $10 tip might be too much.

The bill is almost always presented face down, as if to create some sort of illusion or surprise, and the waiter will say 'There's no rush with this, just whenever you're ready.'

I employ what I call the 'Round, Ready and Run' technique. My policy is to wait until I'm completely ready to leave. You don't want to put the money down and then linger, because the waiter will see the small tip and may say something. They're onto this too, often hovering around waiting to pick up the money. But I wait until I'm about to leave, round up and then move off quickly. For example, for a bill of $38.50, I'll round up to $40, put the money in the bill wallet (always in there so they can't see what you've left), and leave in a brisk but not hurried manner.

I didn't have any issues at all in America using this method. The same couldn't be said for Mexico. In Acapulco a couple of years earlier, an angry waitress chased me down the street to ask for a bigger tip.

She didn't get one.

'No es compulsario,' I said to her.

And in the end, that's the nub of it. Tips are not compulsory and if the Yanks expect tips every time, in my view, they've got to earn them, because I never give tips as a matter of course for bad service.

14

THE IMPALA

'We're on a road to nowhere, come on inside.
Takin' that ride to nowhere, we'll take that
ride.'

—'Road to Nowhere', Talking Heads

The first thing I did when I saw the mighty Mississippi River was piss into it. It wasn't for the purpose of ceremony, but because I was desperate. We were near a small town called Winona. There was some sort of governmental shack next to the river that had a sign on it:

According to common decency and Minnesota law,
it is illegal to urinate into the Mississippi
River.

But by the time I saw the sign, it was too late.

'River snake, river snake,' Lucy yelled. I changed my gaze from across the river to into it. Swimming just a few feet in front of me was a thick snake, about a metre long. It had black and yellow stripes on its back. It stopped in front of us, assessing the scene, then turned.

'There's another one,' Lucy said. She was excited.

A second snake, smaller than the first, swam up and the two intertwined, in some sort of courtship or copulation ritual. After a few minutes they disengaged and swam off up the river.

We got back in the car and drove off.

Some later research revealed that the snakes were cotton-mouths. Also known as a water moccasin, they are a type of viper that can deliver a fatal bite.

The Greyhound routes in the New England area were not very extensive, so we'd hired a car in Boston, a Chevrolet Impala. Our very own Dog.

The man at the car hire office attempted the usual up sell—roadside insurance, pick up insurance, break down insurance and a host of others that I didn't fully understand. We had general insurance and I declined the rest.

'What if you get a flat tyre?' he said. 'Or lose your keys? That's common. Or even lock them in the car? That'll cost you $300.' He must have been on a commission.

I didn't take anything that he offered, but he made his money on the drop off location. Because we were leaving the car in Chicago, an exorbitant penalty fee was charged.

After weeks on the Dog, it was refreshing to have the freedom of a car, to be able to stop when we wanted and eat where we wanted. The Greyhound drivers all stop at specific places along their routes. It tends to be a Burger King or other fast food outlet and it never varies because the driver gets his food for free as a goodwill gesture.

But with the Impala, we were able to get food from supermarkets, and Walmart was our company of choice. Most towns had a Walmart, and whilst they varied in size, they were generally enormous with every foodstuff money could buy.

Every town in America, no matter how small, also seems to have an airport. As you drive across the country, huge towers can be seen in the distance. They must stand 100 feet high and signify the presence of a town. They have a large bulb on the top that has the name of the town written on it. These monstrosities look like water towers and they're generally white, except in Texas where they're blue, just to be different.

In remote places, you'll see the town marker tower from miles away and get excited that there might be a place to eat there or something like that. But quite often, the town will consist of nothing but a few houses and a petrol station. And an airport. There's almost always an airport.

From Boston, we drove up through New Hampshire and Maine and into the White Mountains of Vermont. The verdant countryside was beautiful, with pines and hills and rivers with rapids and rocks.

We drove along a quiet stretch of highway in the woods, following a creek, and as dusk was approaching, I saw some movement next to the water. I stopped the car and we got out and walked into the bushes. There was a moose drinking on the other side of the creek. It was a magnificent creature, albeit ungainly, almost Frankenstein-like, as if a bunch of unrelated body parts had been cobbled together. It looked up at us, and sensing danger, turned and trotted to the cover of a thicket of trees.

We stayed the night in Vermont in a wooden lodge that was run by lesbians, and the next day visited a maple syrup factory as well as the original Ben and Jerry's ice-cream factory, where we did a tour.

From there we headed into the eastern side of Canada, stopping in the very European city of Montreal, before driving the monotonous trek past Toronto and down to Niagara Falls. The only thing to see in that eight hours of stark driving was a multitude of dead racoons on the side of the road.

The driving was slow going in Canada, as, like their American neighbours, the Canadians can't drive for shit. We found the drivers throughout America to be terrible. They are timid and cautious and are sticklers for the speed limit, usually driving at ten miles per hour under it. There are many road signs advising that the speed limits are constantly monitored by overhead aircraft, so perhaps this scare tactic has worked. We didn't see any aircraft patrols at all, and in fact, whilst there are many rules and threats about speeding in America, virtually none of them are monitored or enforced and there are certainly no speed cameras.

The caravans and the RVs are the worst. A lot of those drivers are retirees with nothing to do and all day to do it in. They amble along at their own pace, without a care in the world. Each RV has a different name painted on it—Raptor, Cougar, Falcon, Grey Wolf—desperately trying to add to their contrived sense of freedom and adventure. The man will drive with one arm casually resting out the window to portray a free-spirit, his middle-aged woman, with purpose-fully grey hair and no bra, sitting dutifully by his side and hating every minute of it.

I found them particularly vexing.

'This is ridiculous,' I yelled to Lucy after being trapped behind one for half an hour. It was a common occurrence. 'I fucking hate caravans. It's these slow vehicles that cause accidents because of the frustration of other drivers.'

'I'd like to shoot out its tyres and watch it career off the road,' Lucy said.

'Yeah and see it explode in a ball of flames. How satisfying would that be?'

Mind you, everybody's tough when they're in a car.

Niagara Falls was very impressive. I'd seen many photos of it over the years, but to see it in person was something else. We caught a boat out onto the water that took us next to the falls and got us very wet, despite the fluorescent blue plastic ponchos that were provided.

Everyone said it was better from the Canadian side, which is where we were. I could see people across on the American side and it didn't look any different for them. The same was said at Iguazu Falls in South America, which sits between Argentina and Brazil. 'You've got to see it from the Argentinean side,' the zealots said. But when you're on a boat in the middle of the water, there's no difference.

A refreshingly quick border control took us into New York. We were glad to be back in America. A large sign read 'Welcome to New York—the Empire State'. I had no idea what that meant. It was also the motto on the New York car licence plate.

Every state in America has a licence plate motto, some more glamorous than others. Alabama's is 'Sweet Home Alabama', New Hampshire's is the threatening 'Live Free or Die', and Arkansas, a place that nobody from outside America can pinpoint, has 'Land of Opportunity'. Iowa is the inspired 'Corn State', while Kentucky is 'It's That Friendly'. North Dakota is 'Discover the Spirit' and Maryland is the simple yet sensible 'Drive Carefully'.

But it's not just the American drivers that cause problems on the road. There are a number of other hazards to contend with as well.

Not only do time zones change as you cross into certain states, so do the speed limits. Driving on the exact same road, the limit will suddenly change from seventy-five to fifty-five, and the only difference is the passing of a 'Welcome to Missouri— The Show Me State' sign.

The road signs are generally done in numbers. Highway 10, Interstate 95, or just 25. Often there are no city names on the signs, only the numbers. It would be impossible to navigate without a map.

There is also roadwork everywhere in America. There are reduced speed limits in these areas, but the strange part is, there's rarely any roadwork going on. There'll be trucks and machinery parked by the road, flashing lights and red traffic cones in their hundreds, but no workers. I think the Yanks like to show the appearance of road work so they can reduce the speed limit, which is lowered solely for the protection of the traffic cones.

Then out of the blue, on an open highway, a set of traffic lights will be strung across the open road. And they're always red, even if there are no cars anywhere else.

And then there are the ten-lane highways. The Americans love them. Just to bypass a small town, the lanes will start multiplying. Then, for no apparent reason, they'll become congested with cars without you noticing, like how a bar fills up when you're drunk. And then you sit there and you never know how long it's going to last. Americans spend more time sitting in traffic than anyone else in the world.

Fortunately, there is a lot of music on the radio to pass the time. If you can get away from the Christian and Country channels, there are many others to suit every taste. A lot of them are dedicated to specific artists—Just Elvis, Seriously Sinatra and E Street Radio. And there are decade-specific channels ranging from the 1920s up to the present day.

Once back in America, we started crossing the country— New York, Pennsylvania, Ohio, Michigan, Indiana, Wisconsin, Minnesota, Iowa and Illinios. A lot of the scenery was the same. It was mainly farming land, with vast plains of crops and small houses built right next to the road. That was the case throughout America. People have all this land in incredible locations, but their houses are tiny and are right next to the main road. Whilst small and badly placed, the houses were almost always immaculate. But their barns weren't. Most properties in the rural areas had big red barns with peaked roofs. And most of them were so decrepit that they were about to collapse.

It wasn't just us crossing America. There were trucks too. Thousands of them. At one point, the road in front of us was filled with nothing but trucks. Their licence plates are from all over America as they haul goods from east to west and back again. They are required by law to travel ten miles per hour under the speed limit. They are also required to stay in the slow lane. They adhere to the first law, but not the second, making for more vexation on the roads.

The petrol stations aren't straightforward either.

Quite often we'd stop at them when we didn't need petrol, but so we could use the toilet. A lot of them have the 'Restrooms are only for customers' sign up, but we'd do what I called the 'Wee, Browse and Go' technique. There's not much to it really. You walk in and go straight to the toilet, without making eye contact with anyone. On the way out, you look around the food or magazines in the shop, pretending you're going to buy something, but at the last second you decide against it and leave. It worked well.

Getting petrol is a little more complicated.

Petrol must be paid for up front, either by swiping a credit card at the pump, or by paying inside with cash first. What confused me was that I never knew how much money was needed to fill the tank. I'd put $20 in, then if the tank wasn't full, go back inside and get another $10. It wasn't until I'd done this on about twenty occasions, that someone told me you can get change—if you give them $50 and the tank fills at $40, you go inside and get $10 back. Either way, a lot of trips inside are required.

We were in a two-star town in the middle of nowhere in Iowa and stopped to get petrol. Two rednecks were sitting next to each other outside, not speaking. They stared at me as I went in to pay.

'Can I get $30 worth please?' I said to Kenneth, the old man who ran the station. His name was embroidered on his overalls.

'I tell you what,' he said. 'Just go out and pump the gas. If you fill the tank and pay with cash, I'll give you a discount. A big discount.'

'Okay, thanks,' I said, and went out and filled up the tank.

'How much is it?' Lucy said from within the car when I'd finished.

'It's come to $42,' I said. 'But he's going to give me a cash discount.'

'That's good.'

I went back inside.

'Hello again,' he said. 'Okay, that'll be $41.60.'

America is a big country. We'd driven 3,400 kilometres in six days and didn't seem to put a dent on the map. But despite the many tribulations of driving yourself around America, it's always going to be better than being on that wretched Dog.

15

THAT TODDLING TOWN

'Chicago, that toddling town. Chicago, Chicago, I'll show you around. I love it.'

—'Chicago', Frank Sinatra

My first impressions of Chicago were not good.

We'd driven in along an impossible ten-lane highway where we were forced to pay a $2 toll every five minutes. Then after we'd dropped off our hire car in the city, I waited out on the street, while Lucy went to the bathroom.

I saw a badly dressed man looking at me from across the road. His body language was all wrong. Someone should do a Mugger's Handbook for these idiots. He looked at me, quickly looked away, then eyes to the ground, before slowly looking back at me. It's all so obvious. He walked across the street, gazing at the tops of the buildings, before appearing at my side. I'd seen this procedure done innumerable times in South America, culminating in a gun being pulled on me down a side street in Buenos Aires one day. You could see it coming a mile away. Their routine was no different wherever you were, and with a few simple tips, they'd meet with far more success. On this occasion in Chicago, I made the mistake of looking at a map, which gave him an excuse to approach.

'Need any help?' he asked. His clothes were tattered and unwashed, as was his hair. He had grime on his face.

'No thanks.'

'Here, let me have a look,' he said. He stepped in closer and grabbed my map, touching me on the arm. I was conscious that all our bags were on the ground around me, too many for me to contain alone.

I'd always found this state of affairs somewhat of a conundrum. The aggressive approach may scare them away, but may also incite an attack. The polite approach may defuse the situation, but may give them encouragement.

I chose aggression.

'Don't fucking touch me,' I snapped. 'Give me the map.'

'Well, sooorrry,' he said as he stepped back.

But he hung around behind me, only a few metres away, and I could feel him looking at our bags, waiting for the slightest opportunity to pounce.

Lucy returned and we walked to the subway station. The vagabond followed us, always keeping a safe distance. As we got to the station, two other similarly attired men came up to us.

'Need any help?' one of them said.

I just growled at them and we walked into the station.

We bought tickets and boarded the train. Our carriage was full. I counted thirty-six passengers and we were the only whites. A number of them looked homeless and nearly everyone was staring at us. It was an intimidating journey. We got off at the end of the line and three young men followed us from the train. Our hotel wasn't far from the station and we walked there quickly and went inside, leaving the youths to mill around out on the street.

After checking in, we went up to our room and turned on the television while we unpacked.

'For God's sake,' I said. 'Not Paula Dean again.'

Paula Dean had been haunting us throughout America. When it wasn't Keeping Up With The Kardashians on television, it was Paula Dean. She was a middle-aged lady from Georgia who we'd first heard about in Savannah. She'd made a fortune from her own cooking show and the many spin-off products—$35 million in the prior year alone. She had curly grey hair and was overweight, probably from eating the food she made, which was known for its fat content—fried cheesecake with cream was one of her specialties. She really hammed up her Southern accent, constantly saying 'y'all', and I couldn't help but think her off-screen twang wasn't quite as pronounced. We'd had enough of her.

Lucy picked up the remote control. It wouldn't change the channels and the electronic guide had Paula Dean on for the next three hours.

No, my first impressions of Chicago were not good.

But things quickly improved.

Our hotel was actually very nice. The room was mainly wooden, with French drapes, large windows and covered furniture. It was situated in Oak Park, an affluent outer suburb of Chicago.

We walked out into the sunshine. Oak Park was more like a village, with boutique shops, art galleries and quaint outdoor restaurants. We visited the home where the architect Frank Lloyd Wright once lived and saw streets of houses that he'd designed, with their circular turrets, peaked roofs and wide lawns.

Lucy did some shopping, while I went to Ernest Hemingway's birth home, as well as a nearby museum that was dedicated to the author.

We met back at our room, before having a steak dinner and a few drinks at the hotel bar and grill.

The next day we explored the city of Chicago.

My knowledge of Chicago was limited solely to gangster movies and Frank Sinatra's eponymous song. But I found it to be a very impressive city.

The thing to do in Chicago is the architectural boat cruise and that's what we did.

The tour guide was a teenage girl and she explained everything there was to know about the city.

'The name Chicago is derived from a Native American word meaning 'wild onion' or 'wild garlic' because of the plants that grew on the banks of the river,' she said. 'And, contrary to popular belief, the 'Windy City' nickname is not because of the weather, but due to a 19th Century rivalry between Chicago and Cincinnati, the Cincinnati journalists referring to people from Chicago as 'windy' because of their big talk and bluster.' She knew a lot.

The weather certainly wasn't windy when we were there. It was a bright and hot day as the boat took us along the river, winding through the incredible array of buildings, before reaching Lake Michigan in all its glory.

The Great Chicago Fire of the late 1800s led to the largest building boom in the history of America and precipitated the first steel-framed high-rise building that started the skyscraper era across the country.

Even now, Chicago's skyline is among the tallest and most dense in the world, and when seen from the river, the architecture is breathtaking. The Wrigley Building, Willis Tower, Trump International Hotel and Tower, Tribune Tower, the Fine Arts Building. It feels like you've been transported back to the 1920s. It's beautiful.

The other thing to do in Chicago is eat pizza and we did that too.

Chicago is famous for its deep pan pizza. The crust on them is literally three inches thick, with the toppings on that. We found a pizza place on State Street and ate there until we were almost unable to walk. Paula Dean would have been proud.

By the time we made it back to our hotel, it was after dark. It had been a long day and we lay on the bed.

I looked across at Lucy. She was crying.

'What's wrong?' I said. 'Are you alright?'

'I'm just exhausted, that's all,' she said. 'I'm so tired I feel sick.'

That was all she said, but I woke up in the night and she was still crying.

'Are you okay?' I said to her. I looked at the clock. It was 3am. 'Have you slept?'

'It's nothing,' she said. 'I don't know what's wrong with me.'

'Come here.'

I pulled her over and stroked her head. We lay like that for two hours, before dozing off to sleep.

I awoke to the sound of the 6am alarm. We had to get out of bed early to catch the Dog to St. Louis. We packed up and left the room and went down to reception to check out of the hotel.

'It says here that you only owe $11,' said the woman behind the desk. 'But it should be $111.' She was well dressed and about fifty, but didn't have quite as much going for her as she imagined.

'I don't owe anything,' I said. 'I paid it all when I checked in.'

'I know you paid some,' she said. 'But you still owe $111. You see, you were supposed to be across the road in our motel, but you've been staying here in the hotel.'

'Well, that's neither here nor there,' I said. 'I didn't ask for that and I'm not paying for it.'

She didn't respond, just turned to a man standing next to her. He was about my age.

'Look, that's fine,' he said. 'We do upgrades all the time. There'll be no charge for the hotel.'

'Thank you,' I said.

The woman was not happy that she'd been overruled. She looked shirty, a veiled look of contempt in her eyes.

'Well,' she said. 'You heard my boss. That'll be $11 then.'

'No. I paid everything at check-in. I don't owe a thing.'

'Look,' she said. 'I've already let you off $100 as you were meant to be in the motel. So now you just owe $11.'

'I know what you think. I heard you the first time.'

'Then I'll have to telephone my colleague who checked you in.'

She rang the man and spoke in mumbled tones for a few minutes and then hung up the phone.

'He confirmed that you owe $11,' she said.

'What did he say?' I said. 'Verbatim will suffice.'

'That you owe $11.'

We were in a rush to catch the Dog and I could see that she was not going to back down after the embarrassment with her boss. I threw $10 on the desk.

'That's all you're getting,' I said. 'I trust that handles the matter.'

'Fine.' She snatched the $10 bill and put it in a drawer. 'But just so we're clear, you were meant to be in the motel, not the hotel. Do you understand?'

'Yes,' I said. 'It's not a subtle point you're making. But just so we're clear, you shouldn't try to blame other people for your ineptitude.'

16

THE TEXAS EAGLE

'*I hear the train a comin', it's rollin' round the bend...*'

—'Folsom Prison Blues', Johnny Cash

The Greyhound from Chicago to St. Louis is always full. We knew that going in. And we did all we could to ensure we got a seat. But it wasn't enough and it was never going to be.

We arrived at the bus station at 7am for the 9am departure. Normally an hour before is all you need and all that is allowed, but the earlier the better, we thought.

'Two tickets on the 9am to St. Louis,' I said to the standard ticket counter attendant. There is no point using 'pleases' and 'thank yous' with the Dog employees. State the facts clearly and simply and move on.

'What type of ticket you waaant?' She made no eye contact.

'We've got Discovery Passes.'

'That bus sold out.'

'Because we have Discovery Passes, or generally?' It wasn't the first time we'd been discriminated against because we held a Pass.

'It sold out.'

'Would you mind checking anyway?' I said. She hadn't even looked at the computer screen.

'I'm telling you, it sold out.'

'Well, what should we do?'

'Next bus is six hours after thaaat,' she said. 'You can come back then if you like. And not more than an hour before. You way too early now.'

'Can I reserve seats on that bus now?'

'No. Come back an hour before.'

'It's a shocking system isn't it?' I was becoming frustrated. 'Are we likely to get seats then?'

'You might get on,' she said. 'Won't know until 2pm.'

'But you know this bus is booked out and it's two hours before.'

'Look, come back an hour before,' she said. 'If that don't suit ya, get the hell out of here.'

'Thanks for your help,' I said. 'Have a nice day.'

'Next,' she yelled.

I couldn't face that harridan again, so I asked another employee if there was anywhere to leave our bags. We thought we could leave them at the station and then poke around the city for a few hours to pass the time. She just looked at me and, without saying a word, pointed at some lockers in the far corner of the waiting room, before turning away.

We went over to the lockers, but they were all taken. After twenty minutes of standing there, trying to come to terms with the idea of waiting at the station for six hours, someone emptied their locker and we went to use it. It would only fit one of our bags and, in any event, cost $4 an hour. To leave all our bags for six hours, we would have to wait for two more lockers to become available and the total cost would amount to $72.

'Let's try the train station,' Lucy said. 'They might have cheaper lockers.'

'Anywhere but here,' I said. 'I'd like to take a flame-thrower to this place.'

We walked to Union Station, which was only ten minutes away. But the lockers were equally expensive there.

'Christ,' I said. 'What the hell are we going to do?' I was at the end of my tether.

'Why don't we see how much the train is?' Lucy said.

'Good idea,' I said. 'You're always thinking, you lovely little thing.'

We went up to the ticket counter, more out of interest than with any realistic hope. A middle-aged lady was there. She smiled at us.

'Good day,' she said. 'How can I help you?'

It felt like some sort of joke. Like we were being filmed for a comedy show or something.

'How much are two tickets to St. Louis?' I asked.

'Just a minute, sir. I'll have a look for you.'

She typed on her keyboard for a few seconds, then looked back at me, still smiling.

'There's a train leaving in an hour, sir. The Texas Eagle. Tickets are $52 each.'

'We'll take two,' I said. There was no point checking with Lucy.

The woman printed off two tickets and handed them to me and I paid her.

'Give these tickets to the conductor when you board from gate 6,' she said. 'Thank you very much and have a nice day.'

'Thank you,' I said. 'Very much. This is far better than Greyhound, you know?'

'Yes,' she said. 'I've heard that before.'

A scene in many movies, Chicago's Union Station is stately and impressive, with brass railings, polished wooden benches and high ceilings. I posed for a photo on the set of steps that had been used in *The Untouchables*. An old man was watching.

'That's a great photo,' he said as I walked down the stairs. 'Really great.'

'Thanks.'

'You have a great day, sir,' he said.

He was laughing and very gentlemanly. The old-timers, both men and women, are generally polite and friendly. They are meticulous about small courtesies. It's the other ages that tend to be the problem.

We boarded the Texas Eagle and were shown to our seats by a steward. Whilst we were set to get off in St. Louis, the train was bound for Texas, hence its name.

Our seats were roomy and comfortable, there was fully functioning Wi-Fi, and the staff were helpful, not acting as if they were doing us a favour.

The Eagle rode down the middle of America, through the length of Illinois and into Missouri. We passed farms of crops, as well as shotgun shacks by the side of the line that couldn't have been worth a penny. We saw families of Amish driving between fields in horse-drawn carriages. I always thought that the Amish all lived in a specific area, but they are all over America. Wherever they are seen, everyone else looks at them like they're aliens.

An hour into the seven hour journey, we discovered the dining cart and its well-stocked bar. Lucy went and bought a Budweiser and a gin and tonic, was ID'ed, and came back with a smile. We drank them and I went and got some more.

It was a great trip down the middle of America. We laughed and chatted and drank the whole way. By the time those glorious big steel wheels rolled in to our final stop, the sun was setting over the Gateway Arch of St. Louis and we were drunk.

17

WHAT SEEMS TO BE THE TROUBLE, OFFICER?

'We drove eight hundred miles without seeing a cop, we got rock and roll music blasting off the T-top'

—'Darlington County', Bruce Springsteen

He must have only been fifty yards in front of me and I was doing at least eighty. He was standing in the middle of the road, dressed all in black. I hit the brakes and the wheels locked, skidding the car to a stop a short distance from the man.

It was a cop. There was a brief pause while he looked at me and me at him. Then he slowly walked up to my side of the car, his right hand resting on the gun off his hip.

I wound the window down and looked at his face. He was wearing dark aviator-style sunglasses.

'What seems to be the trouble, officer?' I said.

'I don't mean to be funny or smart,' he said. 'But can y'all see me alright? I'm not sure you can see me from within the vee-hickle.'

'It was a little hard,' I said, quite relieved. 'With you in black against the black road.'

'I thought that might be the case. It's just that I'm clearing this accident here and I have to be out on the road.'

On the side of the highway were the remnants of a three car pile up. The cars were being hooked up to tow trucks and there was shattered glass on the road.

'Maybe one of those high-visibility vests might help,' I said.

'You're dead right about that, sir. We need to do something. It weren't long back that poor ol' Billy Joe passed on.' He looked up at the sky and crossed himself.

There'd been a sign a little earlier stating that the highway was in honour of Officer Billy Joe.

'Thank you very much for your time, sir,' he said. 'Y'all have a nice day now.'

'Can I ask you a quick question?' I said.

'Sure can. Shoot.' An interesting choice of word in the circumstances.

'Why is it that all the police in America wear that type of sunglasses?'

'Well, I don't rightly know,' he said. The look of a confused dog came over him. 'Just like them, I guess.'

'Oh, okay,' I said. 'I thought they must have been standard issue.'

'Nope,' he said, then nodded, as if he'd got to the crux of a long-standing puzzle. 'It's just that we like them.'

We were in Tennessee and it was obviously a treacherous

stretch of highway. Every few miles there was an electronic sign above the road advising that there had been 425 deaths. When we drove back a day later the number was up to 428.

Perhaps that was the reason there were a lot of cops out that weekend. We drove all around Tennessee and the police were out in force. The same was true in Virginia and along most of the east coast. Every few minutes there was a cop car waiting on the side of the highway, partially hidden, or pulled up behind an unfortunate motorist, the policeman standing at the window of the offending vehicle, just like in the movies.

On the other hand, we drove for two weeks through Wyoming, the Dakotas and Montana and didn't see a cop at all.

The standard American policeman fits the stereotype perfectly. They never smile, are usually dressed in black like they're part of a SWAT team out on a raid, and without exception, wear dark or mirrored Aviator sunglasses. They eat a lot of doughnuts as well, or look as if they do, because they are generally fat. Most are bordering on obese. They waddle along, quite often with some sort of limp, and I could never imagine them giving chase on foot, let alone apprehending a suspect. A lot of them are fairly old as well, and we never once saw a woman police officer.

Then there are the cop cars. Every kind for every town. State trooper, state police, constable, highway patrol, sheriff, local police—these are the titles emblazoned on the side of the cars. I never got to the bottom of what meant what, or the difference between any of them. The cars were invariably painted with blacks, browns or blues and looked like they'd come straight from a 1970s police show. In the Rocky Mountains of Colorado they were pick-up trucks, but the design was just the same.

We stopped one night in Tennessee at Bull's Gap, near to where Davy Crockett was born. I asked the receptionist at our hotel where the nearest convenience store was. Five miles, she told me. If a Tennessean tells you something is five miles, double it. We experienced this in Memphis when we were told it was one mile to town. After forty minutes of fast-paced walking, we still hadn't made it. And at Bull's Gap, the convenience store was eleven miles away. When we got there, it was shut. The receptionist probably knew that, but because we hadn't posed that exact question, she didn't think to tell us. That's country folk for you.

'What a nightmare,' Lucy said.

'Yeah,' I said. 'It's more like an inconvenience store.'

'Everything seems shut.'

There was nothing open at all, and our hotel didn't serve food. It was 7pm and we had driven all day and needed something to eat. We found a McDonalds and it was the only thing open. We had no option.

As we were approaching the restaurant, I saw a policeman standing just inside the door.

'There must be some kind of trouble,' I said to Lucy.

'I don't think so,' she said. 'He's just waiting for his dinner like everybody else.'

And so he was. He was a typical cop, big and fat, who loved to eat. They all love to eat. Maybe it's the nature of the job and always being on the move, but they love to eat, and it's always fast food. We went inside.

For a number of years I've had a theory that women are getting better looking. It is based on sexual selection, a revolutionary concept introduced by Charles Darwin in the 1800s. The males of many species compete fiercely for the females, who sit back and wait to be courted, before selecting the most appealing mate. This has resulted in the males becoming more ornate and aesthetically pleasing in order to set themselves apart and impress the females. It is these males who are selected to reproduce, thereby passing on their genes and making their offspring even better looking. Prime examples are the colourful feathers of many male birds, the huge antlers on the elk and the mane of the male lion, compared with their female counterparts, who appear more drab. Sexual selection is predicated on the fact that the male is the aggressor and has to court the female, who does not need to impress. This has been the case throughout history with the human species. But in modern society with the advent of the women's liberation movement, women have become more proactive, approaching and actively seeking out suitable mates. The sexual predatory nature of the modern woman has meant that men have been able to pick and choose to a greater extent, selecting the most attractive partner. And just as it works in the animal kingdom, my theory is that this has resulted in women becoming better looking.

Bull's Gap in Tennessee is not the place to case study this theory. In Bull's Gap the women are breathtakingly ugly. And the McDonalds was their headquarters. They all looked inbred and angry, as if the world owed them a favour. It was a Friday night, and most of them wore ample make up and clothes that were far too scanty. Then there were the truckers and redneck men sniffing around trying to take disadvantage of them. It was a haven for them as well.

Everyone was staring at Lucy and me, like we were from another planet. I'm sure the only thing that stopped us from getting killed was the presence of the cop. But then he got his food, sat down and started devouring it.

'My God, look at her,' I said to Lucy, as quietly as I could. 'She could scare a hungry dog out of a butcher's shop.'

I was referring to the woman behind the till, who was about to serve us. She was obese, dour-faced, and she was not friendly.

'Yes, next,' she barked at us.

We placed our order.

'You'll have to repeat that,' she spat.

I did.

'Again,' she said.

I said it again and it seemed to register with her.

'Now wait over there,' she said, pointing at the wall. 'Next.'

We stood over next to the wall. Everyone kept watching us. The cop was busy eating.

'I bet she's come straight from the Greyhound counter,' Lucy said.

'She'd certainly fit right in there,' I said. 'I must say though, I'll be happy if we get out of here alive.'

Our food was announced and we walked up to get it.

'Eat in or take away?' the woman yelled at us.

'Take away,' we said in unison, and snatched for the food.

As we were bustling out the door, the cop was lining up for seconds.

We spent the next two days driving around Tennessee, West Virginia and North Carolina. We drove 1,770 kilometres in that time. We went to the Jack Daniel's distillery in Lynchburg, which was very well done out—professional and commercial and not rustic like the advertisements portray—before crossing into the Great Smoky Mountains, a sub-range of the Appalachians.

The scenery in the mountains was breathtaking, with knobbly oak trees overlooking the vast timbered plains below. Walking to one look-out point we heard some movement in the undergrowth, and right next to the path was a female black bear and her two cubs, digging in the ground, a chipmunk watching from the safety of a branch above.

On the way back to Nashville, we stopped at a Subway fast food restaurant. It was in the middle of nowhere, just off the highway.

'Where y'all coming from?' said the teenage girl who served us.

I told her we were from England.

'By golly,' she said. 'That sure is a long way from here. Now I tell ya, you must go to the Chattanooga aquarium. It's well and truly amazing.'

'But we're a long way from the sea,' I said.

'It's amazing,' she said. 'How long you got away from home?'

'Three months.'

'That's amazing. You're so lucky.'

'I can't complain,' I said. 'But sometimes I still do.'

'How long you been gawn for?'

'Four weeks so far.'

'Man,' she said. 'I just couldn't do it. No way could I do that. I just wouldn't want to.'

'No way I could serve Subway sandwiches to people every day in Backwater, USA either,' I felt like saying, but didn't.

She gave us our food and we said goodbye. As we were leaving, we passed six cops who were on their way in for lunch.

18

MEGA-DOG

'I love my dog as much as I love you. But you may fade, my dog will always come through.'

—'I Love My Dog', Cat Stevens

After the Dog ride from Hell that took us from St. Louis to Nashville, we had to do something. We didn't have the nerve or the stamina to face another Dog so soon afterwards, nor to go back to the Nashville Greyhound station for that matter.

We needed to get from Nashville to Memphis, but the train line didn't run there and we didn't want to hire another car. Whilst riding on the Dog, we'd seen another bus company called Mega-Bus. It was a big blue double-decker style of bus with tinted windows. It looked expensive, but we were desperate.

I checked it out online. I was able to book an exact bus at a time that we wanted and even reserve seats. Tickets weren't needed. I was given a reservation code and all I had to do was present it to the driver and he would check it off a list. What's more, it cost $9 instead of $80 for the same trip on

Greyhound. It all seemed too good to be true. I assumed there would be a catch, that it would be dire, but how much worse than Greyhound could it really be? I booked it.

We arrived at the designated pick up point an hour before the scheduled departure. I knew we were early, but we had to leave the hotel so I thought we might as well wait for the bus, it being our first time.

There was a group of twenty people waiting in the sun by the roadside. Because of the Nashville Country Music Awards, the usual bus station in the centre of town was closed. But something didn't seem quite right. There was discontentment in the air. People were milling around discussing things, all with earnest faces. Some were on their phones. Things didn't look good. I thought I'd better check.

'Are you here for the 2pm Mega-Bus?' I said to a woman standing near us. She was one of a group of middle-aged black women.

'Wha you say?' she spat at me.

I repeated my question.

'Hell no, we here for the twev o'clock.'

'The twelve o'clock?' I said.

'Tha's right.'

'But it's one,' I said.

'I know what time it is. Our bus is late. I don't think it comin' at all.'

I reported back to Lucy.

'This is not looking good,' she said.

'No,' I said. 'Not a good start at all.'

A few minutes later, someone who had spoken to the bus company reported to everyone that the 12pm bus had broken down and it wasn't coming, nor was any replacement.

The group of women sat in silence for a few minutes before conferring.

'Wha the hell we gunna do?' one said.

'We can't fly,' another said. 'We ain't got the money.'

'But I got hotel reservations I just can't cancel.'

One rang her husband in Chicago. Despite it only being an eight hour drive away, it was clear from hearing one side of the conversation that he wasn't going to help out in any way.

'Excuse me ladies,' I said. 'An option might be Greyhound. They've got a station in town.'

'Greyhound,' one said. 'Heeeell no.'

The group continued to sit in the blazing sun for the next hour, thinking that if they waited long enough, it might not be true.

When the lack of hope finally registered, one of them phoned Greyhound and arranged tickets on the next bus to Chicago. They then trudged away, without thanks or comment to me, that inherent dislike yet again.

Despite some genuine misgivings, at 2.05pm, our Mega-Bus rolled in, just slightly behind schedule. An enormous bus driver who resembled Fat Albert got out. I gave him my reservation code and he motioned us on to the bus. He was friendly enough, until he picked up Lucy's 30 kilogram suitcase and hurled it under the bus as if it were a handbag.

'Now give me yours,' he said.

'You grab some others,' I said. 'I'll put mine in.'

Still ambivalent about our choice of transportation, we walked up onto the bus. But it was a revelation. We climbed up to the top level (Greyhound is always single) and had two seats each (Greyhound rarely has spare seats), right at the front of the bus, a perfect view of the highway before us. The air-conditioning was at a pleasant temperature (on Greyhound it's always too hot or too cold or there isn't any), there were functioning seat belts (they don't exist on Greyhound), and the Wi-Fi actually worked (it doesn't on Greyhound). The bus set off, and unlike Greyhound, no rules or regulations were announced. And the clientele seemed far less threatening. For once we were not scared for our lives. And for once we were in complete comfort.

'This is amazing,' Lucy said.

'I know,' I said. 'There's got to be a catch. This only cost us $9.'

'It's ridiculous. How can Greyhound compete?'

'Compete?' I said. 'With this sort of competition, I have no idea how Greyhound even exists.'

It wasn't the Mega-Bus. It was the Mega-Dog. And it took us all the way to Memphis in style.

19

THE CITY OF NEW ORLEANS

'Good morning America how are you? Don't you know me, I'm your native son. I'm the train they call The City of New Orleans.'

—'The City of New Orleans', Willie Nelson

I sat in seat 1 on the City of New Orleans train. That was the name of the train. The line ran the length of America— 900 miles from Chicago to New Orleans. The train was very comfortable, with big leather seats and plenty of leg room. Far superior to the Dog. I'd got there early. I had seats 1 and 2. Lucy's ticket was for seat 2. It was 6.35am. I'd got a cab from the Memphis hotel room, the room that Lucy had left the night before, and it had only taken five minutes to get to the station. The train wasn't scheduled to depart until 6.50am and I knew it wouldn't leave early. I kept looking out the window, craning my neck trying to see down the platform and to the ticket office where people were gathering for the trip. I never really thought there was any chance of Lucy turning up at the station, but the mind can play tricks. I decided there was no point looking again. I turned again. I couldn't help it. I kept watching the platform. I had Lucy's ticket, but she'd find a way to get on. At 6.45am a taxi pulled up and a girl got out. She had blue jeans on and a yellow vest top, one of Lucy's outfits. My heart increased a beat. She had long and dark hair, but it wasn't Lucy's long, dark hair. It wasn't Lucy's body.

Lucy had phoned me the night before from another hotel in Memphis.

'I'm here,' she said. 'I thought I'd let you know. That you'd want to know.'

'Thanks,' I said. 'You can still come with me tomorrow.'

'I can't,' she said, then paused. 'I'll think about it.' Some hope.

'Okay. I hope you do. I've got your ticket. I'll be at the station at 6.30 and the train leaves at 6.50.'

'Okay,' she said. 'I've got to go.' She hung up.

I kept looking at the girl on the platform, somehow thinking that she might turn into Lucy.

Just before 7am the conductor blew a whistle and waved an orange flag. The old metal wheels creaked on the tracks and the train laboured away from Memphis, slowly picking up steam. Seat 2 remained empty. I was alone.

I watched blankly out the window as the pine trees sped past, along with my hopes. The train cut through Mississippi, where shotgun shacks lined the side of the tracks. By the time the train reached the bayou swamp and a sign read 'God Bless Louisiana', we were in New Orleans and ten hours had raced by, just like the last two years had. A wasted two years.

I walked out of the station and into the New Orleans sun. There was a taxi queue out next to the road in the heat. You could see the heat coming up from the bitumen. A Mustang Man—at least, he would have been in his youth; he was seventy-five or so now—was standing by the road with a crutch in one hand. His other hand gripped a cellophane-wrapped custard pie. He was not letting go of that pie. He was marshalling the taxi queue, telling which people to get into which cab and directing the taxis to the curb. He wasn't employed by anyone.

A woman behind me was muttering loudly to herself.

'He's ordering the cabs,' she said. 'He's in charge. This is the line. I'm behind this man. This lady's behind me.'

I turned to looked at her. She was a middle-aged woman with a moustache. She was fat. They were all fat. I turned away to stop myself from retching. I got in the next cab. The driver was a black man of about fifty.

'Where you heading, sir?' he asked.

I told him.

'Hell, man,' he said. 'That's a mighty fine hotel you're staying in. Hell, sir,' he corrected.

We drove for a few seconds and he didn't put the meter on. Cabbies invariably put the meter on immediately and when they don't, they are usually trying a rort.

'Is this on the meter?' I asked.

'Ten dollar standard fare, sir,' he yelled. 'It's all written there on the window. $10 from the bus station.'

'Ah, that old chestnut,' I said. The standard fare from air-ports, train stations and bus stations is such bullshit and I've never got to the bottom of the reasoning for it. It's always overpriced.

'Yes, sir.' He was yelling every word.

'How's the weather here?' I asked. 'I saw on the TV that there'd been some rain.'

'Rain,' he yelled. 'Hell, man. Yesty we had five, six inches. Man, it rained. Rained. But in patches. That's called isolated, you know?'

'What about now?'

'Now? Now, it's not raining.' It wasn't raining.

'Yeah, but the next few days?'

'Hell, man. I wouldn't know. How would I know?'

He drove on.

'See that street we just crossed?' he said. 'That's the start of the French Quarter.'

'Is that Canal Street?'

'Yeah. Canal Street. Start of the French Quarter. The French Quarter. It's the best Quarter. Hell, man, there's Bourbon Street. Bourbon Street. French Quarter is safe too. Lots of policemen walking round,' he yelled, emphasising the 'oh' in 'policemen'. 'You think you're talking to a normal person. Turns out it's a policeman.'

'Are they undercover?'

'Yes, sir. Undercover, uniforms, every damn thing. Yes, man. Yes, sir.'

'Which way's the river?' I asked.

'This way's the river,' he said, pointing down the road in front of the cab. 'The Mississippi River. Yes, sir. You climb the stairs at Du Monde's over there and you can see all the way to that river, the Mississippi River. The Mighty Mississippi.'

'Du Monde's?'

'That's right. You're in a real good hotel. Real good. And you're just across from Irene's restaurant too. Irene's. Hell, man, you'll be able to smell the garlic in the air from Irene's tonight. Yes, sir.'

'Sounds good.'

'Is this your first time here?' he said, looking at me in the rear view mirror as he drove.

'Yeah.'

'What's that?'

'Yeah. First time.'

'Man, you're gunna love it here,' he said. 'You're in a real good hotel. Lovely people in that hotel. Here we are.'

He pulled up to the curb in front of my hotel. I handed him $10. No tips with the fixed station rate.

'Thank you, sir,' he said. 'Thank you very much. You enjoy your stay now. You're gunna love it here in N'Awlins, I can just tell. You're gunna love it.'

But he didn't know half the story.

20

BREAKING POINT

'I gotta take a little time. A little time to think things over…'

—'I Want To Know What Love Is', Foreigner

Twenty-nine states in and Lucy left. It was 10 June, less than half way through the trip.

Lucy and I had got on fairly well during the tour. There'd been a few incidents and a lot of tears, but nothing anything serious. Lucy cries easily. Then came Memphis. We'd been there for two days. The night before we'd walked into Beale Street in silence. There was no apparent reason for the silence, but Lucy was in a black mood. Her black moods build up, just like a storm and you can feel the weight of humidity. It slowly builds to a hurricane—all violent and tumultuous—then it clears, just as quickly as it came, usually after she sleeps for a couple of hours. But the black mood was definitely there as we walked into Beale Street.

The next day we went to Graceland and Lucy started crying uncontrollably because of the lack of food options.

'We haven't had a decent meal for days,' she said.

'You had the best steak of your life last night at Beale Street,' I said, amazed with her comment.

'I didn't even want that.'

'It was the most expensive meal on the menu,' I said.

'Whatever.'

After Graceland we went back to our hotel. Lucy went to the room while I spoke to the receptionist about finding a grocery store. When I got back to the room, Lucy was crying angrily. The room smelt strongly of perfume.

'What's wrong?' I said.

'I was trying to get something out of my toiletry bag and my perfume fell and smashed. Be careful, there's glass on the ground in the bathroom.'

'It doesn't matter,' I said. 'You can get some more perfume.'

'It was really expensive.'

'Don't worry about it. You can get some more.'

'Get out of my way,' she yelled. 'I'm leaving.'

'What are you talking about?' I said. I could see that she had packed her bags. 'Get out of my way.' I was standing in the doorway.

'I'm not letting you go while you're like this,' I said.

Lucy became frantic, crying and screaming.

'Get out of my way. Get out of my way. I have to leave.'

'You don't have to leave,' I said. 'Sit down. You'll be alright.'

'You can't keep me here,' she screamed and started punching me in the chest. 'Move away, now. Move away.'

'You're not leaving until you calm down. It's too dangerous out there. Where are you going to go?'

'Anywhere. Anywhere but here.'

'That's ridiculous.'

'It's not ridiculous. Get out of my way. I'm leaving.'

She was trying to pull me away from the door, hitting me

and then grabbing at the handle.

'You're not leaving until you've calmed down.'

'Fine,' she said and sat down on the bed. She stopped crying, as if she'd flicked a switch.

'Why are you doing this?' I said, sitting down on the bed next to her. 'What's the reason for this?' I went to put my hand on her shoulder, but it was definitely hands-to-yourself time.

'I'm calm,' she said. 'Can I leave now?'

'You don't want to do this,' I said.

'I do. Can I leave now?'

'Do whatever you want,' I said. 'But you'll regret this.'

'No I won't,' she said. She picked up her bags, and stormed out of the room, slamming the door as she left.

I looked at the door, flummoxed. It was so sudden, so unexpected.

I lay on the bed and turned on the television to ESPN. The Chicago White Sox were playing the Texas Rangers. I opened the fridge, got a beer and took a long swig. I could still hear the sound of the slamming door in my head.

'Well, that was very strange,' I said softly to myself. 'Very strange.'

I finished the beer and opened another. There was no point in not drinking. I relaxed back and watched the game. The smell of Lucy's spilt perfume lingered in the air.

It's very easy to be blasé during the day, but alone in the dark at night when the demons come, it is an entirely different thing altogether.

21

N'AWLINS GROOVE

'Do you know what it means, to miss New Orleans?
And there is something more, I miss the one I
care for, more than I miss New Orleans.'

—'Drop Me Off in New Orleans', Kermit Ruffins

New Orleans has distilled the essence of groove. N'Awlins, as
the locals call it, is one cool city.

I walked out on the street from my hotel and the first
person I passed was an old man with a verve in his step.

'How you doin' on this fine morning, my friend?' he
drawled in a deep southern accent.

'Good thank you, sir,' I said, before turning to watch him
swagger away along the cobbled pavement. It was my first
day alone.

On the state licence plate (or license plate, as the Yanks
spell it), Louisiana is referred to as the 'Sportsman's Paradise'.
I don't understand why, but it is certainly a paradise of some
kind. Whilst Baton Rouge is the official capital, New Orleans

is the cultural capital. The key region of NOLA (New Orleans, LA), one of the many names the city is known by, is the French Quarter. Set on the usual grid system of most American towns, it's an easily navigable area of about ten by five streets and sits adjacent to the Mississippi River, where paddle steamers and ferries still run through the dirty waters. The French Quarter is filled with bars and restaurants in colonial-looking buildings. Palm trees line the front street and Jackson Square, the pedestrian plaza where buskers and street performers hang out, is the central meeting place. Bourbon Street runs through the middle of the French Quarter and is the famous road that the annual Mardi Gras parades down.

I wandered the streets of the French Quarter, poking in and out of the many artesian-style stores. In one tourist shop I bought a New Orleans T-shirt and a vintage metal sign advertising Cajun spicy sauces. I also got a magnet as a small gift for Lucy, just in case. Lucy likes to collect magnets from the main cities.

'Do I get a discount for buying this much stuff?' I asked the young man behind the counter in the store.

'No, no discount, sorry,' he said. He seemed unusually shy for his breed. 'You only get discount if you buy two of one thing. Like two T-shirts. Then you get discount. But you buy different things, so no discount, sorry.'

'Jesus,' I said. 'Did you invent that policy just then?'

He laughed.

'You did didn't you? You just invented it?'

'I give you $2 discount.' He was still laughing.

'Okay, thanks,' I said.

A lot of the souvenirs in all the shops had 'The Big Easy'

written on them. The whole town referred to The Big Easy. There were Big Easy daiquiris, Big Easy gumbo, Big Easy Tours and Big Easy posters. The derivation of the moniker varies. Some say the town is known as that because of the ease of finding work in New Orleans in the early 20th century. Others claim it originated during the Prohibition era, when the city was rife with speak-easies, owing to the government's inability to control alcohol sales in the city. It was also known as one of the cheapest places in America to live, leading some people to call it the Big Easy.

Whatever the reason, the Big Easy is a very friendly place. Most locals, who are nearly all black, or 'coloured folk' as they say, will come right up to you to talk on the street. Most conversations are unsolicited, and give the feeling that there's no attempt to extract anything, but purely because the people are friendly.

But there's an edge to the city as well. As I wasted the morning away, walking from store to store, I was followed by three men. They were washed out Mustang Men—filthy, with old torn clothes, no hopes and bad intentions. I saw them a couple of times on different streets, then caught a glimpse of them plotting something on a corner, partially concealed by a road sign. I was in a store and came out without them seeing me. They were loitering nearby, then upon seeing me, pretended to play a harmless game of knuckles with each other, looking at the ground, trying to appear nonchalant, the usual fenestral mugger's routine. As I walked past, one yelled out at me.

'You got a dollar, man? Just a dollar.'

They were across the street, but started walking towards me. I looked at them hard, trying to appear undeterred, trying to look tough. They were white, genuine dirt trackers.

I'd been told by many locals how dangerous N'Awlins was, how you must be careful, even during the day. It wasn't worth taking a chance. I ducked into a restaurant and sat down. The Mustang Men crossed the street and stood outside, glaring in through the window for a minute, before moving on in search of another victim.

The restaurant had a warm feel to it. There was a lot of wood. I quickly forgot about the men. I ordered jambalaya, a local dish of rice, seafood and spicy sausage. It came with vegetables, the first I'd seen in four weeks in America. I laced the food with Tabasco sauce. Tabasco sauce is on every table in New Orleans. The meal was superb. Almost as good as Lucy's—she'd made it for me in England.

The waitress walked past me as I devoured it in quick time. She was a fat white girl.

'Everything good there with you, sweetie?' she said with a twang of the south. 'Sure looks like it.'

'Yep, pretty good,' I said, as I swallowed the final mouthful.

I kept thinking how much Lucy would love New Orleans—the atmosphere, the people, the food. Everything.

After I'd finished the jambalaya, I left the restaurant and went into Jackson Square. There were buskers playing jazz and young men hanging around in groups, like young men mostly do. There was a section of the square that held an array of palm and tarot card readers. A sign in front of one bedraggled man read 'Tarot by Michael, the Realistic Mystic'. I kept walking.

But no matter how much I walked, browsing in souvenir shops and taking in the streets, I couldn't take my mind off Lucy. God, I missed her. Her face, her laugh, everything. It'd only been a day and a half. That morning I'd awoken in my hotel room, my second morning alone. The hotel was of a

French design. There was a sandstone courtyard where a pool was surrounded by sun lounges and fountains. My room was quaint, with carved wooden furniture and patterned drapes and cushions that matched. I thought how Lucy would love it as well. It was early and I had turned my computer on to check my emails. I opened my Hotmail account. I searched amongst the spam, but there was no message from Lucy. The day before when I arrived in New Orleans, there was a message from Lucy. My heart had raced when I saw her name, as only she can make it race. I opened it. It was timed at 6.30am. Lucy was never up that early. I was about to board the train from Memphis at that time.

The email read: 'I wish I was on the train with you. I see it has arrived early so there is no chance for me to get there before it leaves. It's probably better for me to go home anyway. Can you email me to let me know what you are doing? I wish I were there with you.'

It gave me a glimmer of hope. I'd emailed straight back and told her to get on the train the next morning for the best oyster and seafood, cocktail and jazz night of her life. But I'd not heard anything back from her, and as I ambled around the vibrant streets of New Orleans, going nowhere in particular, feeling a little fuzzy, a little numb, I wondered if I'd ever see Lucy again.

22

THE BAYOU

'Wish I was back on the Bayou. Rollin' with some Cajun Queen. Wishin' I were a fast freight train, just a chooglin' on down to New Orleans.'

—'Born on the Bayou', Creedence Clearwater Revival

I was lying on the bed in my New Orleans hotel room, having a beer and watching another baseball game. I'd walked around the city all morning and felt I had the gist of it. It was about 6pm and I figured I'd relax and have a couple of beers in the room, before heading out to a few bars.

There was a knock on the door. I ignored it, annoyed. I had the 'Do Not Disturb' sign out. I always had it out. One of the few downsides of travelling the world and staying in upmarket hotels is cleaners. I despise cleaners. They rustle outside the door and harass and apply pressure. I often forego the cleaner, as they invariably arrive exactly when you don't want them to.

There was another knock at the door.

'For fuck's sake,' I said and got up. I looked through the

peephole, but there was nobody there. I opened the door.

It was Lucy. I looked at her. There were tears in her eyes. I couldn't believe it.

'I couldn't stay away,' she said.

'I'm glad you came,' I said. 'Really glad. Come inside.'

I grabbed her suitcase and pulled it inside. I shut the door. We stood facing each other. There was an awkward silence.

'I'm glad you came.' I didn't know what else to say. 'Come here,' I said.

I leant forward and hugged her hard.

'It's good to see you,' I said. 'I missed you.'

'I missed you too.'

We didn't speak for a few minutes, just hugged.

'Do you want to go and get something to eat?' I said. 'I was thinking oysters.'

'Can we go to Acme?'

We got ready and headed for the Acme Oyster House on Iberville Street. We walked past a salsa and chilli sauce store near Jackson Square. There were free tasters with corn chips, the various dips lined up along a bench in the shop. We love hot sauce. The hotter, the better. We went in.

'What's the hottest one?' Lucy said to the man behind the counter.

'This one,' he said, pointing at the final sauce, a dark habanero-based salsa. 'But it's very hot. Be careful.'

Lucy put a small amount on a corn chip and bit half.

'Oh God,' she said. 'That's too hot. Argh, argh. You have this.' She handed me the other half and I ate it.

'It doesn't seem too bad,' I said, piling a heap more onto

another chip and putting it in my mouth.

I have a very high tolerance for hot chillies. After three months in Mexico, I couldn't find a sauce hot enough. In one restaurant in Palenque, I ate a full bowl of their hottest sauce and asked for more. Our waiter went into the kitchen and must have told the rest of the staff, as a group of three men wearing chef hats came out peering at me from a distance. Since then, I've considered myself somewhat invincible when it comes to chillies. I even got to the point where I was cutting up habanero chillies, the second hottest in the world, and putting them in my Corona beer bottles, just to add some zest.

So I had that chilli-piled corn chip and then another.

'My mouth's on fire,' Lucy said as we left the shop.

'Yeah, it's pretty hot,' I said. 'Strong after taste. It's building up.'

'My mouth's still hot,' Lucy said. We were about 100 metres past the shop.

'I don't feel all that good,' I said. We crossed a street. 'My stomach's starting to hurt.'

'Are you okay?' Lucy said. 'You look pale.'

'I can't see properly. Everything's blurry.'

Lucy put her hand on my arm.

'Don't touch me,' I said. 'I've got to sit down. I can't breathe properly.'

We made it to the other side of the street and I keeled over and slumped down to the curb. I didn't know where I was. I was wiping my brow, but the pain was getting worse. An hour after reuniting with Lucy, I was sitting on the ground of a grimy street in New Orleans, sweating and delirious with chilli fever.

We were next to an ice cream shop. Lucy went and

bought a large tub full. She fed it to me. I couldn't co-ordinate my hands. I had no strength. I finished the tub. Lucy bought another and I ate that too. The pain alleviated, and then as quickly as it came, subsided completely.

'How are you feeling?' Lucy said.

'I think I'm okay. God, that was spooky. I couldn't move there for a minute.'

'You do get yourself into some scrapes, don't you?'

'Sometimes,' I said, then paused. 'Why'd you come back?'

The question took her by surprise. There was a delay before she spoke.

'I woke up yesterday at 6am and thought how much I wanted to see you. I was going to rush for the train, but looked on the Internet and saw that the train was early and that I wouldn't make it. And I thought I was miles from the station, but it turned out I was only a few minutes away.'

'It left on time,' I said. 'A few minutes late actually.'

'I would have made it.'

'That would have been good. I was watching for you, hoping you'd come, but I didn't think you would.'

'I'm so sorry about what happened,' she said.

'Me too.'

'Then I was going to get a flight down yesterday and beat you down here,' she said. 'But I was so tired. I needed to sleep and I thought it was better to get the train today.'

'It doesn't matter,' I said. 'I'm just glad you're here.'

We walked on towards Acme Oyster House. It was only a few minutes away. There was a long queue out the front, going down the street. Acme is an institution in New Orleans. We gave our name to the waitress and waited at the end of the twenty-strong line.

'I need a beer,' I said to Lucy. 'To get rid of the taste of chilli.'

'You could get one from that shop over there,' Lucy said.

'Have this one,' said a man just in front of us. 'I've just cracked it, but you can have it. I'll share this one.' He motioned towards his wife, who was in the queue next to him and was holding a beer of her own.

I thanked him and took the beer. I drank it quickly. A few minutes later the waitress yelled out.

'Lucy. Lucy,' she said from the door of the restaurant.

'Yes, here,' Lucy said.

We walked past the beer provider and the rest of the people in the queue and into the Oyster House. What's more, we were directed to the bar, without a doubt the pole position in the place.

'I wonder what we did to deserve this,' I said to Lucy.

'Who cares,' she said. 'This is excellent. What shall we get?'

'Oysters.'

There were men behind the bar, dressed in white aprons, shucking oysters with stub knives as pieces of shell flew into the air.

I ordered a dozen fresh oysters. They gave them to us on a bed of rock salt. They were huge. We put lemon and salt and Tabasco sauce on them. They were fresh and good. We washed down their salty, metallic taste with cold beer. We got a dozen more.

We sat and chatted in the Acme Oyster House for hours. It was like our first date. It was good to have Lucy back.

Heading back to the hotel, we decided to check out Bourbon Street. It was packed with beer-swilling revellers spilling out of crowded bars. Live bands were playing in most of the bars and the music was deafening as we walked down the neon-lined street. It wasn't late, but it felt like 3am.

'I'm too old for that,' Lucy said, as we passed a particularly loud sweat box.

'I was always too old for that.'

We passed the gay area of the street, signified by the rainbow flags hanging from windows, and walked through the red light district. Scantily-clad whores stood out on balconies, displaying themselves as an enticement to the drunkards. One place was called 'Barely Legal' and there were pictures of twelve year old girls in the window.

'Call me old-fashioned,' I said. 'But I find that a tad unsavoury.'

'It's disgusting,' Lucy said. 'It can't be legal can it?'

'Who knows down here,' I said. 'But they seem to be getting a fair bit of business.'

We walked to the end of Bourbon Street and away from its seedy clutches. Meandering back to our hotel in the warm still night, we wandered a couple of blocks in the wrong direction, into an area we shouldn't have been. It was dark and quiet. I kissed Lucy on a street corner. I didn't care where we were. It had been a good night and it was good to have her back.

The next morning we got up early to go to the bayou, the wet swamp lands an hour from the city. We'd arranged a tour and a mini-bus arrived at our hotel to pick us up. The bus driver introduced himself as Little Bill. Bill was white and he was not little. He was describing points of interest as he drove. And he kept listing his traits.

'I'm one of those people that if I don't know the answer, I'll usually find it out,' he said. 'But I know most answers. For example, I'm one of those people who can tell you where any burger joint is in the city.'

'I can't stand people who continually list their traits,' I said to Lucy. 'But I bet he knows the burgers joints alright.'

'That's because he's probably in them most of the time,' Lucy said.

Little Bill continued with his commentary. A couple of middle-aged women were yelling out questions and then saying 'wow' to every answer.

'There are some real talkers on this trip,' Lucy said.

'Yeah,' I agreed. 'And they're all middle-aged women. There's nothing worse than a middle-aged woman who thinks she's a character.'

'They're always so loud in America,' Lucy said.

'They should not be allowed to raise their voices. The tone and the pitch, it just doesn't suit volume.'

Little Bill went on with his monologue.

'If you look o'er yonder,' he said. 'That's where Katrina caused a whole heap of destruction. Lot of destruction in the city. The poor folk got their houses repaired. But it's means tested.' He was starting to sound angry. 'A lot of good people who can't afford the repairs are still without houses. Government won't pay for them 'cause they got too much money. My brother ain't got much money, but hell, the government means tested him and won't pay.'

'He's on a rant with this one,' Lucy said.

'Yeah, he's getting a bit aggressive,' I said, as the tirade went on. 'I must say though, I agree with him. There should be no social welfare. It weakens the species. Goes against our instincts. Every man for himself, I say.'

Little Bill was just finishing his speech when we pulled into The Swamp Shop.

'Don't get bit now y'all,' he said as we got off the bus.

We went into The Swamp Shop and registered for the tour. The tour cost $60 per person, but I had two $10 off vouchers. The man behind the counter looked scruffy, like he had been born on the bayou and hadn't washed since. The arithmetic was clearly beyond him, even with the use of a calculator. He was punching numbers in, pressing 'clear', then punching more in. In the end he asked me what we should pay.

We walked outside and into the sun and got on the airboat. It held about fifteen people and had an enormous fan on the back for propulsion.

'I'm Lil' Lex, your guide. And I'll charge you extra for every blow job you get today,' said the driver of the boat in reference to the airboat propellers.

The boat loaded up and we set off.

We passed catfish traps and blue crab pots as the bayou forked into two—one branch going to the Gulf of Mexico and the other to the Mississippi. Lil' Lex manoeuvred the boat through narrow estuaries and under fallen tree branches until we were in the depths of the swamp. Live oak trees lined the banks. They were covered with hairy moss, giving them an eerie appearance, like they belonged in a ghost story.

Lil' Lex cut the engine and pulled the boat in to a grassy bank.

'Alright, folks,' he said. 'Welcome to the Louisiana swamp. If you've got it, now's the time to smoke it. What happens in the swamp, stays in the swamp.'

He cupped his hands to his mouth and started yelping like a terrier dog.

'There are three rules in the swamp,' he said. 'Yelp, yelp. Rule one—everything out here tastes like chicken. Yelp. Rule two—never stand in the boat while we're moving, and, yelp, yelp, Rule three—if you hear a banjo playing, I'm getting the hell out of here.'

'He looks like the sort of bloke who has a banjo of his own,' I said to Lucy.

'What's with the yelping?' Lucy said.

'Probably calling to his swamp buddies so they can all have a go.'

Lil' Lex suddenly froze, like an animal that senses a predator nearby. He was listening hard.

The head of an alligator appeared in the water about twenty metres from the boat. Then another. Then one only a few metres away.

'Here they are,' Lil' Lex said, getting out of the boat. He pulled some pieces of chicken out of a bucket. Two large gators, about ten and twelve feet long, climbed up onto the bank and started charging at Lil' Lex, snapping their jaws.

'Don't worry y'all,' he said. 'They can't even see me. They can only see the chicken. They can't see a pi-erson.'

He was holding the chicken out above the alligators, who were jumping in the air and snatching it out of his hand.

America has more 'deaths by reptile' than any other country in the world, and it was little wonder why.

'I'm pretty sure the gators can see him,' I said to Lucy.

'Maybe they can see persons, just not pi-ersons,' Lucy said.

Lil' Lex then leapt onto a small gator that had come up on the bank. It was only a few feet long, but he clutched it in his hands and then jumped back in the boat. He fed it a couple of marshmallows and then passed it around the boat to anyone who wanted to hold it.

'He's so scared at the moment,' said Lil' Lex, as Lucy held the little gator. 'That his heart has virtually stopped. He's only just breathing. Has no idea what's going on.'

Lucy passed it to me, I held it, then passed it on. Lil' Lex then let him go into the water, throwing a few more marshmallows after him, which were snaffled up by a larger gator.

Once we got back to the city, we walked through the French Market. There was a heavy Chinese influence working the stalls there. The only person who wasn't Chinese was an old bald black man talking to a woman from across a table. When he was alone, I went up to him.

'Excuse me, sir,' I said. 'What do you do?'

'I recite inspirational poetry.'

'Oh,' I said. 'I thought you were a mystic. I saw Michael the Realistic Mystic in the square yesterday. I thought you might be like him.'

'No, I'm not Michael.'

'I know that. But I thought you might be a mystic or fortune teller of some sort.'

'No, sir,' he said, smiling. He had big white teeth. 'I'm a pastor and a poet. Let me recite you a poem. I'll do it reeeal slow.'

'Maybe later,' I said. 'We've got to go.'

'I'll do it reeeal slow,' he repeated. 'Please let me.'

'No.'

We left.

We walked down to the banks of the Mississippi and caught a ferry ride across and back. Then we went in search of food.

The day before I'd seen a little place called The Gumbo Shop. It was a good-looking dark wooden joint with a well-stocked bar. We found it and went inside and sat down.

'My name's Charles and I'll be looking after you folks today,' said a smartly dressed black man of about forty-five. 'Can I interest you in a cocktail to start with? We make the best cocktails.'

'Thanks Charles,' I said. 'Maybe later on tonight.' It was 2pm.

'Alright then. I'll give you a minute and then be back for your order. Our speciality is crab. And gumbo and jambalaya. We do a great jambalaya, I tell ya.'

We both ordered the jambalaya. It was delicious.

Charles came to check on us. He was a good waiter.

'How y'all doin' here? How's the food?'

'Very good, Charles,' I said. 'It's excellent.'

'Good, good,' he said, drawing out the words. 'Man, you sure gettin' it down. Hell.'

We finished and got the bill and I handed it to Charles with a heavy tip.

'Thank you,' Charles said. 'You need any change, my man?'

'No Charles, you keep it.'

'Thank you. Thank you, sir.'

'Thank you, Charles,' I said. 'See you later for a cocktail.'

'Yes, sir,' he said. 'You come to me for a cocktail. I gotcha covered. I'll make you a Hurricane. You gotta have that before you do anything, man. Then I'll make you a daiquiri. We do fresh daiquiris. Strawberry, mango, passionfruit, lime.

So good. You'll love them.'

As we were leaving, Lucy turned to me and smiled.

'Those fresh daiquiris sound good,' she said. 'Let's go back in and have a drink.'

We walked back into The Gumbo Shop. Yes, sometimes Lucy and I got on pretty well.

23

FUNDAMENTAL
BIOLOGY

*'You and me baby, we ain't nothin' but mammals,
so let's do it like they do on the Discovery
Channel'*

—'Discovery Channel', Bloodhound Gang

'Why do guys always approach me as soon as I'm alone?'
Lucy asked me when we were in New Orleans. 'Even when
they have wives, as soon as they're alone, they come straight
over to me. What's the point? What are they trying to
achieve?'

'It is a fundamental theory of evolutionary biology that
the male of any species seeks to have sex with as many
different partners as possible so as to increase his chances of
procreation. This includes humans. A man's reproductive
success depends on how many women he has sex with. The
more mates he has, the more likely it is that his genes will
live on. By imposing monogamy on men, the modern world
has attempted to use moral codes to contradict this innate

urge. This conflict between a man's physical biology and society's standards has resulted in confusion. Were you looking for a scientific explanation or were you just making conversation?'

'Thanks for that,' she said with a grin. 'But it's just so annoying. I don't see what they get out of it.'

'I don't see the point either,' I said. 'But they'll be trying to have sex with you.'

'Do you really think so?'

'Definitely. Men rarely talk to unknown women unless they're trying to have sex with them.'

It had happened a lot over the past two years with Lucy. Lucy is beautiful and men stare at her a lot. And they do approach her when they get the chance. A year earlier we were on a boat in Thailand. Lucy went up onto the deck to get some air and saw a middle-aged man and his wife sitting nearby. The wife went inside and the man came straight over to Lucy. He asked her what she was doing and then started talking about himself—his successful business, his houses, his money. Then he gave Lucy his card and said she should look him up if she ever needed any help in the business world—he said he had a lot of contacts. As his wife came back up on deck, he eased away as if nothing had happened. Then in the St. Louis train station Lucy was waiting outside for me while I went to the toilet. She mustn't have been alone for more than a minute and a man went up to her and started talking. As soon as I came out he walked off. He was in his fifties too. They were always older. What chance did they think they had? A fifty year old with a wife nearby approaching a gorgeous girl in her twenties. Absurd.

'Why are you talking about this?' I asked. 'What happened?'

'It was on the train from Memphis to here,' she said. 'I had two seats to myself and across the aisle was a man and his wife. I'd seen the man staring at me throughout the journey.'

'Mid-fifties?' I said.

'Yeah, something like that. Anyway, his wife walked off to go to the food carriage, I think, and he stood up and leant right over me and said 'Do you mind if I just take a quick photo out the window?"

'Not a bad opener.'

'Then he sat down on the seat next to me and introduced himself.'

'What was his name?' I said.

'I can't even remember, but he said he was an ex-marine and now he was in security. He kept checking for his wife at the door the whole time.'

'What else did he say?'

'He said New Orleans is very dangerous and that he should have brought his gun, but he forgot it. Then he said 'You look like one of the Kennedys. You know, the Kennedys, JFK Junior and that lot. Like you're really rich.'

'What a sleazy prick.'

'Yeah. Then he asked me where I was staying.'

'Really? What did you tell him? We're not going to have Sleazy Marine knocking on our door tonight are we?'

'I told him I wasn't sure,' Lucy said. 'But that I was staying with my boyfriend. I must have said 'boyfriend' ten times.'

'That never deters them.'

'Then he said his wife was leaving that day and I could

151

stay with him if I needed to.'

'Maybe you should give him a call,' I said. 'We can both turn up on his doorstep. Save us a night's accommodation.'

'I didn't get his number.'

'That's a shame.'

24

THE DOG IS
SCRATCHED

'The dog days are over, the dog days are done.'

— 'Dog Days Are Over', Florence and the Machine

It turned out that the horror bus journey from St. Louis to Nashville was in fact our last time on the Dog. I didn't really think it would be at the time, but whenever we went to catch another one, an obstacle would present itself and some other mode of transport seemed a more agreeable alternative.

When I arrived into New Orleans by myself, I sat waiting for my bag to be brought off the train. I saw that the Greyhound ticket office was in the station as well, so I thought I'd go through the charade again. I walked up to the counter.

'I'm leaving from here to Austin in four days' time,' I said. 'Can I book a ticket on that bus please?'

'What sort of ticket?' she asked.

'I have a Discovery Pass.'

'You're too early,' she said.

'I know,' I said. 'But a man in Key West booked me on a

bus for two days later.'

'Can't do it,' she said. 'I won't do it.'

'Okay,' I said and turned to leave.

'If you turn up the night before you can get a ticket as the bus to Austin always sells out,' she said.

'Isn't it only an hour before?' I asked.

'The night before will be fine,' she said.

'What about the morning before?'

'That's fine too. Turn up then and you'll get a ticket. But now's too early.'

'Really,' I said. 'Thank you. I could have used that tip a month ago.'

'Move on please,' she said, afraid that she was being too helpful. 'Next customer.'

I recounted the story to Lucy a few days later.

'It was a good tip,' I said. 'I wish we'd been told that at the start of the trip.'

'So was the woman behind the counter friendly for a change?' Lucy asked.

'No, she was angry. Middle-aged and angry. The usual.'

'And fat?' Lucy said.

'Is there any other kind?'

'Do you think we'll get tickets?'

'Who knows,' I said. 'It's fifty/fifty I think. No more.'

'I heard someone on my train say that the Greyhound buses in the south are far more dangerous than on the east coast. I don't know if I can face another Dog trip at the moment.'

'Maybe we should look into a hire car instead,' I said.

'That'd be good.'

The hire car was $200 for one day, but we agreed that the thought of a Southern Dog was too much to bear, so we booked it.

The woman at the car hire place in New Orleans was clearly a former Greyhound employee. We just couldn't seem to escape the clutches of the Dog. She was angry and unhelpful. And fat. I'm surprised America is a world leader in so many fields, given the average body-mass-to-brain ratio. I suppose they were just lucky to be blessed with an arable country and good natural resources.

The technology at the car hire place was ridiculous as well. It was completely archaic. The woman was unable to tell us what the final cost would be and the print out she gave us was one of those 1980s spreadsheet-style pages, that has holes down the sides and prints line by line.

But as we set off for Austin, Texas, we were just thankful that we weren't on the Dog. A few minutes into the trip, Lucy looked over at me.

'What are those marks up your arm?' she said.

'What marks?'

'All there,' she said. 'They're everywhere. On your leg too.'

I looked at my arm. It had twenty or more bites on it, all in lines. So did my leg, and my other arm and my stomach. I don't know if it was psychosomatic, but then they started itching. Itching badly.

'Christ,' I said. 'Have you got any?'

'I don't think so.'

I looked at Lucy.

'There, on your neck,' I said. 'There's four there.'

Lucy examined herself and found an array of other bites.

She went into a blind panic.

'I think they're bed bugs,' she said. 'They're all in lines, and that's how they bite.'

'But you've been checking the hotel beds,' I said. 'We can't have got them from there.'

Ever since South America, where bed bugs are prevalent, Lucy had painstakingly checked every hotel bed we'd been in and never found any bed bugs.

'Why have the bites suddenly appeared?' I said. 'I can't stop scratching them now. They're so itchy.'

Lucy went onto the Internet on her mobile phone.

It turned out that the odious little bugs were super creatures. Feeding on human blood, they often live in bedding and mattresses and can survive a laundry wash. They can live for a year without feeding, and will seek out a human host from some distance, climbing from under a mattress.

'It says here that the bites can take nine days to manifest,' Lucy said.

'Where were we nine days ago?'

'The Greyhound. St. Louis to Nashville,' she said. 'This website says they're associated with the poor and immigrants.'

'Greyhound for sure.'

'And this forum says that bed bugs are often found on the seats of Greyhound buses and can be carried there on people's clothes.'

'We just can't seem to escape that mongrel,' I said.

'That's definite, then,' Lucy said. 'I'm not getting on another Dog.'

'Neither I am.'

As we drove away from New Orleans, we even threw our Greyhound Discovery Passes away, well before their expiration date, just to seal our fate.

But it felt like the Dog was in the back seat of the car, breathing on our necks. We drove for 850km across the swamps of Louisiana and into Texas, scratching ourselves the whole way.

25

GOD BLESS AMERICA

'They say there's a heaven for those who will wait. Some say it's better but I say it ain't.'

—'Only The Good Die Young', Billy Joel

America is full of religious freaks and the word of God is everywhere.

God cannot be avoided. He's on television, the Internet, road signs and the radio. His word is written on the sides of trucks and on car bumper stickers. And it's not just in the Bible Belt, the traditional God-fearing region of the South, it's everywhere.

I was on a plane flying to Flagstaff, Arizona. Lucy and I had been allocated separate seats by the liar at the check-in counter and I was jammed in against the window next to a big fat ogre. He was wearing a suit and was breathing and sweating hard. He turned on his iPad and began reading. I was reading along with him. The title on the first page was 'New World of Holy Scriptures' with the heading 'Draw Close to God'.

'Christ,' I thought. 'The bastards have brought mobile technology to their pathetic cause.'

The article was an in-depth analysis about why Jehovah Witnesses go door knocking, with comments and quotes from various leaders of the Church. I never got the answer to that perennial question as the selfish cad saw me reading over his shoulder and angled the screen away so I couldn't see it. Meanwhile, the hypocritical prick took up two-thirds of our seats, as well as the entire arm rest, and kept reading as we were landing, despite the announcement to switch off all electrical items. I guess when you're reading the word of the Lord, an exception can be made.

Of course, like in all guises and areas that religion exists, hypocrisy is rife in America. Close to nearly every roadside billboard about God, is another advertising an adult super-store. America produces more pornography than any other country. There are adult superstores dotted along every major highway in the US, warehouses just off the road catering to every need of the perverted church-goers in terms of toys and outfits. Surely at least a couple of the sacred commandments must be broken with that coupling. Or perhaps the superstores aren't there to attract the celibate Christians, but merely strategically placed as an enticement to the Mustang Men to pick up a little something special for Christmas when driving back from an out of town bender.

God's roadside signs are just as brazen and obvious as those of the superstores. Fear and implied threats comprise their general tone. 'Ready or not, Jesus is coming,' read one sign in West Virginia, while another just outside of Yosemite National Park read 'This is a test of your loyalty to God'. The test was not explained, but I'm sure those in the know would have somehow been made aware. A 'God is watching us!' banner in Texas felt more judgemental than protective, and 'The only hope for America is Jesus' seemed a little desperate. Yes, there are rules and scripture on enormous road signs all over the place and they usually carry an implied or direct threat. We saw one sign that was thirty feet high on the outskirts of Denver, Colorado. It simply listed out the Ten Commandments. Driving west of Chicago there was a sign just off the road for 'Highway Evangelist' and a toll-free 1-800 phone number. The caption read 'You need God. He will save you. Call now!' The Yanks effectively don't pay for phone calls. Virtually every business has a toll-free 1-800 number.

On the off chance you miss these roadside signs or don't have a mobile phone to get your driving fix, the public have taken up the cause as well, displaying timely quotations on their vehicles. Many cars have subtle stickers of that Jesus fish symbol, while others have bumper stickers with helpful reminders such as 'Found Jesus Yet?', 'Christ is The Answer' and 'Christ is the King'. Many simply read 'God Bless America'. Some people have the Jesus fish symbol on their actual car number plate. It's not a sticker, but is painted on and part of the plate. Presumably, this must be arranged through the transport department. One car had no numbers or letters on its plate at all, just the words 'God bless Our Nation'. The motto on all Alabama state plates is 'God Bless

America'. Quite a few commercial trucks have Bible quotations written on the back. A lot of them merely refer to 'John 3:16' with no other text. I looked it up. Sometimes referred to as 'the Gospel in a nutshell', the verse reads: 'For God so loved the world that he gave his one and only Son, that whoever believes in him shall not perish but have eternal life.' I had no idea how that related to hauling frozen goods across America, but it was only the truckers that were spreading this word.

And if you happen to be a blind driver, there's no need to fret. The word of God is not hard to find on the radio. In fact, it's hard to avoid. Christian radio makes up around one in three channels. The other two are generally Country stations, or a mixture of Christian and Country. Some are Christian Country. Driving in Oregon we decided to have a break from the iPod and tried the radio. The first three FM stations, and six in the first nine, were Christian. A number of these were religious ranting stations, with the usual threats and aggression to keep the mob in check. We listened to one for a few minutes. There was a man yelling, punctuating the prophecy with pregnant pauses. It was almost as if the heathen was in the car with us.

'To live a Godly life you must be persecuted,' he screamed. 'Jesus said this. You may be persecuted by your family or you may be persecuted at your work. But you will be persecuted. It will happen. You might be persecuted at work, but you'll be rewarded in Heaven. You might miss out on a promotion at work, but you will be promoted in Heaven.'

'Cogent arguments,' I said to Lucy, who couldn't stand it anymore and was reaching for the radio to change the channel.

Religion is advertised constantly on American television as well. One organisation was called Christianmingle.com. It was a dating agency.

'Good news for you single Christians out there,' said a cheesy young preacher wearing a suit and standing too close to the camera. 'We have thousands of young Christians out there just waiting to meet you.' The ad ended with the catchphrase, 'Find God's match for you'. Perhaps they should have teamed up with an adult superstore.

God really is all around you in America. When you're not getting inundated via the media, you're getting hammered in your car. And you're not safe on foot either. We saw many people with god-bothering slogans blazoned across their T-shirts or caps. Most caps simply read 'I Love Jesus', or the more pithy 'Jesus', unless I was mistaken and there were a lot of people by that name. Waiting for a flight at an airport in Austin, Texas, a woman sitting near us sneezed. She was assaulted from all directions, even at a distance, by strangers saying 'God bless you'. In that same airport I overhead a discussion between two people who were getting to know each other.

'Have you got a husband or boyfriend?' one lady said to the other.

'No, I don't,' she answered. 'I'm in a committed relationship with God.' Like most religious nuts, she was rather ugly, but I was tempted to direct the lonely soul to the Christian Mingle website.

Should the barrage of religious advertising somehow pass you by in America, there is absolutely no excuse for not attending church in person. Chestnut reasons such as not being able to find a church that caters to your strain of faith do not wash in America. In the Texan desert I saw a rickety old barn with a cross on the top and a sign out the front— 'Cowboy Church'. In Monument Valley a sign in the middle of the desert was for a 'Coven Church', presumably catering to the witches in the region. In Cody, Wyoming, there was a list of churches in a brochure about the town—for a population of only 9,520, thirty churches were listed. Mariposa in California has a population of 2,173. A large sign by the side of the road in the middle of town headed 'Churches of Mariposa' listed the following churches—Apostolic Power House, C. V. Church of Christ, Church of Jesus Christ of Latter Day Saints, Grace Community, Lutheran, Midpines Bible, Ponderosa Basin, St Josephs Catholic, Assembly of God, Christian Science, Circle of Hope, Hillside Baptist, Mariposa Christian Fellowship, New Beginnings, Seventh-Day Adventist, United Methodist, Cathey's Valley Baptist, Church of Christ, First Baptist, Lighthouse Fellowship, Mariposa Revival CTR, New Life Christian Fellowship, St Andrew's Anglican and Living Water Pentecostal Church of God. The information booklet at our hotel also listed these churches, as well as Church of Jesus Christ of LDS, First Baptist Church, First Spiritualist Church, Kingdom Hall Jehovah's Witness, Little Church in the Hills and Cathey's Valley United Methodists Church. It went on to say 'For other churches in the area please refer to your local Yellow Pages'.

Just before we left America, I saw a female sprinter who was preparing for the Olympics interviewed on television.

'What will you be thinking when you kneel down to run that race in London, the culmination of your entire career, everything you've ever trained for?' the interviewer asked.

'I'll be thinking what I always think when I kneel down,' she replied, smiling. 'I'll be praying to God, to not only win, but also praying to his glory.'

Yes, the poor bastards of America have been brainwashed alright. And they're all going straight to Hell.

26

LONE STAR BELT BUCKLES

'Lone Star belt buckles and old faded Levis and each night begins a new day...'

—'Mamas Don't Let Your Babies Grow Up to be Cowboys', Willie Nelson

Everything is bigger in Texas. And if you ask a Texan, everything is better. The country, the pick-up trucks, the women, the beef. The catchphrase 'Bigger is better in Texas' is everywhere. As we crossed into the state, there was a road sign—'El Paso 857 miles'. Even the speed limit was higher—seventy-five miles per hour, the highest in the country, compared with a meagre fifty-five in the East.

The Texans do their best to create this separate identity for their state—the Lone Star State. The symbolic single star of Texas is all over the place. It's on the cement of highway overpasses, on buildings and on most road signs. It's even on the sewer manhole covers. It's hard to find a sign without the word Texas on it as well.

And there are Texan flags everywhere. Most of America flies the US flag on its streets and in front of its houses, but in Texas it's the Texan flag. The only other place where the state flag can be seen a lot is in Tennessee.

The most common beer is called Lone Star, 'the national beer of Texas'. The folks down there don't even consider Texas a state, it's a nation.

Yes, the Texans are obsessed with Texas.

I met a couple from the Lone Star State whilst in Vietnam the year before.

'Are you from the US?' I asked them when I heard their accent.

'No,' they replied. 'Texas.'

And there is no state where God is more present than in Texas. There are churches aplenty and numerous God-fearing signs by the road side. Intermingled with the religious signs are patriotic ones. 'Don't mess with Texas' is a common phrase. We drove past one sign that simply quoted Davy Crockett—'You may all go to Hell and I will go to Texas'. Perhaps it was a religious sign as well.

But I had to admit, there was a certain romance to the state. Driving out into the big sky of Texas, you felt a sense of adventure and freedom. And heat. It was 100 degrees Fahrenheit and the sun was shining brightly.

'The car temperature gauge has just hit one hundred,' I said to Lucy.

'I'm just glad we're not on the Dog.'

'Imagine the heat on it,' I said. 'And the stench.'

It seemed that we could never fully escape the Dog. We turned the radio on, and after three preacher channels, landed on a station called The Dawg. It played the usual modern country twang. There was nothing but God and Country as we drove towards Austin.

And traffic. Passing Houston, the highway grew to twelve lanes as roads overlapped roads like a looping roller coaster. We came to a standstill a number of times, for no other reason than the volume of traffic, and the driving was not easy.

Just as all things in Texas are bigger, so are the egos of the men. The pick-up truck drivers are the worst and there are a lot of them in Texas.

Pick-up trucks are almost impossible to pass. The reason for this is that the drivers of them are absolute fuckwits. The pick-up is the Texan equivalent of the Mustang and the most common model is the Chevrolet Silverado. Whenever I tried to pass one, always having to undertake as they just sit in the fast lane, the driver would glare at me and speed up, straining to keep his fragile ego intact. On the odd occasion that I did manage to get past, I would inevitably be re-passed a minute later, the pick-up then cutting sharply in front of me.

Austin is a clean and vibrant city, with lots of restaurants and cafés. I'd heard that the best looking women come from Texas. Whilst they weren't perhaps as fat as elsewhere in America, I didn't find that to be the case. In fact, it was hard to pin-point the area that did have the best looking women in America, because nowhere did. We travelled the entire country, to every major city and nearly every town in between, and in our whole time in America, only saw a handful of attractive girls.

But apart from their redneck highway brethren, the people of Texas were remarkably hospitable. Whilst most people in America had been polite—they always called me 'sir'—with the exception of New Orleans, we hadn't found them to be all that friendly. In Texas they were.

We dropped our car off in Austin in the morning and needed somewhere to leave our bags while we looked around the city. There was a Sheraton Hotel nearby.

'Would we be able to leave our bags with you?' Lucy said to the man at the desk. She gave him a smile as big as Texas.

'Absolutely,' he said. He put tags on our bags, wheeled them to the storage room, then called us a taxi. Later that day, when we came back to collect our bags, we waited in the air-conditioned bar, using the Internet and having the complimentary soft drinks and bar snacks.

In Austin we went shopping for a few things. We went into an Apple store to buy a cord for the iPod.

'Where y'all from?' said the attendant. He then asked us all about our trip and where we were going. It was the first person who'd shown any genuine interest. He then gave us some recommendations about where to eat and what to do.

'It's pretty hot at the moment here isn't it?' I said to him. I was dripping with sweat.

'Hell, you got it at a good time,' he said. 'It's not too hot now. It's normally very muggy.'

We then bought a wildlife book at a bookstore.

'Off to do some animal spotting?' the young woman said to us.

She then discussed Yellowstone National Park at length, telling us the best places to go and what we might see.

People who heard our accent in bars and restaurants all

asked us where we were from and if we needed any help.

Even the bus driver to the airport had a big chat to us and let me off half the fare. Then at the airline check-in we were given better seats, and the woman didn't even do any of that fake typing that they usually do behind the desk.

And on the plane the friendliness continued.

'Howdy y'all friends and neighbours,' said the pilot just after we'd boarded.

People were trying to find their seats, walking up and down the aisle. They'd read their boarding passes, then stare at the seat numbers, then look back at their boarding passes, completely flummoxed. One couple, with a particular look of bewilderment on their faces, just stood there, helpless.

'Can I be of assistance?' said a man in a flight uniform.

He looked at their boarding passes and showed them to their seats, just a few feet away.

'I'm your captain today,' he said with a smile. 'I hope you have a great flight.'

He then went back to the cockpit and flew us to Flagstaff, Arizona. We were doing anything we could to avoid the Dog.

When we landed and were getting off the plane, the pilot was standing at the doorway, bidding the passengers goodbye.

'Fare thee well,' he was saying as people walked past.

'Good flying,' I said. 'I like your style.'

'Thank you, sir,' he said. 'I sure had some fun today. I hope you did too. And I sure do hope you come back to Texas real soon.'

27

MILITARY MEN

'I'm the daughter of a military man. It's a way of life and I understand.'

—'Military Man', Jessie James

The biggest shock for me about America was the complete and utter obsession the country has with the military and the reverence it holds for those who have 'served'.

If you have served in America, you are considered a superior citizen and are treated like royalty. The entire nation is proud of you and you are proud of what you've done. Nobody hides the fact that they have been part of the military. They all shout about it. And why wouldn't you? The country treats you like a demigod. Any Military Man's car is emblazoned with their credentials. A lot will have stickers on their rear window—*US Navy, Retired United States Army Colonel*; it's almost name, rank and serial number sort of stuff. Others take it further and get their achievements formally imprinted on their car number plates. *Purple Heart Winner* was one I saw. Another was *Honorably Discharged Veteran*. Presumably the former would be of more help in a highway pile-up situation. Other plates do list the rank. *US Navy—Petty Officer* was one inscription. These guys must actually go to the transport department, provide the requisite evidence and ask that their plate be marked.

Driving around the country, it's hard to go for more than an hour without seeing a road or highway dedicated to some group of veterans or another. Coming into Flagstaff, Arizona, the Interstate 40 is the 'Purple Heart Lane'. I drove a number of 'Korean War Memorial' highways and the Vietnam ones are innumerable. Just after leaving Yosemite National Park we passed a sign that read 'You are entering Mono County— Where we Honor Veterans'.

The Yanks definitely put their money where their mouth is where the military is concerned. America spends more on the military than the next twelve countries combined, exports more arms than any other country, and has the most foreign bases.

Whilst they hardly seem to need them, the media is saturated with advertising campaigns for the military as well. One television ad entitled 'Heroes Work Here' features men and women in their battle dress and continually repeats the words 'Hire excellence. They'll get the job done. Hire veterans.' Marine Corps Jobs Centres (spelt Centers) are all over the place pushing for jobs as well. The most seen ads are for the marines and are on roadside billboards throughout the country. There's a series of them, featuring a good looking black bloke, dressed in his uniform and saluting. The catch phrases vary, but the theme is the same—to be a marine you have to be committed, courageous, elite, a superior being. 'Be better than yourself, be a marine'; 'Dedicated to a sense of honor'; 'Dedicated to a life of courage'; 'For Our Nation. For Us All. The Few. The Proud. The Marines' and 'It's a Commitment—The Marines'. It's all presented in a very romantic way. There's little wonder every Yank is clamouring to be a part of it.

And if the pride of serving and the esteem in which you're held wasn't enough of an enticement, the preferential treatment and monetary discounts for absolutely everything would be. Most public car parks have spaces reserved for military personnel who can park for free. That's probably why they get their number plates imprinted. But that's the least of it. They get large reductions on bus fares, museums, hotel bookings, and even in some clothing stores. It's significant as well, often being 50% off or even completely free. We did an alligator tour on the bayou in Louisiana for $60. The army boys only had to pay $20. To get into Universal Studios in Los Angeles they don't pay the $80 fee, but are advised to phone in to discuss a fair rate.

When we went to the Grand Canyon we bought an annual pass that allowed us entry to all the country's national parks. The sign at the paying station read 'Annual pass $80. Active Military Personnel $0'.

I asked the ranger who we bought our pass from about it.

'Well, they deserve it,' he said. 'Incredible people. They deserve it for serving.' That's the attitude of everyone in America.

'Why's that?' I said.

'They've served. You serve, you deserve,' he said. 'Mind you. It's only for active personnel. I'm a Vietnam vet and I don't get it. I don't get much at all.'

'Really,' I said. 'You do fairly well don't you?'

'Not so much,' he said. 'All we get is all our schooling paid for, a cheap house loan, a free burial, quite a bit of free parking and a lot of respect. Respect is the main thing.'

'And discounts on pretty much everything,' I said. 'Hotels, museums, entry fees, cheap cinema tickets.'

'I suppose so,' he said, shrugging his shoulders. 'Are you active US military or not?'

'No.'

'Which military are you in, sir?'

'I'm not in the military.'

'Really,' he said. 'Not in the military at all. There's no discount then. Only active US military.'

'Yes, I know.'

We drove through.

'What's this 'served' shit they go on about? 'Served this', 'served that',' I said to Lucy. 'I'm pretty sure being in the military is a paid job, isn't it? It's like they're doing the country a favour. They haven't been conscripted. It's absurd.'

They really do see it as far more than just a job. Corporate America has bought into the obsession as well. Budweiser advertises that if a certain make of its beer is bought in enough quantities, it will donate $2.5 million to military families.

And they don't miss out at the airport either. At the gate when the boarding call is made—'First class and business passengers, as well as families with small children, are invited to board now'—'US military personnel' are added to the pre-boarding list.

They even have specific churches for those who have

served. In Montana, there was a 'Soldiers' Church', mixing the country's two favourite pastimes.

Of course, the military has agencies to manage all of this. Throughout America there are branches of the Department of Veteran Affairs everywhere. In Wyoming I actually saw a car with the department's name on the side, driving the country dealing with the affairs of veterans. The question is, what affairs do they need to deal with? Prosthetic maintenance perhaps, but most of the time I'd imagine it's a team of accountants managing the array of discounts that have been received and negotiating for more.

28

THE DESERT DOG

'I've been through the desert on a horse with no name, it felt good to be out of the rain...'

—'A Horse With No Name', America

I threw the coin high into the air and watched it fall into the abyss below, quickly losing it in the glare and the expanse.

'What did you wish for?' Lucy asked.

'Can't say.'

'Come on. Tell me.'

'Nope,' I said. 'Then it won't come true.'

'I think I know anyway,' she said.

'Is that right?' I said.

'Was it that my moods would get better?'

'I can't give any clues either,' I said, smiling. But she knew. And what was the difference, anyway? I didn't really think it'd come true.

We were standing on the edge of the Grand Canyon in Arizona. There were layers of red and orange in the walls of the cauldron that stretched in every direction. The Colorado River could just been made out as it carved its way through the bottom of the enormous gorge. A condor hovered above, its black and white wings tilting up on the thermals, before swooping away.

I was expecting the Grand Canyon to be large, but its enormity is incredible. I walked up to it nonchalantly, without thinking about all that much, another day another sight. But when I first saw it I was speechless. It's an awe-inspiring vision, more impressive than any other I'd seen, including Machu Picchu or the Great Pyramid. People misuse the word awesome. Awe means reverential fear or respect for a holy being. If something is awesome, it has a God-like power or presence. The Grand Canyon is the closest thing to awesome that I've witnessed. I found it difficult to stop looking.

But I did stop and we left and went back to our car. Lucy had been getting photos of the car licence plates for every state. She was still missing a couple from the east coast, as well as Hawaii and Alaska. Car parks at national attractions were a good place to get them. A man saw her photographing Delaware.

'I've got Vermont over there if you don't have it,' he said. 'I assume you're collecting plates.'

Lucy thanked him and photographed his plate.

'Excuse me,' yelled another man. 'There's a car next to mine with Pennsylvania if you need it.'

The people of Arizona are very friendly. We found that in Flagstaff where we picked up our car.

We'd flown into the town at 1am and caught a cab to our

hotel. The cab driver chatted away, as did the hotel manager. People spoke freely, happy to discuss their lives. The cabbie had been driving a truck across the country when it broke down near Flagstaff. He made it into town to get the truck fixed and never left. That was three years ago. A number of people told us similar stories. A lady working in the Walmart had come on a holiday from New York and didn't go home.

The next day we went to a Starbucks. There were thirty cars queued up for the drive-through service and the store was packed, with a line of people reaching out the door.

'Thank you very much for coming in,' said the woman behind the counter when she served us. It was a beautiful sunny Sunday and she was stuck inside serving a never ending queue of people. She had a genuine smile. 'You have a terrific day now ya hear.'

The man at the car hire place was equally helpful. In fact, when we dropped the car back thirty-two days later, he was so impressed with the 9,000 kilometres that we'd driven, that he shook my hand and gave me a discount, laughing as he told his colleagues.

Our car was a Chevrolet Malibu. It was very comfortable and rode smoothly. We called it Mal, our Desert Dog.

We drove out from Flagstaff and followed Route 66 through Winslow and out to the Grand Canyon. From there, we headed through the desert to Monument Valley.

The Arizona desert was magnificent—vast spaces filled with millions of tufts of grass and rocks and red dirt. We passed groups of cyclists competing in the 'Race Across America'. The heat was scorching, and one man was kneeling on the ground, his bike lying next to him, as he vomited into the dust. A nearby cross marked a lone grave in the desert. The conditions were tough.

We crossed into Utah on Route 163 and into Monument Valley. Immense red and jagged monoliths rose from the desert floor all around us, as if they'd been painted on the sky. It was beautiful. We stopped the car on the side of the highway and watched the sun set, the crimson light shimmering across the valley. There was nobody else around.

I grabbed Lucy's hand.

'This is awesome,' Lucy said.

'Yes it is,' I said. 'It is truly awesome.'

It was the second correct usage in one day.

It quickly grew dark and we drove away, looking for somewhere to stay for the night. Next to a lonely stretch of highway was a red 'Vacancy' sign flickering above a place called Bob's Motel. We pulled in. The motel looked shut, although there was a man sitting by himself outside one of the rooms.

'Can I help you?' he asked.

'We're after a room,' I said.

'The office is around the front, I think,' he said.

He obviously didn't work there. I assessed the man more carefully. He looked like a redneck. There was a Mustang parked in front of his room. I looked at the front of the motel and couldn't see any office.

'No, no, my bad,' he said, collecting his thoughts. 'It's around here. Around the other side.' He stood up and pointed past his room.

'Come on,' he said. 'I'll show you.'

There was a sense of controlled impatience.

'Come on,' he repeated. 'I ain't gunna bite. It's just

around here.'

I stood there for a second in silence, surveying the scene. It wasn't right. I was in the ring alone with the bull.

'Just a second,' I said. 'I'll just get our bags.'

'It's just around here,' he said, taking a step towards us.

I looked at Lucy. She was pale.

'Walk normally back to the car,' I whispered to her as we turned.

'Please get me out of here,' she said.

'Just walk to the car and get in.'

By the time we got to the car, the man was only five metres away.

'I'll just get my stuff,' I said to him.

I got in the car and locked the doors. I looked up and he was standing next to the car. He had the look of an unsuccessful rapist. I started up the car and sped off, through the dirt of the car park and onto the highway.

'Oh my God,' said Lucy once we were at a safe distance. 'I can't believe that. He looked bloody dangerous.'

'That was like a scene from a movie,' I said. 'He didn't look like he had much of a social compass. Did you see the Mustang parked there?'

We slept the night in a hotel in Bluff, and the next day pressed on through the Utah desert. We had lunch at a busy little town called Moab. Eddie McStiff's Brewery looked good and we went in for a drink. I ordered a beer and a gin at the bar.

'Where are you going to sit?' asked the bartender.

'Not sure,' I said. 'But I can take the drinks.'

'I'm sorry, sir,' he said. 'But I have to know where you're

sitting. You see, if you sit at a table, I can't serve you alcohol unless you order a meal.'

'That's strange,' I said. 'Why's that?'

'Utah State law,' he said. 'I can't serve alcohol unless it's with food. But you can sit at the bar and just drink.'

'We'll sit at the bar then.'

There was a sign on the wall that read 'Driving under the influence of alcohol is a serious crime that is prosecuted aggressively in Utah'.

We had the drinks and left for Arches National Park. It was a clear day and there was nothing but sun and sky and desert. The dramatic landscape changed constantly, the rocks sculpted by the wind. The Utah car licence plate matches the scenery, with oranges and blues blending into each other like a painting.

We made it to the Park. The wind was hot and dry, and opening the car door was like opening the door of an oven.

We walked to the rock formations that had been hollowed out by the wind erosion. They are the key attraction of the area and were not all that impressive, although we'd been spoilt. There was a pair of prairie dogs eating some grass next to the path. A group of middle-aged Americans were taking photos of them.

'What are they?' one lady said to nobody in particular.

'Prairie dogs,' I said.

'Really,' she said. 'They're so cute. Aren't they cute?'

'They sure are ma'am,' I said. 'Damned good eating too.'

'Oh, I see,' she said.

We walked back to our car. A gang of bikers had arrived. They were standing in the car park, putting on hiking boots and the mandatory bandanas, preparing for the zealot hike into the desert, just so they could say they did it. One man had a camera on his helmet to record the event.

A big butch woman with unwashed, stringy hair was in the group.

'I don't travel to find myself. I travel to create myself,' she said.

'It's all about the journey, not the ride,' said one of the men, as he was taking off his leather jacket. 'I go wherever the road takes me and when I reach the top of the mountain, I keep climbing.'

'Hell yeah,' said the butch woman. 'I was born lost and take no pleasure in being found.'

'Good God,' I said to Lucy. 'Listen to these dickheads, will you?'

'Unbelievable,' she said.

The bikers of America pretend they're rugged and tough, but they are such losers. For starters, they're frightened of the road, always going under the speed limit and too timid to overtake anyone. A lot of them are ex-military and think riding a bike is a religion and they do everything they can to exude the freedom they pretend they're chasing. They wear their tattered leather jackets, with pictures of skulls and slogans like 'Live to Ride' on the back, and their Nazi-style helmets, and go off riding to nowhere with a bunch of other similarly-minded morons who think they're living the dream as well. The fact is, there are Harley Davidson shops in every second town that cater to the weaklings, who probably watch

Easy Rider every Saturday morning before they set off.

It's all so contrived. We saw one biker on his knees by the side of the road, photographing his Harley like it was his girlfriend, the desert scenery in the background.

There are thousands of bikers in America and whenever one passes another coming the other way, they each put a hand out low to the ground as a wave of acknowledgement and respect. This happens every time and in every part of the country. Such camaraderie. Such losers.

We left the Arches and continued through the desert as the land changed to a moonscape through towns called Yellowcat and Rabbit Valley. These towns were tiny—no services and only a house or two—but each had a Welcome Centre. Virtually every town in America has a Welcome Centre that contains maps and leaflets setting out the key attractions. Presumably some simply tell the visitor that there is nothing whatsoever to see and advise them to move on immediately.

Different areas of America have cornered the market for different essentials as well. The niche of the desert was fireworks. Every ten minutes there was a huge sign advertising a fireworks barn. Big Daddy's Fireworks, Blow 'Em Up Fireworks or Frank's Fireworks would appear a mile later as an enormous warehouse on the side of the highway.

Beef jerky, the tasteless chewy dried meat, was another item heavily pushed in the desert region. One large sign with a picture of the foodstuff had the words 'Super Fresh Jerky'.

'It's really fresh,' Lucy said. 'Except for the six months of air drying.'

There were also quite a number of indoor shooting ranges in the desert towns. We stopped in at one of them. It looked like a 'ma and pa' type of outfit. There was a sign on the door as we walked in—'When there's lead in the air, there's hope'.

'Howdy folks,' said a man of about fifty with a skin head. He was wearing a red lumberjack shirt. 'You can call me Bill. What would you like to shoot today?'

'We were wanting to shoot a pistol if possible, Bill,' I said.

'That's no problem,' he said. 'We got pistols, assault rifles, machine guns, anything you like really. Come take a look.'

He walked us into a warehouse. There were people lined up, shooting down lanes at targets. There were no instructors there. People were just shooting as they pleased. One man turned to talk to another, his gun moving with his body, the business end pointing across the other shooters.

'Health and safety doesn't seem a high priority here,' I said to Lucy. 'Do you want to leave?'

'Yes please,' she said.

'Thanks all the same,' I said to Bill. 'But we might give it a miss.'

We turned to walk out.

'Hey, mister,' yelled Bill. 'Don't go. Please don't go. The family that shoots together, stays together.'

We left and drove on through the desert.

29

ROCKY MOUNTAIN HIGH

'He climbed cathedral mountains, he saw silver clouds below, he saw everything as far as you can see.'

—'Rocky Mountain High', John Denver

The drive into Aspen, Colorado along the Top of the Rockies highway is breathtaking. It is breathtaking not only because of the remarkable scenery, but also because the road is narrow and winds alongside a precipitous cliff face where there are no safety barriers at all.

We drove above the snow line, climbing to 4,300 metres as we crossed the tectonic plate of the continental divide, sharp pains jabbing in our stomachs from the altitude. Perhaps predicting a calamity, a bird of prey circled above the thousands of pines trees, all uniform and standing at attention like soldiers, different shades of green signifying the ranks.

We stopped and got out of the car at the top of a peak

that overlooked a stony creek of rapids. A young deer was drinking from the bank. The dulcet sounds of John Denver coming from the car stereo filled the air. I held Lucy's hand and we kissed at the top of the Rocky Mountains.

We had driven through the towns of Parachute, Rifle and Battlement on our way towards Aspen. The foothills of the Rockies were like piles of grey sand that had hardened. Then they turned into bare mountains of rock, jagged on top like a comb with some of its teeth snapped off. And then the pines started appearing. They were sparse at first, and from a distance looked like a teenage boy's stubble, but they quickly thickened to make the mountains fully green.

Old wooden telegraph poles followed the road through the hills as we wound along the line of the Colorado River, its waters bright blue and pristine, with trees growing right up to the gravelly banks.

The sun was bright, as bright as in the desert, and we had the car roof open. The wind blew back our hair and, with a bit of luck, I hoped it would blow away the heavy mood that filled the car. We had been arguing a lot for a few days about little things, nothing in particular, and we were trying to smile through the problems that lay just beneath the surface.

The night before we'd slept a few hours away in Grand Junction. We'd had trouble getting a room there, despite it being a Monday night, because there was a school swimming meet on in town. We'd had a similar problem in La Crosse, Wisconsin with a teenage athletics competition. There was always something to jack up the hotel prices.

Lucy wasn't feeling well and became frustrated when we couldn't find accommodation easily. Then she wasn't happy with the place we ate dinner in. We had been driving some long days and it was beginning to get her down. Her hormones were being inconsistent, as were her moods.

A lot of America was on high forest fire alert and going from Grand Junction to Aspen we saw planes dropping water as plumes of smoke billowed out of the mountains in the distance. In fact, the fires worsened, and a week later 250 homes near Denver were burnt and 32,000 people had to be evacuated. We were lucky and managed to avoid any trouble, as had been the case throughout our trip. There'd been floods in Florida, violent storms up the east coast, heat waves, hurricanes and bush fires, but we'd missed them all, and (apart from in New York) saw nothing but perfect weather the entire time.

Just before Aspen we stopped at Woody Creek and went to the tavern there for lunch. The writer Hunter S. Thompson used to live in the area and the place was a shrine to him, with photographs and memorabilia all over the walls. We had a burger each and a few drinks, before leaving for Aspen.

Aspen is a very upmarket and smart alpine village. You can almost smell the money. There are high-class fashion stores and many art galleries. The people are well-dressed and the houses look expensive. Kevin Costner is a resident, as was Jack Nicholson.

We had a drink at a microbrewery, then walked through the John Denver sanctuary, a wooded area a few hundred metres from town. It followed a shallow tributary of the Colorado River. We stopped on an old wooden bridge and looked into the water below. A cutthroat trout was swimming against the current, camouflaged against the smooth brown rocks, its position betrayed only by the fleck of red under its head. The green pine-covered ski fields of Aspen surrounded us. It was a magnificent and romantic setting. But this time there was no kissing.

30

EARLY IN THE MORNING

'Well, you're gonna miss me early in the morning one of these days…'

—'Early in the Morning', Buddy Holly

Walking back to our hotel in Aspen, a white cat crossed the path in front of us.

'Presumably that's good luck,' I said to Lucy.

She whipped up a smile from a large and varied stock. But it wasn't good luck.

'I'm going to leave in the morning,' she said when we were back in the room.

'But you've been feeling good for the last few weeks.'

She started crying. 'No, I've not been good. I've got to go.'

'Go where?' I said. 'How will you go?'

'I'll get a flight to Denver and fly to London from there.'

'Why are you doing this?' I said. She had taken me by surprise again.

'I have to go. I've been vomiting with stress. I can't stay

any longer.' She lay on the bed and covered her face with her hands. She was crying hard now.

'You have to stay,' I said. 'You have to finish the trip.'

'I can't. I'm exhausted.'

'I don't want to break up, but if you go I think we will.'

'Why do we have to break up?' Lucy said, her eyes red. 'I don't want to. I'll just go home and we can meet there when you get back.'

'I don't think it'll work like that.'

'I can't stay.'

She put her head in the pillow. I was sitting on the edge of the bed.

'Well, you need to think about what you're doing,' I said. 'Because this is a big decision. We've been through too much to end it now.'

'I don't want to end it, but I want to go home.'

'Going home will end it.'

'Why?'

'It just will,' I said.

We sat in silence for a few minutes.

'I really don't want you to go,' I said after a while. 'This is a lot like our discussion in Salvador, but it's about breaking up instead of starting out. Not quite as much fun.'

'It is, isn't it?' Lucy said. 'I'm sorry. I'm going.'

I walked over to the other bed in the room and got in. Lucy stayed in her bed. I turned out the lights.

'You're going to miss me, Lucia,' I said.

'I know. I'm so sorry.'

I lay in the dark, looking at the ceiling and waiting for my eyes to adjust to the night. I thought about what I would do if Lucy left. Finish the trip, that's what I'd do. But without her, it'd be no good. Still, I had to do it. I started thinking about my failed marriage. It'd been four years now. Then Lucy had come and made everything better, almost perfect. And now that was going to be over as well. Happy memories are the worst, and I tried to remember the bad times, the issues that Lucy and I had. But I couldn't. I just kept thinking how I didn't want to lose her. We'd been in each other's pockets for two years. She felt a part of me now. I couldn't sleep and the time passed slowly. I couldn't stop thinking about Lucy—about her expressive face lighting up when she spoke of her cats, about her walk and her talk, her smile. She always did things with a certain style. I didn't want to lose that. We'd resolved the issues from Memphis, but had we just tried to smile through it all, ignoring and masking the inherent problems, problems that were real? Things do not change with a change of scene and our capacity for self-delusion is boundless, especially when matters of the heart are concerned. But there was still hope, I was sure of it.

I looked across at Lucy sleeping. She looked so peaceful, so beautiful. I didn't want to lose her. I would do what I could.

Early in the morning, before sunrise, Lucy came across and lay in my bed. She didn't speak, she just tucked up beside me. I stroked her head. It was a good sign.

But then, without saying anything, she got up, dressed and walked out of the room. She returned an hour later.

'Where have you been?' I said as she walked in the door.

'I went to get some breakfast.'

'What are you going to do?' I said, still hopeful.

'I'm going.'

'Well, I'm going too then. I have a lot of driving to do today, so I've got to get going.'

'Where will you go?'

'North,' I said. 'Like we planned. I don't generally change plans.'

'You could come back to England as well,' she said.

'No. I'm going on. I have to.'

I packed my bags and took them out to the car. When I got back to the room, Lucy was sitting at the table and was on her laptop.

'What are you doing?' I asked.

'Booking my flight,' she said. 'I looked last night. I can fly to Denver at noon and then on to London at 3pm.'

She was completing the booking details. I walked over to her and put my hands on her shoulders.

'Please don't go,' I said.

'I have to. I'm too tired to stay. It's too hectic.'

'It doesn't have to be. We can have a week relaxing in one place. Maybe at a ranch somewhere. You've always wanted to do that.'

She finished completing the flight booking. All she had to do was click 'confirm'. We spoke around in circles for another ten minutes.

'No,' she said. 'I've got to go. I'm going.' She clicked 'confirm'. Nothing. She clicked it again. The page wouldn't load.

'This page has timed out,' she said. 'Now I've got to fill it all in again.'

'You don't have to,' I said. 'Don't fill it in.'

She completed the booking form again and was about to confirm. I put my hand on hers.

'Don't do it,' I said.

'I have to.'

'You don't have to.'

'I do.'

She moved my hand away and was about to finish it.

'If you click that mouse, it will change your life,' I said, trying to sound dramatic. 'Please don't go.'

She looked up at me and started crying.

'I don't know what I'm doing,' she said. 'I love you so much.'

'Then don't go.'

She stood up and I hugged her hard. Her tears wet the shoulder of my T-shirt. I could feel my own eyes welling up. We stood together, embraced in silence. She looked up at my face.

'You're nearly crying,' she said.

'I can't remember the last time I did,' I said. 'I can't say I care for it all that much.'

'I really love you,' she said. 'But I have to go.'

She reached to her computer to finish the flight booking.

'For God's sake,' she said. 'Now the Internet connection's gone.'

'Somebody mustn't want you to go.'

The Internet came back up and her details were still there.

'Look,' I said. 'I've got to go. It's check-out time. I'm going to the car now.'

'Goodbye,' she said. 'I love you.'

She was about to click the mouse again.

'This is your last chance, Lucy,' I said. 'Don't do it.'

'Goodbye.'

'So long, Lucy. I love you.'

I picked up the car keys and turned to walk out the door.

'Wait,' Lucy said. 'Hold on a second.'

'Yes.'

'I was thinking,' she said.

'Yes.'

'About that week in one place to relax? Where would we go, do you think?'

'Anywhere you want,' I said. 'Anywhere at all.'

'Could we go to a ranch?'

'Let's go.'

We drove away. Far away from the pretty little town of Aspen.

31

CRAZY HORSE AND THE WILD WEST

'Out to the west there's a trail that leads somewhere. And a call of the wild that takes some people there. And things get crazy and you have to use that sun. And you wonder if this is the way the West is won.'

—'Wild West', Joe Jackson

The Native American Indians may not be a very intelligent race where money is concerned. Sure, they may have survived off the land for years before the West was civilised, but they haven't done too well at all in modern times. Apart from the American government continually duping them, resulting in most of their land being taken away, they've completely failed to capitalise on the intrigue the white man holds for them.

Throughout America there are Indian reservations that

have towns on them. These towns are saturated by Indian 'trading posts', which are nothing more than shops with tee pees painted on the outside that sell mass-produced tacky crap. Every one of these shops is exactly the same, the Indians not realising that to succeed they need to be unique.

But the pinnacle of their economic ineptitude must surely come in the form of the Crazy Horse Memorial.

Famous for leading a war party to victory against the US Government at the Battle of the Little Big Horn in 1876, Crazy Horse ranks as the most notable and iconic of all American Indians. And he has been immortalised in the form of a monument in the Black Hills of South Dakota. Commissioned by Henry Standing Bear, the memorial consists of a rock carving of Crazy Horse riding a horse and pointing into the distance. But it's not just any monument. This thing is carved out of a mountain and it's gigantic— 195 metres wide and 172 metres high—the world's largest sculpture. At least it was supposed to be. The monument has been under construction since 1948, has cost a fortune, and it's not even close to completion. At present, all that can be seen is Crazy's face and the top of his arm. And you have to look at it for a while to even make that out, like one of those dotted paintings that you stare at cross-eyed before the image suddenly becomes apparent.

And here's the best part. It costs $27 to view the monument, more than any national park in America, the Grand Canyon and Yellowstone included, but because of its size, you can appreciate it far better from miles away on the highway than you can from close up. But the scenery around Crazy Horse is spectacular and it's a beautiful drive to get there, so that's something I guess.

Before arriving at that white elephant on the mountain, we'd driven down through the wide plains of Wyoming—the romance of the West. There was nothing for hundreds of miles but gold and brown grass, healthy cattle grazing and plenty of space. The highway was gun-barrel straight for as far as the eye could see, and we had it completely to ourselves. We saw only the occasional car in hours of driving, the trucks of the East and North being replaced with emptiness. Rickety windmills dotted the landscape as a Union Pacific train carting coal at 5,000 feet snaked along in the distance.

It was amazing how fast the scenery changed from desert to alpine to vast plains, all within a few hundred miles.

We were looking for something to eat and there weren't many options. There wasn't much in Cheyenne, the capital of Wyoming, and what was there wasn't open. Known as a rough gunslingers' town back in the day, Cheyenne appeared very sedate, the people more interested in the numerous ten feet high brightly-painted and spurred cowboy boots that stood in the streets. It was as if a family of giants had got drunk, taken off their boots and left without them.

Having had no luck all morning, at about noon we passed through a two-bit town called Wheatland, and saw a café. Vimbo's Dusty Boots, it was called, and there was a 'Welcome Hunters' sign out the front. We couldn't quite tell if it was open or not, but there was nothing else around so we walked in. We were met at the door by a man who I assumed to be Vimbo.

'Howdy folks. Table for two?' he said.

He sat us down and gave us menus. There were rifles mounted on the walls, as well as deer heads and paintings of horses and boots.

As well as the usual fare of red bean soup and beef, there were Redneck Nachos and Cowboy Cookies available.

After a few minutes, Vimbo came back to our table.

'Are you ready there partners?' he said. The 'ya'll' of the South had been replaced by 'howdy' and 'partner' in the West.

Every head in the place turned to look at us when we ordered. I assumed it was our accents. Either that or our clothing. They were all wearing boots and dusty jeans and we weren't.

'I could really do with a beer,' Lucy said, after Vimbo had left our table.

'Really?' I said.

'Yeah. I've got a real taste for it.'

'You don't normally drink beer,' I said. 'Maybe it's the Wild West. It brings out the thirst in a cowgirl.'

After lunch we headed through real Indian country— Elkhorn Creek, Middle Bear, Horse Shoe Creek—before passing the border town of Van Tassell, population eighteen, and into Nebraska. We were on the Crazy Horse Memorial Highway, presumably named to commemorate his slaying or as a compromise after stealing the Indians' land. Trees started appearing as the plains turned to hills. A lot of the towns we drove through were decorated with covered wagons on the roofs of the houses.

From Nebraska, we crossed into South Dakota. The road changed to the US Marine Corps Memorial Highway, ironic given that the Crazy Horse Memorial is in that state. The State Line Casino was at the border in South Dakota, in the middle of nowhere on the plains.

The long straight roads continued as we went past Dead Horse Creek, through the Badlands and into the Black Hills. Grey rock formations developed into rustic hills, before mountains covered with pines replaced the wide plains. Pronghorn deer ate by the side of the road and hundreds of prairie dogs sat on their mounds of dirt, watching us as we climbed.

The gambling theme continued throughout South Dakota. There were casinos everywhere, and the town of Deadwood was no exception. Every establishment was a casino or had some form of gambling available. Most were full of slot machines, with the odd Black Jack table at the front.

We decided to stay in Deadwood for a couple of days, and checked into the Franklin Silverado, a grand old red-carpeted hotel in the centre of town. When you walked in it felt like going back in time, and I could almost picture the big time gamblers and whores it would have once housed.

Of course, it had a casino in the main foyer, and being small and not very sophisticated, I thought it would be the perfect place to try counting cards. But there were continuous shuffling machines on the Black Jack tables, which negates any counting, so we went for the slot machines.

Lucy played first and won $5 with her opening spin. She was happy and shrieked with excitement.

'Having a bit of luck there are ya?' said an old man with a

lupine smile who had chosen to sit at the next slot machine, despite there being a hundred others that were vacant.

I'd seen him dancing with a woman as we walked in, the white man's overbite on full display.

'That was our first spin,' I said. 'It's going pretty well so far.'

The man pulled down on the lever of his slot machine and the electronic barrels spun.

'Knowing my luck,' he said. 'I won't win a thing.'

'Do you get a lot do you?' I asked.

'Lot of what?'

'Bad luck.'

'I get my share,' he said. 'I don't have any money, but I live well and I'm proud of that. Very proud indeed.'

'It's no shame to be poor, but it's no great honour either.'

'It's no honour,' he said. 'But poverty's only comparative anyway. I'm going to make my money one day soon. And this is the way to do it. I've got a system.'

He lost his first spin and played again.

'A system on the slot machines?' I said.

'That's right. I can't tell you, but it involves betting low and then betting high.'

'Only madmen and drunks bet high on the slots.'

He kept spinning and he kept losing. We were losing now too.

'I'm neither,' he said. 'But I'm going to do it. I'm going to do it and get rich. I have $1,000 to play with today.'

'Are you serious?' I said. 'You can't build a reputation on what you're going to do.'

'Oh, I'm going to do it alright,' he said. 'Get rich and live as a poor man with lots of money.'

'Like Picasso?'

'That's right. I've always admired that great man.'

As is usually true of a man with one idea, he was obsessed and he kept spinning, betting small amounts, followed by large amounts. He won the odd game, just enough to keep him interested, but in the time we were there he lost about $100 I'd say.

I got sick of watching.

'Good luck with the system,' I said.

'Thank you, sir,' he said. 'But I don't think I'll need any luck this time. I've got God on my side.'

We left to get a drink.

'Do you think he's for real?' Lucy said.

'He seems to be,' I said. 'At that rate, he'll lose the lot tonight. A fool and his money are soon parted.'

We walked out on to the street. A sign read 'Historic National Town' and I couldn't fathom how one town was more historic than another. A lot of towns had those signs.

I knew nothing of Deadwood, apart from the HBO television series, but it had one main street running up the centre of town. There were saloons and steak houses and it looked like the Wild West, except for the lights from all the casino machines. Two men staggered down the street with guns, on the way to one of about twenty daily re-enactments of the killing of Wild Bill Hickok. I'd never heard of Wild Bill, until the HBO series that is, but he was very famous in Deadwood. So were Seth Bullock and Calamity Jane (I'd heard of her). The trio were buried in the cemetery on the hill above the town.

We went into the only good bar in town, the No. 10 Saloon. There were animal heads on the walls and sawdust on the floor. Everything was made of wood and it was very dark. It could have been 1870 in there.

Lucy and I had a few drinks. We were getting on so well that it was hard to believe we could ever argue.

A band set up in the far corner of the bar, then started singing Country songs. They were pretty good. Most of the bands we'd seen in America were pretty good. After a few songs, the lead man started talking about the history of Deadwood. Named for the dead trees found on its hills, Deadwood thrived during the late 1800s after gold was discovered in nearby Custer. It quickly gained a reputation as a lawless town, where murders were commonplace. He went on to tell a story of John Wayne getting arrested in the town for having a gun on his hip.

'The Duke was walking through town to do some filming here eight years ago,' he said. 'He was wearing a gun as that was needed for the part. Anyway, the police came and arrested him. Locked him up for a couple of hours.'

'That doesn't sound right, does it?' Lucy said.

'The arrest or the eight years ago part?' I said.

'Both.'

John Wayne died in 1979. We didn't listen to the singer's stories after that. As soon as one lie is told, nothing can be believed. We went on drinking instead and the time passed.

The next day we woke up feeling a little hazy. We needed a good breakfast.

'I'm starving,' Lucy said.

'Me too. I could eat the arse out of a low flying duck.'

We went to the hotel dining room. Lucy got ID'ed at the

door, probably because of the gaming tables that were also in there.

The breakfast was a $10 buffet. We paid half that because we had vouchers from the hotel. It was incredible. Anything you could want was there. I knew we had a long day's drive ahead of us, so I ate up—two six-egg omelettes, a fruit and granola plate, fried eggs and potatoes, six pieces of pizza and two enormous roast beef steaks. Lucy had some fruit and eggs.

'How are you feeling now?' Lucy said as we were walking out.

'Not too bad, but I'm waiting for it all to kick in,' I said. 'I might have overdone it a bit with that last piece of pizza.'

We left Deadwood after breakfast and passed through Custer, a small town with fur trading posts and rustic saloons that advertised buffalo and elk steaks. We were heading for Mount Rushmore. Mount Rushmore is near to Rapid City, and whilst it is geographically almost in the dead centre of America, it is a long way from anywhere else you'd want to go.

It is free to get into Mount Rushmore and this fact is advertised everywhere, on road signs and in tour brochures. What they fail to tell you, is that you are forced to enter the affiliated car park and that costs $11.

'It's a real rort this isn't it?' I said to Hailee, the young girl who was manning the car park booth. 'They say it's free, but there's no other option than to pay the parking.'

Hailee giggled and didn't say anything.

'It's really an entrance fee isn't it?' I said. 'Why don't they just call it that?'

'I suppose it is,' she said, and handed me the parking permit. 'This is valid all year.'

'Well, that should come in handy,' I said. 'We're here almost every day.'

Our guide book recommended that tourists allow at least two hours to fully appreciate the monument. Whilst it was very good, the carvings of the four ex-presidents' faces almost perfectly defined, we were there ten minutes. I couldn't see how anyone could take any longer. We walked up to the viewing point, looked at the mountain, took some photos, and left. There was nothing else to do.

During the few minutes that we were there, I overheard a woman who was standing next to me. She was gazing at the faces like they'd been blessed.

'Oh dear God,' she said to nobody specific. 'It's amazing. Truly amazing.'

I looked at her, but she wouldn't avert her eyes from the sculpture. She was transfixed with the mountain.

'It's almost as if God descended from the Heavens and carved that mountain himself,' she continued. 'It is that beautiful.'

As we were leaving, I saw her getting onto a bus in the car park.

'Rivers Harvest Church' was painted on the side, and under that were the words 'Need Jesus? Ask me how. You need Jesus!'

32

CITY SLICKERS

'Riding on the range, I've got my hat on, I've got my boots dusty...'

—`'I Wanna Be A Cowboy'`, Boys Don't Cry

A wave of water lurched into the raft as we bounced off a series of rocks like a pinball and plummeted down a sharp drop to the next level of the river. The raft bent and slinked to fit the contours of the pass as we nose-dived into another deeper pool before flattening out again.

'Alright, we made that one. Yeehaaah,' yelled Mike, our guide, over the noise of the rapids. 'Quick paddle high five.' From the back of the boat he lifted his paddle in the air to the centre above our heads and we all joined in, shaking hands with the ends of our paddles. There were seven of us in the raft. I looked at Lucy. She was drenched, her wet hair strewn across her face.

'Okay,' said Mike. 'Here we go again. Paddle hard, left, left, left, harder. Now hold on.'

The raft was sucked forward again as a wall of water engulfed the vessel, blinding us for a few seconds.

'Oh yeah baby,' screamed Mike.

'Yeeeahh,' I joined in, but in my mind I was wondering why the hell I'd not listened to a word of the introductory safety demonstration on the bank. I'd been too busy adjusting my far too tight full-body black wetsuit. At least we had helmets on.

We were rafting down the Gallatin River along a fourteen mile stretch that contained grade four rapids. Part of the stretch was where the film A River Runs Through It, starring Brad Pitt, was shot. The minutes seemed like hours, but we eventually made it through the Mad Mile and the river flattened out. It was in the Mad Mile that the scene where Brad and his brother take a wooden boat down the river and it gets dashed on the rocks was filmed.

'Yeehaaah. We did it. We did it, god damn it,' said Mike. Another paddle high five. 'That's the end of the dangerous stuff. Well done y'all. Now just sit back and enjoy this wonderful scenery.'

I took a deep breath and wiped the water from my face and looked back up the river. It really was something. The winding river was peppered with grey boulders as it cut its way through steep pine-clad mountains. I looked over at Lucy. She was smiling. I put my hand on her hand.

'Why's that there?' I said to Mike, pointing at some writing on Lucy's seat which read 'The First Lady Sat Here'.

'Unbelievable,' Mike said. 'It was unbelievable. About six months ago the Obamas came here and the First Lady sat right there. In that exact spot. The kids were in the raft too.'

'Where was Obama?' I asked.

'It was deemed too risky for him.'

'The rapids?'

'No,' said Mike. 'It was deemed a security risk. National security.'

'Why was that?'

'You wouldn't believe what went on. The Secret Service were out here for four months, asking questions of us and the locals, doing surveillance, checking everything. They must have come here twenty times. They shut off sixteen miles of the river and twenty miles of the highway and had security cars and men with guns positioned on the road. They also had four other rafts filled with Secret Service men on the river. And all this for a two hour raft down the river, but it was still deemed too risky for the President.'

'That must have cost a lot,' I said.

'Hundreds of thousands,' Mike said. 'But hell, it was well worth it to have the First Lady on my boat.'

'Were you guiding her?'

'No.'

I looked down the river as we floated along.

'Hey man,' said one of the other guys who was in our boat. Everyone else was American. 'What's the name of that Mexican joint in town?'

'Don't know its name,' said Mike. 'But they do awesome margaritas there.'

'Yeah man,' he said. 'We had, like three there last night. We were hammered.'

Christ, the Yanks and their drinking. They think taking a six-pack to a piss up is a big night out.

'The lady in there,' he went on, 'was telling us about how she caught her husband with some other woman in town.

There was an uproar.'

'How big's the town?' I asked Mike.

'Not big at all.'

'Is there much interaction like that? You know, sneaking from cabin to cabin at night?'

'This is Montana,' said Mike. 'It's a very small area and people come to work for the summer. Sneaking from cabin to cabin is all there is here.'

We got to the end of the stretch, pulled the raft up the bank and got onto a bus to take us back to town. It was full of people from other rafts. Lucy and I sat near the back and all the guides were behind us. They were talking about kayaking down the river.

'It's awesome man,' one said, looking very animated. 'I like, paddle hard, then like settle into an eddy, then attack the rock face. It's like, totally radical.'

Christ, the Yanks and their 'likes'. It's like this, and like that. Once the purview of teenage girls, now half the country talks that way. When will it come to an end?

'Hell, dude,' said a younger guy. 'I like to get right back and come at the tough sections hard. Like real hard. Show no mercy at all.'

These guys were the surfers of the rafting world. They certainly loved what they did, but I was glad to get off that bus and get back to the ranch.

We were staying at the 320 Guest Ranch at Big Sky, Montana, named because of the 320 acres it sat on. Our package was the 'Your Keepin' It Cowboy' deal. That got us a spacious log cabin set at the base of a pine mountain with a crystal clear creek running past that flowed into the picturesque Gallatin River. A family of prairie dogs scurried and played on the grass outside our window. Set at 6,500 feet in the Rocky Mountains, the dude ranch had been there since 1905. The sign as we turned off the road to go into the ranch read 'Howdy Y'all'.

There was a bar and dining room on the ranch, made all of wood, with grizzly skins and moose and elk heads on the walls. The restaurant was always full, most of the patrons wearing cowboy hats, checked shirts and boots. All the women looked like Annie Oakley. At dinner time a local girl with an acoustic guitar sang Dolly Parton songs, whilst the breakfast of sausages and eggs, one of the only decent ones we'd had in America, was accompanied by banjo playing bluegrass music.

The 320 was a genuine dude ranch, with horse riding, lassoing and fishing.

Dude ranches began in the late 1800s in response to the romantic notion of the West. There was an appetite for people to enjoy the freedom and nostalgia of the West, without being exposed to the dangers of the original pioneers. The clientele were people from Eastern cities, known by the cowboys as 'dudes'. As Western movies became more popular, the trend increased to the point where the Dude Ranchers Association was established in Cody to manage the industry.

To get to the ranch, we'd driven through the badlands of Montana, with their grey dirt hills and desolate plains of inhospitality, and into Billings, the most populated city in the state. The capital is actually Helena, but in thirty-three of the fifty states, the most populous city is not the capital.

Billings is a terrible town. Just before the main street as you come into town is the Montana Women's Prison.

'Imagine the bitches in there,' I said to Lucy as we went past it.

Just near to the prison a shop sign read 'Welcome. Deli. Gifts. Guns.' Another read 'Ammunition. All Your Killing Needs Here'.

As usual, all the accommodation was taken as there was an antique car show and a dog show and a monster truck show on in town. We drove on.

Billings was quickly behind us as the scenery turned beautiful. There were fields of green crops with big irrigating machines spraying water into the sunshine and forming rainbows in the sky. Green foothills covered with pines appeared, together with austere rock mountains of snow behind them. There were a lot of deer dead on the highway.

We got to Bozeman, a quaint university town with far more character than Billings, and decided to stay. Our hotel was straight out of the 1960s. Frank Sinatra music was piped throughout the hotel and car park, so when you walked, it felt like you were in a television show.

We went out for a drink at the local microbrewery. I had four pints. Christ, they made me feel better.

'What day is it?' I asked Lucy.

'Saturday,' she said.

'Really,' I said. 'It feels like a Friday.'

'You have no idea what day it is?'

'No,' I said. 'It makes me feel good not knowing. It makes me feel glad.'

The bartender gave me a free sample of a local beer called Moose Drool.

'It's very fruity,' she said as she handed it to me.

'Yes,' I said, taking a mouthful. 'A bit too fruity. You wouldn't want more than a pint of it. Unless there was nothing else, that is.'

We were sitting on stools at the outdoor bar and a large, strong looking girl came and sat right next to me, almost on top of me. She was straight out of the Montana Women's Prison, I thought. She stared right at me. The range was four inches. God, she was hard to look at. She could have hosted an ugly convention.

'It's high,' I said, referring to the bar stool.

'Hi,' she said.

'Hi,' I said.

She looked across at Lucy. They went through similar pleasantries and then the woman starting talking about her husband.

'There's road works at Parachute and Rifle where he is right now,' the woman said.

'Is he in the army?' Lucy asked.

'No, he just works up there on the roads.' Parachute and Rifle were towns.

'Can you go rafting up there?'

'You can,' she said. 'But you have to be real careful because I stood on a catfish and had an infection for five days. The water was dirty. They make good eating. But some people don't like them 'cause they're bottom feeders.'

'Yes, I saw them in the South and didn't fancy them,' Lucy said.

'I just send my husband to the creek at the end of the garden and he catches them. The other day he caught one and put it in the bath with me. It was right in there, swimming in the tub. I was not real happy 'bout that. But my two year old got attached to it. But I said 'no honey, that's your dinner'.'

'So how did you kill it, then? Do you just hit them over the head?' Lucy asked.

'I wish you could. But they're real tough. They don't die. Better off stabbing them in the head. You need to stab them in the head. They don't die easy.'

'Oh, I see.'

'Yeah, so Casey, my girl, was real attached to it, but I stabbed it in the head and fed it to her for dinner. She wasn't real happy 'bout that, but you gotta eat someways, don't ya?'

There was an awkward silence.

'That sounds nice,' Lucy said.

'Do you have any pets?' the woman asked.

'Three cats.'

'Oh, I hate cats,' the woman said, scowling. 'I've got two dogs. Do you want to see a picture?'

She got her phone out and showed us a picture of two pit bulls.

'What breed are they?' Lucy asked, just for something to say.

'Pit bulls.' The woman smiled.

'That's nice,' Lucy said.

'People say 'Oh my God, you've got pit bulls with two young kids' but they'll do anything with my kids. They play with them. They're the sweetest dogs. Totally harmless most of the time.'

'Cute,' Lucy said. 'In England they're not allowed outside without a muzzle.'

'Ah, that's not needed around here. I grew up in a tough area. Really tough area. Me neighbour had a pit bull. It wasn't so good. Real territorial, ya know.'

'I bet,' Lucy said.

We finished our drinks, said goodbye and left.

On our first day at the ranch, we went horseback riding in the tree-covered hills. Lucy had a horse called Hershey and they put me on Spanky. We set off with the smell of leather, horse shit and pines in the air. We were on the Buffalo Horn Trailhead. A sign at the start of the trail read 'Beware. This is bear country.' There were about ten in our group, as well as two girl guides who were each about twenty. I followed Lucy, whose horse was very feisty and kept turning and trying to bite her. We climbed high into the hills. The mountains in the distance had snow on their peaks. Little rat-like creatures fossicked in the undergrowth while bright blue mountain birds flew across our path. We passed a mother moose and its cub seeking cover under a tree, as well as a lot trees covered in the claw markings of grizzly bears.

It was very windy in the hills and we could hear the pine trees creaking. There was a lot of fallen timber on the ground. Then we heard a loud snapping noise and a large tree, at least twelve inches in diameter, came crashing down thirty feet behind us, just after we'd passed. We pressed on into the mountains, but by the time we got back, six more thick trees had fallen on the track, making it impassable. We tried to make it out another way, but trees had fallen there too so we were trapped. We rode as far away from the dense timber as we could and waited for an hour until someone from the ranch came up with a chain saw and cut us out. It was a nervous time as we tried to calm the horses while enormous trees creaked and swayed dangerously in the wind.

On the trip back, as we passed a beaver lodge across a small creek, Lucy broke into a trot. Lucy is much more competent on a horse than me, but I did my best to follow her. But we were quickly brought back into line by the guide, who said we all had to stay together.

It had been a good ride, but there was a ten year old kid on it, slowing us down. If kids can't do something properly, they shouldn't be allowed to do it. That's why they should never be allowed in pubs. They can't drink, so don't let them in.

For the final twenty minutes of the ride, I had a middle-aged woman riding in front of me. I was about to talk to her to pass the time, but I thought that the chances of her having anything of interest to add were remote, so I didn't. Besides, her horsemanship was starting to piss me off. She refused to kick her horse and the pace was very slow.

That night the ranch put on a bonfire barbeque. We were picked up by a wagon led by two wranglers wearing hats, chaps and spurs. Their hair was dusty and the spurs clinked as they slowly walked. Their talk was even slower than their walk.

We passed a second wagon.

'This is where we get out and take everything they have,' drawled one of the horsemen. Everybody laughed.

'Good fun,' I said to Lucy. 'Good clean fun.'

There was a lot of meat at the barbeque and after that, one of the cowgirls brought out the smores. Smores are marshmallows and chocolate sandwiched between two biscuits, and are known as such because you always want 'some more'.

It really did feel like a dude ranch with wagons, running horses, whip cracking and men throwing lassos around a dried cow skull.

With only a few days left on the ranch, we thought we'd try some fishing. The Gallatin is known as some of the best trout fishing in the world. We went to the ranch reception to enquire about it. As we were talking to the woman there, the fishing guide walked in.

He was a young guy, about twenty-two, with brown hair. He was fairly well built and looked very country.

'What can I do you for?' he said, with the exact accent of Brad Pitt from A River Runs Through It.

'We want to do a bit of fishing.'

'I can give you a lesson and show you a few places I like to fish.' He was shy and reserved. He only spoke to me and didn't look at Lucy. He told us when to meet him and then went to leave.

'My name's Andrew,' I said.

'Greg,' he said, putting out his hand. Or he might have said 'great'.

'Okay, Greg,' I said. 'See you tomorrow.'

We walked away.

'Why'd you call him Greg?' Lucy asked.

'I thought he called himself Greg, but he may have said 'great'.'

'I think it was 'great'.'

We met him the next day. It turned out his name was Grey and he was from Alabama. He was a good bloke. A good man in a crisis.

'Greg isn't it?' I said when we arrived at the fly shop.

'No, Grey. Grey, like the colour.'

'Oh,' I said. 'Grey with an 'a'?'

'That's right,' he said. That's the Yanks for you. 'Where y'all from anyways?'

I told him and that we were travelling around America

for a few months.

'Awesome. D'ya go to N'Awlins?' he asked.

'Yeah,' I said. 'Top spot. It's a lot different to other cities in the States.'

'Hell yeah,' he said. 'And Bourbon Street. Hell, there's some crazy Cajuns down there. Crazy Cajuns.'

'Yeah,' I said. 'So do we need to match the hatch today?' 'Matching the hatch' is a fly fishing term that I'd heard about matching the type of fly to the insects that are hatching on the water. I thought I'd throw it in to make him think I knew what I was talking about, if only for a little while. He soon figured out that I didn't. But I took a few cold Corona beers, as well as cut up limes, so my angling ineptitude probably didn't worry him all that much.

He was teaching us to cast at the trout pond on the ranch. It was extremely windy which made it hard, but we got the hang of it in the end.

'Ten to two, ten to two,' he said. 'Keep your arm straight and don't flick it. It's all about rhythm. You need to get the rhythm. It's like poetry.'

He really loved fishing and I could tell he was a purest.

'So you're travelling around all of America?' he said.

'Yeah, and some of Canada,' I said.

'Awesome. You doin' rafting or anything like that?'

'Yeah, we rafted the other day.'

'What grade?'

'Lower whitewater, we did. Grade four, I think.'

'That would have been on the Mad Mile. Gnarly, man. Really gnarly.'

It turned out Gray liked surfing and knew all about Laird Hamilton, the big wave surfer. His goal was to go to Fiji to surf. He certainly had the lingo for it.

'Where do you drink around here?' I asked him.

'Just in my cabin. I'm kinda on a rum and noodle diet as I don't have any money.'

'What beer do you drink?'

'American beer is horse piss,' he said.

'I'm hearing that.'

'Your best bet is the microbreweries. They do pretty good beer.'

'Have you seen any grizzlies here?' I said, changing the subject.

'Nope, not seen any yet. Don't really want to either, unless I'm looking through binoculars.'

'What sort of animals do you get in Alabama?'

'Nothing really,' he said. 'A few deer. And hogs. I love huntin' hogs.'

'Me too.'

We shared pig hunting stories and then he took us to the river to show us a few fishing holes.

'I've got a couple of beers if you want one,' I said.

'You don't need to do that,' he said.

'It's no problem.' I handed him a Corona and a piece of lime.

'Well, thank you very much. Takes me back to Mexico.'

'It's good with the lime,' I said.

'Great way to end the day,' he said. 'I'm only nineteen, so I can't buy 'em. America is way too strict when it comes to liquor. I mean, if you can fight in a war, you can have a beer, right?'

'I reckon.'

'You know what,' he said. 'You can use the rods for free. Save you thirty bucks. Just get a licence and that's all you'll need.' He seemed very appreciative of the beer.

'Thanks very much,' I said.

He left and I went to get a fishing licence. The questions for it were ridiculous. The usual name, address and that sort of thing, but then height, weight, eye and hair colour and about ten other questions. It cost $30 and twenty minutes. Lucy and I then went fishing.

We walked down to the Gallatin River to the best place Gray had shown us. We fished from the bank, casting into a side estuary where the water eddied around some rocks. Lucy hooked on about five times, but the fish spat the barbless hook every time. One was so big it almost pulled her into the water and she was unable to lift the tip of the rod up. It then snapped the line. We fished for an hour or so, but they had gone off the bite, so we went to the saloon and had a burger and some beers. Lucy was very keen to fish again. I wasn't, but I was casting in my sleep that night. Ten to two, ten to two. Poetry.

The next day we drove to town. Lucy wanted to get her nails painted at a salon there. On the way back to the ranch, we stopped in at a local fly shop. There were only men in the rustic wooden cabin. There were huge mounted trout on the walls. A man wearing a flannelette shirt and a stubbly beard came over to us.

'What can I do you for, sir?' he said to me.

'Not me, mate,' I said. 'She's the one.' I pointed to Lucy, whose finger and toe nails were bright pink. Her hair was flowing. It really did look like she'd just stepped out of a salon.

'I'm looking for a fairly large wet fly,' Lucy said to the man. 'Yellow and black, if you've got it, as well as a couple of different dry ones. What's hatching on the Gallatin at the moment?'

The man was taken aback, paused and then stuttered a little, but got himself together and he and Lucy started talking technical fly fishing. She bought a handful of different flies and we left.

Lucy fished alone and with me for the next two days. She hired a rod again and got her own Montana fishing licence. She quickly became a very proficient caster and was astute at matching the hatch with the flies and even tying them on. But she didn't catch anything.

'Are many fish being caught at the moment?' I said to one of the ladies who worked at the ranch.

'Let me tell you this,' she said. 'My boyfriend always catches a few. Every time he goes out and he never misses. But yesterday he fished all day and got thunked.'

'What's thunked?'

'Means he caught nothing. Not a bite. It's just too hot. They're not biting in this heat.'

But that didn't deter Lucy. On our last night at the ranch we went to the main restaurant and had an incredible dinner of beef and elk. The elk was dark and rich. After dinner we had a few more drinks in the saloon bar over a game of chess and two games of pool. It was getting late and we started walking back to our cabin.

'Let's go for one more fish,' Lucy said. 'There's still a bit of light.'

'Okay,' I said. 'I'll get a couple of beers while you get the rod.'

Ten minutes later, we were back on the Gallatin, Lucy still dressed for dinner in a flowery red dress and jewellery.

Lucy flicked lures like poetry into the rapidy waters while I sat and watched, drinking icy cold Summer Honey seasonal ale, made by the Big Sky Brewing Company.

Lucy turned back to me after a series of casts. There were tears in her eyes.

'What's wrong?' I said. 'It doesn't matter. They say it's too hot to catch any at the moment.'

'Don't be stupid, it's not that,' she said. 'I just don't want to leave Montana. I don't want to go home. I love it here so much.'

'It almost feels like we live here, doesn't it?'

'Yes it does. How is that beer?' she said, wiping her eyes.

'Good,' I said and gave Lucy a sip.

'Oh, I like that one,' she said. 'And I love you. I feel like we've fallen in love all over again this week.'

33

BURGER KING

*'In the daytime I'm Mr Natural, just as healthy
as I can be. But at night I'm a junk food
junkie, good Lord have pity on me.'*

— **'Junk Food Junkie', Larry Groce**

A close third behind the American obsession with God and
the Military, is their obsession with burgers. They say the
national pastime is baseball, but really it is burger eating. Or
perhaps it's burger eating at the baseball.

America has easily the most fast food chains of anywhere
in the world. A quick search of Wikipedia revealed that 157
chains originated in the US, compared with twenty-six in
the UK and thirteen in Australia. There are the national
chains, such as McDonalds and Subway, then the different
states have their own distinct ones, a lot of which I'd never
heard of. There was Starvin' Arvins in Arizona and Popeyes
in Texas. In addition to Taco Bell, which is everywhere, the
Spanish speaking areas of the country are inundated with
similar chains. There's Taco Bueno, Taco Cabana, Taco del
Mar, Taco John's, Taco Mayo, Taco Tico and Taco Time. I

didn't go in to any of those, but I'm sure they all served an array of burgers as well.

And then there are the specific burger joints. Ones like Burger King and McDonalds are ubiquitous (it is said that you're never more than twenty miles from a McDonalds), but then there are the more niche burger chains, with their imaginative names. All that seemed to matter was that the word 'burger' was in the title. Back Yard Burgers, Fatburger, Five Guys Famous Burgers and Fries, Hesburger, In-N-Out Burger, MOS Burger, Blake's Lotaburger, Burger Street, Burgerville, Cheeburger Cheeburger, Cheeseburger in Paradise, Crown Burgers, Good Times Burgers & Frozen Custard, Griff's Hamburgers, Halo Burger (combining with God, no doubt), Milo's Hamburgers, Smashburger, The Original Hamburger Stand and Whataburger.

Whatajoke, more like it. I challenge anyone to find an American restaurant of any class or description that doesn't have a burger on the menu. From the upmarket starched white table-clothed establishments, to the grimy street cafés. They all have burgers. And a lot of them have nothing but burgers. Many a time we traipsed from place to place looking for something to eat that wasn't a burger. It wasn't always easy.

In Austin, Texas I was craving a steak. And I'd always wanted to have a big, juicy Texan steak. We found a place called The Prime Rib Steakhouse. It had a menu posted out the front that had a number of steaks on it in varying cuts and sizes. It was perfect, so we went inside. We had to wait thirty minutes for a table before sitting down.

'With a wait like that,' I said to Lucy. 'The steaks must be good.'

I perused the menu.

'I can't see the steaks,' I said. 'Can you?'

'No,' Lucy said. 'Seems to be mainly burgers.'

'Seems to be all burgers.'

There were no steaks on the menu at all, but it was replete with burgers, twenty types of burgers, in fact. All I wanted was a steak. We'd been talking about it for a week. The waitress came over. She was wearing a red checked shirt, old jeans and boots.

'You all set?' she said. That's the standard line from waitresses.

'I'm after a steak, but can't see any on the menu,' I said.

'No, we don't do steak, we only do burgers.'

'But there are heaps of steaks listed on the menu out the front.'

'What menu?' she said.

'The framed and laminated menu at the front door,' I said.

'I've not seen it.'

'You can't really miss it.'

'Oh,' she said. 'That must be out of date. We only do burgers.'

'Out of date,' I said. 'How long have you worked here?'

'Six months.'

'Incredible,' I said. 'Anyway, give me the biggest burger you've got.'

Lucy ordered a burger as well, and then the waitress left.

'Unbelievable,' Lucy said after she had gone.

'I know. It's like we're in a burger vortex and can't escape.'

The burger arrived and it was big. I was hungry and I devoured it.

'Holy cow,' said the waitress when she came back to check on us a few minutes later. 'You have really slayed that burger, partner.'

The tables were booths lined up against the wall. A man from the next booth must have been listening and turned and looked at us.

'You were after a steak, hey?' he said in a broad Texan accent.

'Yeah,' I said. 'It's all I've been thinking about.'

'The burgers are good though aren't they?' he said. 'I gather with that accent you're not from around here.'

'No. Australia originally.'

'I work for an Australian. Here in Texas. He's got a pie shop.'

'You don't see many pies in America,' I said.

'No, there's none. He's starting up a new market.'

'Well, that should do well with you Yanks,' I said. 'Make a change from burgers anyway.'

The thing that amazed me the most about the burgers in America was their quality. Given that every restaurant serves burgers, a perfectly competitive economic market exists. Should any place increase its price or reduce its quality, consumers can easily source their products elsewhere. Despite these anti-monopolistic conditions, the burgers are generally pretty terrible. The first good burger I had was a buffalo burger in a small town called Grand Junction, Colorado, six weeks into the trip. The buffalo burger (actually, bison) tends to be less fatty and has a gamey flavour. Bison burgers were very prevalent in the West of the country.

The meat in the American burgers is often passable, it's the bun that ruins them. The bread is that white sugary sweet crap, and as any burger aficionado will tell you, it's all about the bun. And then it's further spoilt by the cheese they smother it in. Most American cheese is an orangey colour, completely flavourless and has the texture of partially melted plastic.

But you never just get a burger. They are invariably accompanied by a mountain of greasy chips (that the Yanks call fries) that serve purely as a vehicle for salt, as well as a carbonated soft drink in a large cup. I don't know why the Americans bother with the different sizes for their drinks, as everybody orders the supersize. And it's enormous. The smallest size is bigger than a large in England, and the supersize requires two hands to pick it up. They then go and get a refill. Americans are the most obese people in the industrialised world and they drink the most soft drink, averaging more than 600 'sodas' a year each.

They are not particularly fond of their greens either. You'll never see a burger served with salad or vegetables. It wasn't until we got to New Orleans, thirty days after arriving in the States, that I ate either. And it was just a small side helping with a dish of jambalaya. The only thing that stopped me from getting scurvy in America was two full fruit smoothies a day from Walmart.

Yes, if you go to America, be prepared to eat burgers in great quantities. If you don't like burgers, don't go. Unless you want to starve, that is.

34

YELLOWSTONE

'Searching for a little bit of God's mercy, I found living proof.'

—'Living Proof', Bruce Springsteen

Highway 191 runs from Montana to Wyoming and all the way into Yellowstone National Park. Yellowstone is a vast wilderness of lakes, rivers, plains, gorges, geysers, waterfalls, glaciers, animals and pines. There must be more than ten million pines. It is a vast wilderness of breathtaking beauty.

Opened in 1972, the world's first national park is in a volcanic basin that is flanked by rugged mountains. Lodgepole pines cover around two-thirds of its 2.2 million acres. The altitude of the park ranges from 5,000 to 11,000 feet. It is an incredible wildlife sanctuary, with sixty-seven species of mammals and 320 species of birds.

Upon entering the park we drove at the speed limit of forty-five miles per hour. It was never faster because the Yanks refuse to speed. The road was single-lane and it was very

225

hard to overtake. There was little point anyway, because after overtaking one car, you quickly came upon another going equally slowly. After only a few minutes of driving, we suddenly slowed to five miles per hour. The traffic was backed up for miles. We'd heard about the likelihood of this and there was nothing we could do about it. After twenty minutes of crawling along, we rounded a corner and discovered the reason for the slow pace. A lone male bison was trudging across a wide grassy plain and people were stopping to watch. The bison was large and brown and covered in thick bushy hair. Its shoulders were robust and its back sloped down to lower hind quarters. It had strong curled horns and large dark eyes. It was a majestic beast. The bison took its time across the grass, before wading a river and lumbering up the far bank and across the distant plain. We took the requisite photos and drove on. A few minutes later we saw where the bison was heading. Around the next bend in the road was another plain filled with bison. There must have been over a hundred in the herd, the calves being protected by a ring of adults.

We then came across another lone male bison and stopped. I got out of the car and walked up behind a tree to within five metres of him. He snorted at me, but I thought little of it. Later in the Visitors' Centre, we watched a video of a bison attacking and tossing a man like a fighting bull would. There were also leaflets being handed out to people which read:

Warning. Many visitors have been gored by buffalo. These animals may appear tame but are wild, unpredictable and dangerous. Do not approach buffalo.

The animals are actually bison and not buffalo, but not even the official park literature could get that right.

I walked up to the counter in the Visitors' Centre and spoke to the man there. His name tag said 'Phil' and he was about sixty and was dressed all in khaki with a wide-brimmed hat, like Smokey the Bear.

'Can you tell me what the best time to see the animals is?' I asked him.

'Well, I'd like to help you out, sir,' Phil said. 'But I've just about given up. Those animals just ain't playin' by the rules anymore.'

'Morning or night would you say?'

'Hell, I couldn't say. As much as I hate to say it, look for groups of people and find those with big cameras. They'll be shooting the best animals.'

'Okay, thanks.'

'And look for the elk. The bears will be watching the elk. And there are buffalo everywhere.'

'Why do people call them buffalo when they're actually bison?'

'Hell, I couldn't say that either,' he said. 'Happy hunting partner.'

Just near to the Visitors' Centre was Old Faithful. Apparently it is the world's most famous geyser and the park has the world's largest concentration of active geysers. Every ninety minutes, and right on cue, it spewed out gas and steam one hundred feet in the air to the cheers of the throng of thousands.

We continued driving around the enormous park. We stopped at the Yellowstone River and walked across the bridge. The scenery was mind blowing. Large cutthroat trout, native to the area, were spawning in the water, stationary as they fought against the current. Clusters of pine trees grew on small river islands in the water of azure blue. Snow-capped mountain peaks were in the distance. Next to the river there was a huge male grizzly bear moseying along a pasture foraging for shoots and berries, oblivious to us looking on. Still, I didn't get out of the car. Flying above was a bald eagle, its bright white head prominent in the sky.

Going past a lake that looked the size of an ocean, we saw trumpeter swans, white geese, osprey diving for fish, pelican and green-winged teal. A yellow-bellied marmot scurried across the road in front of us, followed by a very lively looking deer that we almost hit. Fly fishermen, dressed in dark green waders, flicked lures into the water.

And then there were the bugs. Millions of bugs. You encounter a lot of bugs when driving in America generally, but we were assaulted like never before in Yellowstone. They were the size of small birds and they hit the windscreen hard and in great numbers. It was like we were in a life-sized video game.

We kept driving, searching for the elusive wolf. The place to see them is in the Lamar Valley. The road there took us over a mountain range to the grassy plains below. But we saw no wolf, only elk. Most of the elk were female, but there were two fully-grown bucks with impressive multi-pronged antlers. We wound down our windows to get photos, but it was dusk and the mosquitoes hummed around us like sewing machines, so we quickly moved on.

And all day we saw bison. There were a lot of them. And

the cars kept stopping to photo them. If one car stopped, every car would stop, the people stricken with the herd mentality of the bison themselves.

As the end of a long day approached, I developed a thirst. It had been a stressful day's driving, winding slowly around bends, unable to overtake selfish drivers going ten miles under the speed limit. And then there'd been the groups of losers on motorbikes, all in their custom leather jackets, hogging the road in pairs of two and scaring everything within earshot with their revving engines of freedom.

We'd seen a DUI truck and twenty ranger cars doing a road block on the way in to Yellowstone, no doubt trying to catch picnickers who'd been drinking in the park on a Saturday. But that was hours earlier and I thought it was worth the risk. I've never been a big believer in creeds, and I needed a beer. I'd brought a six-pack and had them on ice in a champagne bucket from the hotel. I had one. It was good.

Half way through drinking it we came into the town of Mammoth, still within the park. A male bison was crossing the road at a zebra crossing between all the cars, as if searching for a car park. Elk were feeding on the median strip in town. I drove closer to them to get a photo. I pulled to the side of the road and had a swig of beer. Red and blue lights flashed up ahead. It was a park ranger. They have the same powers as police. He drove up to me, blocking my path, then motioned for me to wind down my window. I handed my beer to Lucy under the level of the window, and she concealed it in her jumper.

The ranger wound his window down and levelled at me a most cynical eye.

'What do you think you're doing?' he said to me, in a voice exactly like Gomer Pile.

'Pardon?' I said, playing dumb.

'Do you know what you're doing is highly illegal?'

'What's that, sir?' I knew I was done, but I thought I'd let it play out.

'You cannot park here,' he said.

'Sorry?'

'You cannot park here. This is a one-way street and you're going the wrong way.'

'Oh,' I said. 'Sorry about that.'

'Please remove your vehicle at once,' he said. 'And have a nice day.'

'Will do. Thank you, sir.'

He drove away. I finished my beer, turned the car around and moved on.

We passed through canyons of waterfalls and cliffs, before crossing the continental divide at over 8,000 feet where ice remained unmelted. Thermal pools of bright turquoise glowed in the twilight as gas seeped from the ground, bringing with it a deep smell of sulphur and an eerie mist in the night.

The diversity of scenery and ecosystems in Yellowstone is incredible. It is a vast wilderness of breathtaking beauty. We drove around its scenic, winding roads all day, for a total of fourteen hours, in complete silence as Lucy's black mood descended upon us, heavy like a thick blanket.

35

RIDE 'EM COWBOY

'Just rope and throw and brand 'em, soon we'll be livin' high and wide...'

—'Rawhide', Frankie Laine

The bull came out of the chute fast, pounding its front hooves into the dirt while it kicked its back legs out hard. Jacob O'Mara was lying back on top of the bull, his feet in the air, trying desperately to hang on for eight seconds. The Louisiana man's hat flew off as his right arm jolted back and forth violently, the rump of the bull hitting into O'Mara's head as he grappled for balance. AC/DC's Thunderstruck was blaring out across the stadium. O'Mara had only been on the manic bull for a couple of seconds before he was flung head first into the steel door of the chute and into the dust of the ring. He was the first contestant in the blue ribbon event of the Cody Stampede, the bareback bull riding.

We'd driven into Cody, Wyoming that afternoon, the scenery changing from the pine-covered mountains of Montana and Yellowstone, to striking hills and canyons of dirt and clay. It was real cowboy country and it wasn't hard to envisage an Indian riding over a ridge at any time. And Cody is a real cowboy town. Sheridan Avenue, the main street, is replete with saloons and everything Wild West. Country music emanated from nearly every door, but Cody is more of a cowboy town than Nashville. Well, more of a redneck town, anyway.

Cowboys are really just lower class rednecks more than anything, and there are rednecks aplenty in Cody. There were men chewing on sticks as they moseyed around the town. Redneck central. A sign outside one shop had pictures of guns on it and the words 'We Don't Call 911'.

We were looking for something to eat and walked past innumerable bars and eateries, including The Hungry Bear, El Vaquero, Wyoming Rib & Chop House, Buffalo Bill's Irma Hotel, Sunset House, the Hungry Cowboy Café, the Silver Saddle Saloon and the Rawhide Coffee Company. Of course there were a lot of boots shops too—The Boot Barn on Stampede Drive, Wayne's Boot Shop, the Custom Cowboy Shop and the Wyoming Buffalo Company. Cody is Indian territory and many trading post shops display native art and animals furs on the walls. Buffalo Bill is very prominent in the town, a museum dedicated to him on the main street. He was instrumental in founding the town in the late 1800s. We walked past the Dude Ranchers Association and the Six Gun Motel and into the Silver Dollar Bar, where nightly boot, scoot and boogie dancing was advertised. Our guide book had guaranteed it had the best burgers in the West. They looked crap, so we left and ended up eating at the

Proud Cut Saloon and Steakhouse. Naturally, the predominate item on the menu was burgers, so we both got one, adding Johnny Midnight's black peppercorn sauce and Coyote Ketchup in ample quantities. There were antlers and animal heads and skins on the wooden walls of the bar.

'How can I help y'all?' said our waitress. Cody saw a return to 'y'all' being said indiscriminately. We ordered and our burgers arrived. The burgers weren't bad, but as we left we saw some free samples in the salsa shop next door. We love free samples and there were a lot in there, nearly as many as in that nut shop in Savannah. After my episode in New Orleans, I avoided the tasters for 'The Hottest Fuckin' Sauce' and 'One Fuckin' Drop At A Time', but what I did have was good.

There is a gunfight re-enactment in the Cody main street six days a week, advertised in one town brochure as 'Free Old West melodrama, with characters depicted including Buffalo Bill, Wild Bill Hickok and Wyatt Earp'. The brochure went on to say that 'The intent of the Cody Gunfighters is to keep alive the spirit of the Old West with free family fun in the Western flavour'. We walked past one of the gunslingers on the way back to our car, two six-shooters hanging off his belt and his spurs clinking as he walked.

Then it was time to head out to Stampede Park for the rodeo. The rodeo is called the Cody Stampede and it's the richest rodeo in the world. It runs from 1 to 4 July. Now in its ninety-third year, the top 800 riders from the Professional Rodeo Cowboys Association compete for $300,000 in prize money. Cody is known as the rodeo capital of the world and an enormous sign to that effect features across the rodeo stadium. In fact, there is a rodeo every night in Cody throughout June, July and August. But the Cody Stampede is the big event.

The rodeo is a big deal in Cody, and there were brochures and leaflets throughout the town advertising it. We picked a few up.

'Bring your hat and boots and watch a cowboy or two eat some dirt,' one headline read. 'Cody is Rodeo!' read another (that is also the town slogan). 'Cody is well-known as the 'Rodeo Capital of the World'. It has the longest running nightly rodeo in the US and many of the current national leaders and Cowboy Hall of Fame inductees started their careers at the Cody Nite Rodeo. There are Wyoming Junior Rodeo Association events on as well and it is guaranteed to capture your imagination with ladies precision events, men's bareback and saddle bronc riding, bull riding, tie-down roping, team roping, steer wrestling, cowgirls barrel racing, the children's calf scramble, and rodeo clowns to entertain the crowd. What's more, spectators are invited to stay back after the rodeo for contestant autographs.'

I went to the reception of our hotel and asked the lady there how to get to the Stampede.

'Hell,' she said. 'Just follow the traffic.'

'Okay, thanks.'

'Have you got tickets?' she asked. 'Cause if you ain't got tickets, you ain't gettin' in.'

We had tickets. They were $18 a piece for the grandstand, the only place to sit, apart from the 'Buzzard's Roost', the premier seating above the bucking chutes. Season passes were also available.

We drove out to Stampede Park, directed by a cop in a car marked 'Sheriff', parked and went through the gates. There was a bull named Hollywood just inside the gates. You could pay $10 to sit on him and get your photograph taken. But the bull was so still that Lucy thought it was a fake initially. One of the brochures I'd read promised 'Rodeo stores with T-shirts and everything cowboy', but there were only a couple of terrible T-shirt stands and some horrendous hot-dogs and popcorn, both pre-made in bags. One shop had an entire shelf dedicated to copies of 'The Cowboy Bible'. I opened a copy. It was just a normal bible.

We made our way into the arena. The crowd gathered in the stands with a murmuring of anticipation. Everybody, the men, women and children alike, wore cowboy hats. The hats were made of straw and were a yellowy-white colour, as opposed to the dark felt of Nashville. The men wore big metal belt buckles featuring six-shooters, horses or bulls, where the size of the buckle is undoubtedly inversely proportional to the dick size of its wearer. Ushers sporting ten-gallon hats directed people to their seats. Buxom girls wearing far too little clothing for their weight had wooden boxes strapped around their waists containing cans of beer covered with ice.

Country music was being played loudly, courtesy of the BigHorn Radio Network, but all eyes were drawn to the big screen which stood at the end of a fence-enclosed field of dirt about the size of half a football pitch. A cameraman was zooming in on couples in the crowd and when in close, a pink border of love hearts appeared around the screen and the words 'Kissing Cam' were displayed. The couple on screen would then kiss, to the delight and cheers of the crowd. This happened umpteen times, until one man on screen rejected the kiss of the woman next to him.

The theme from *The Magnificent Seven* was played as a voiceover advertised the latest pick-up truck available on the market. Pictures from all angles appeared on the big screen. 'It's comfort and elegance meet style and power in this, the ultimate in pick-ups. Go y'all and have a look at it after the show. It's parked over near gate 1.'

There was a brief pause. 'Ladies and gentlemen,' said the voiceover. 'Your announcer for tonight's event, coming to you all the way from Texas, is the one and only, Randy Schmutz.'

With that, Randy, dressed in a bright pink shirt and an enormous white hat, rode out on a horse onto the dirt of the arena. He had a microphone in his hand.

'Well, thank you, thank you very much,' Randy said. 'Now, ladies and gentlemen, tonight we are here to celebrate the cowboy tradition and our freedom which is only maintained by those who've served this great country in the United States military. Will those of you fine people who have served this wonderful nation please be upstanding.'

About one in five people in the stands stood. The rest of the crowd clapped.

'Thank you,' said Randy. 'Now please be seated while the rest of us stand and applaud you for what you have done for us and the rest of the world.'

Four soldiers in full military regalia then rode out onto the arena and saluted. The crowd cheered some more. Meanwhile, a military video was played on the big screen. It looked more like a horse branding documentary to me, but the four soldiers were staring at it saluting, as were most of the crowd, so I gathered it was somehow army-based. A Star-Spangled Banner the size of a tennis court was then escorted past the grandstand, carried by thirty military personnel in uniform.

'And now,' said Randy, once the military genuflection was over. 'Let's bow our heads and say a prayer.'

Everyone in the crowd bowed their heads.

'Our heavenly Father, we thank you for letting us live in the greatest country in the world. We thank you for our blessings, for our families and friends who are gathered here tonight to celebrate this great United States of America. And Father we thank you for the men and women who serve this great country and allow us to have the freedom that we do. Father, we are very mindful when we look at this great arena, that we are looking at one of the roughest playing fields in the world. We ask you to please ride alongside our cowboys and cowgirls tonight and protect our riders, protect our livestock and protect the rodeo fans. Let us all travel in grace home and please forgive us when we fall so short. We ask these things in Jesus' name. Amen.'

The crowd repeated 'Amen' in unison.

'God bless you all,' Randy said. 'And God bless our president, Barack Obama, the first black president in the history of this great nation.'

'Obama's mother is a white woman from Kansas,' I said to Lucy. Randy went on before she could reply.

'Now we're going to sing the greatest song in the world. To lead us for our national anthem, this, is Shelby McNeal.'

Shelby, dressed in full cowgirl garb, walked out onto the dirt with a violin and started playing the *Star-Spangled Banner*. The crowd remained standing, and everyone to a man sang the words with feeling.

'And now,' said Randy at the completion of the anthem, amidst cheers from the crowd, 'I want you to take a look at the skyline and coming in from the west, ladies and gentlemen, that is a 1943 B-25 bomber making its way over here.' A plane, which I gathered to be as Randy described, did a fly-by over the stadium.

'And I'd like to ask you one more time,' Randy yelled. 'Are you proud to be an American?' The crowed hollered and whistled and the noise was almost deafening. 'Outstanding,' he said. I failed to see the connection between the plane and national pride.

'Before tonight's events get under way,' Randy continued once the cheering had subsided, still sitting on his horse in the middle of the dirt ring. 'We're going to thank our sponsors. And our sponsors are going to be displayed by some very pretty ladies.'

From one end of the arena rode girl after girl, all dressed in bright pink, galloping past the main grandstand, each with a flag in their hand, advertising the sponsors. Randy commentated with a scripted marketing spiel for each company. 'And here come our friends at Wrangler. You won't find a better pair of jeans for the tough country in which we live.'

'Here comes Miss Cody Stampede. And here we have Miss Rodeo Wyoming.' Randy was getting noticeably excited as he bounced up and down on his white horse. 'Now this is Miss Rodeo America. Yes, Miss Mackenzie Carr. Some very pretty ladies here tonight, folks. Very pretty ladies.'

The formalities complete, it was time for the competitions to begin. The theme song from Bonanza was played and fireworks were lit along the arena fence.

The first event was the men's bareback bronc riding.

'Here we go, folks,' said Randy. 'It's round two. The boys competed last night and we have Steven Depp and Cody Ryers in the lead. But first up, we have Ethan Assmann and he'll be riding Bartender.' A number of the cowboys seemed to be named after the town.

Assmann came out of the chute and was flung from side to side as the unbridled stallion jumped and kicked out its back legs violently. Assmann leaned right back, almost lying on the horse, whose hind quarters thumped hard into the back of Assmann's head with every jerk.

In seeming breach of the immutable laws of physics, Assmann lasted a full seven seconds before he was tossed to the ground.

Orin Larsen was up next. Orin was from Idaho and had won $10,000 to date for the season. He rode the bronco for the full eight seconds and scored seventy-two. The number was put up on the big screen and the crowd jeered.

Tucker Zingg came out third. He was riding Sign Language and scored well, as his horse kicked its hind legs out viciously. Tyler Nelson had some trouble inside the bucking chute, but hit the lead with a seventy-nine. Chase Erickson from Helena, Montana scored seventy-five.

'Now we have the great Chris Harris from Texas,' yelled Randy. 'Chris is talent and toughness personified and has won $1 million in prize money in his career.'

Chris's horse came careering out of the chute aggressively. He was thrown from the horse to the ground and tried to roll to safety, but was trodden on as the horse kicked to the dirt.

'Uh oh,' yelled Randy with a laugh. 'A little love tatt there for Chris.' Chris got to his feet and limped to the bullpen, as two mounted wranglers in the ring lassoed the loose horse and ushered it out of the arena.

'How are you finding the rodeo?' I yelled in Lucy's ear, trying to get above the noise of the crowd.

'I love it,' she said.

'It really is the boldest thing I've ever seen.'

I looked at the woman next to me. She was about eighty. She had the rodeo program and was marking the score of each contestant next to their names.

'I can't understand anything the people around us are saying,' Lucy said. 'There's so much lingo.'

'You'd need the Rosetta Stone to decipher a lot of it,' I said. 'Or at the very least a redneck dictionary.'

The twelve contestants had ridden and the first event was complete. The rodeo clown came out. He was dressed like a typical clown with the red nose and make up and everything and began engaging in some tedious banter with Randy. There was a Texan man sitting not far from us, who had been yelling out loudly every time a rider from Texas competed. He had a bald head and a bushy moustache. The Texan had obviously not gone unnoticed by the clown, who singled him out.

'Good Lord,' yelled the clown, pointing at the man, who then appeared on the big screen. 'That is one redneck dude. Man, you've got enough moustache for six men. Maybe you should put some of it on your head.'

The crowd laughed, but the Texan did not look happy. He stared at the clown and bellowed like a wounded bull.

'That is a helluva yell you got there, sir,' said the clown, before Randy stepped in.

'Next up,' said Randy. 'We have the big men of the Rodeo. It's steer wrestling time. Now these big men tip the scales at 200 or 220 pounds. K.C. Jones is up first.'

A young steer came bolting out of a chute. K.C. rode after him, then dismounted at pace, before hurtling up to the steer. He jumped on the steer's back and grabbed it by the horns, twisting its head hard to the ground until the rest of its body followed. The steer safely secured to the dirt, K.C. jumped to his feet and the crowd cheered. The entire act had taken 4.2 seconds. K.C. was a big man and he lumbered through the dust and out of the ring.

Seth Morgan came out next and got to his frantic steer quickly, but lost his grip and the steer scampered away and out of the ring. It was a 'no time'. Seth sat in the dust disconsolate, and then threw a handful of dirt to the ground.

Wade Sumpter, an ex-college footballer of some note who chose rodeo for his career, a move that, according to Randy, had paid off big time, mounted his horse and prepared to compete. Wade was the final competitor and he wrestled his steer down in 3.5 seconds to win the event. He swaggered off to loud cheers from the crowd.

The favourites in the team roping spectacle were Arky Rogers and Clint Summers. But it was Chad Master and Clay Cooper who won the event, managing to each lasso a steer from horseback, one around its neck and one around both legs, in 5.1 seconds.

Chuck Schmidt opened the saddle bronc riding, which was the same as the opening event, except that the horses wore saddles. Blaze Hannaker rode second, and he was followed by his brother Colt. I could barely imagine the intelligence of the parents of those two brothers. The great Jesse Bail, who'd won $1.7 million in bronc riding, won the event with a score of eighty-two, before limping out of the arena.

As a break in proceedings, two little Mexican kids showed off their impressive skills in rope twirling, in a cowboy slant on rhythmic gymnastics.

The next event involved lassoing, throwing and then hog-tying a steer. The first contestant threw the lasso, but missed the steer altogether.

'A swing and a miss,' cried Randy into his microphone. 'Why don't you all holler 'Ah, shucks'.' The crowd did. The contest was won at the death by hot favourite Monty Lewis, who managed to secure his steer in 7.8 seconds.

The comparatively tame cowgirls barrel racing was the penultimate event of the evening. It involved cowgirls galloping on horses around barrels, the fastest time winning once a penalty of five seconds was added for any barrel knocked down. Most girls turned too tightly and knocked over a barrel.

The brightly-dressed cowgirls cleared from the dirt, it was time for the blue ribbon event.

'How many of you are ready for some bull riding?' yelled Randy. The crowd cheered wildly.

After Jacob O'Mara's demise into the chute's steel door, Chad Halstead came out on a bull named The Pacifier. Randy said that Chad was a champion bull rider and he did ride well, making the full eight seconds.

Bull riding is somewhat of a Catch-22 sport. The rider needs to stay on the bull for eight seconds for a qualifying ride, but a difficult bull that is hard to stay on is needed to score well with the judges. An eight second ride on a tame bull will score lowly.

Townsend Prince was the next rider to be hurtled off his bull prematurely. Like all riders, he had a personalised song playing when he came out of the chute—George Thorogood's *Bad To The Bone* was his choice. I consider myself somewhat of a country music aficionado, but I didn't know half the songs being played. Everybody else did. Some teenage girls sitting in the row in front of us were singing and jigging along to them all.

Friday Wright II came hurtling out of the chute, but stayed on for the full eight seconds to score an impressive eighty-two (the maximum score available was never divulged). I could only assume Friday's father, Friday I, named his son as a joke to divert some of the shit he had copped all his life on to his unfortunate offspring.

'Next up,' said Randy with excitement in his voice. 'We have the amazing Wesley Silcox, the world champion.' That is to say, the American champion. 'He strapped on the gold buckle a few years ago and has worn it with pride.'

There were competitors from all around the West of America—Texas, Colorado, Utah, Oregon, Montana, Wyoming and even a couple from Louisiana. The crowd comprised similar origins. Randy listed out the key American states, imploring those from each state to stand and cheer. He didn't bother asking if there were any foreigners in the crowd. I'm sure we were the only ones.

Wesley was the final rider of the night, and he came out of the chute with his right arm flailing above his head. He rode the full eight seconds and he rode well.

'Ladies and gentlemen, what a ride,' yelled Randy. 'What a ride. We saved the best for last. And here comes the score. Oh my God, it's a ninety-one. Ninety-one. Incredible.'

The crowd was on its feet, cheering hard.

'And that completes tonight's proceedings,' said Randy, suddenly subdued. 'See you tomorrow night, when we'll do it all over again. Good night and God bless America.'

We didn't hang around to get autographs.

36

BORN ON THE FOURTH OF JULY

'Some folks are born to wave the flag, ohh they're red, white and blue...'

—'Fortunate Son', Creedence Clearwater Revival

Americans are obsessed with America and being Americans. They are an extremely patriotic nation and it's little wonder they are so successful in the sporting arena. It's hard to find a bar that doesn't have live baseball or basketball on at least five televisions. They're obsessed with sport and winning.

And the brainwashing starts young. When we were staying at a ranch in Montana, we were woken every morning at 6am by a group of teenagers jogging past our cabin chanting 'Go USA, go USA.'

The Americans love their physical country as well. I'd heard that very few Americans held passports. In fact, two out of three Americans don't, and can't even go to Canada. This figure is well down in recent years. In 1989 only 7% held passports. A common question posed to them is 'What are you afraid of?' The fact is, they're not afraid. America is a big country and the diversity within it is incredible. In one day's driving we went from the desert of Monument Valley to the pines and ski fields of Colorado. Anything you could ever want in terms of scenery is within their borders— deserts, canyons, mountains, beaches and cities. And if they want to go off the mainland, they can head to the Hawaiian Islands or the wilderness of Alaska. They could fly to a completely different style of holiday every year and there'd still be places to go two decades later.

Travelling around the States I noticed that nearly all the tourists are Yanks. In our whole trip, the only foreign tourists we met were a pair of Dutch. That was it. If you walk around the parking lots of any major sight in America, you will see licence plates on cars from all over the country. The same is true on the roads. There will be marginally more from the home state, but you're almost as likely to see a Floridian plate in Arizona as you are in the Sunshine State. I walked around a parking lot in Nashville, Tennessee and counted cars from thirty-five of the fifty states. There were probably only a couple of hundred cars there. The exception to this seems to be Wyoming and Colorado, where the majority of plates are local. I never got to the bottom of the reason why.

Americans are a very proud people. At the Cody rodeo, with all its patriotism, I saw a man wearing a T-shirt with an American flag on it. The caption under the flag read 'Unflammable—Now and Forever'. Of course, 'unflammable' should have been 'inflammable', but that's the Yanks for you. Disrespect the flag or their anthem at your peril. No two things are more important to Americans. Apart from burgers, perhaps.

The American flag is everywhere. Drive the highways and you will see it flying from most businesses. On an average suburban street of one hundred houses anywhere in the country, you will see sixty Star-Spangled Banners flying from front porches and from poles on the street generally.

And their houses are immaculate. Most town streets look like they've been prepared for an inspection. The houses all look recently painted and the lawns and yards are perfect.

Whatever criticisms one might have of the Americans, a lack of self-respect would never be one of them.

We spent the Fourth of July holiday in a sleepy town called Jackson in Wyoming. Many mistakenly call the town Jackson Hole, which actually refers to the entire valley, where skiing is popular in the winter. It was like a cross between Cody and Aspen, with picturesque mountain scenery. The dramatic ice-streaked Teton Mountains are a backdrop to the town and every picture looks like a postcard. Jackson is a country town with plenty of shops full of wooden furniture, moose heads and wolf skins. It also has hundreds of T-shirt shops. Every second shop seems to be one. There are a lot of art galleries as well, but very few bars. There were only three noticeable bars.

Despite being the tenth largest geographically, Wyoming is the least populated state in America and the car licence plates have few numbers on them, such as '11—940'. The '11' denotes the county and the second the car sequence number. The second number is never very high. There are that few people—just over half a million.

It being their national day, the Americans are obsessed with the Fourth of July and the multitude of celebrations that it entails.

We walked out into the sunshine of Jackson at 10am and onto Broadway, the main street. The Fourth of July parade was well under way. The population of Jackson is about 9,500 and at least 8,000 of them were at the parade. Grandstands filled with people lined the street. Old couples were sitting in deck chairs that they had brought for the event. Everybody was dressed in Americana—star-spangled T-shirts, American caps and people draped in flags. Everything was red, white and blue. Even the dogs were wearing American flag bandanas. A lot of the town's stores had signs in their doors which read 'Happy Fourth of July. God Bless America'. Everyone was God blessing America.

Float after float came up the main street to raucous applause, as two announcers commented on the festivities, effectively advertising local businesses with the usual pre-arranged marketing spiels.

'Here comes Teton Motors,' one of the announcers said as a brand new pick-up drove slowly along. 'Get right along there and get yourself a high quality motor. They're even open today.' The crowd cheered. Various local guest ranches went by, then came the Jackson Hole Baptist Church.

'They'll answer all of your big questions,' the second announcer said. 'Why I am here? Where did I come from? Where am I going? They'll answer it all for you.'

'Here comes trouble,' he continued. 'It's none other than the Jackson Hole Juggernauts. It's the most fun you'll have on eight wheels at the roller derby. Watch the girls battle it out in this ultimate tension-reliever as they smash one another to pieces. A-ha, there's Geena, the Queen of Mean.'

Geena was a stocky and ugly woman, with a head like a bucket of smashed crabs, and looked as if she could tear your arms off. She smiled and waved to the crowd.

'And here we have the Jackson Rodeo Queens.' The announcers were taking turns. The Queens were dressed in the colours of the day and were throwing confetti from horseback. Other floats squirted water pistols at the admiring crowd. Everyone was smiling and laughing. And applauding. The Yanks love to clap.

'Holy Toledo,' one of the announcers yelled. 'I've just been advised that it's Paul Compton's birthday today. Can you imagine sharing your birthday with our proud country's national day? Incredible.'

Bagpipes and flautists then marched up the street, followed by a multitude of fire engines.

'Here come the fire trucks. The Jackson Hole Fire Department, ladies and gentlemen. Stay safe out there folks.' More fire trucks came.

'And now, the Jackson Hole Airport Fire Department.' More cheers. 'And after them we have the helpful folks at the Search and Rescue. By God, do they do some great work out there.'

'And now our final entry for the day,' said the first announcer. 'And please remember that each of these entries will be judged by our panel, are the town street sweepers. Thank you coming out today. Happy birthday and God bless America. Be safe out there.'

The crowd went berserk as the street sweepers drove slowly off into the distance, cleaning as they went. Most people stayed in their positions, looking around as if expecting something else to happen. But it didn't and they gradually thinned out. Tammy Wynette's *Stand By Your Man* came out over the loud speakers.

We never did hear the results of the parade. Perhaps they were to be published in the local newspaper. It was going to be a difficult decision. All the floats were equally abysmal. But the crowd loved them, maybe because it was warm and sunny. But it was warm and sunny every day.

Lucy and I wandered away from the parade street to find something to eat. We went into the Great Harvest Bread Company and got a sandwich for $9. I gave the cashier a twenty and she handed me $1 change.

'I gave you a twenty,' I said to her. 'You need to give me another ten.'

She looked in the till. 'You did indeed,' she said. 'I'm very sorry.' She handed me a $10 bill.

'You need to give me this, then,' she said, taking the $1 bill from me.

'No,' I said. 'I gave you twenty. It cost nine. So you give me eleven.'

'That can't be right,' she said in a panic. 'It just can't be.'

'It is,' I said, and took the $1 bill from her.

The sandwich was excellent. They make good food at the Great Harvest Bread Company, but they're not too bright.

We went back to our hotel room for a rest from the street fun, and turned on the television to watch the Fourth of July International Hot-Dog Eating Competition in Coney Island, New York. Naturally, it was an all-American event. The crowd to watch the proceedings was enormous as they stood on the sand and basked in the sun, eager to view some gluttony.

The women's event was up first, with Sonya Thomas, a skinny forty-five year old woman of Asian descent, out to defend her title. She is known as the Black Widow because of her ability to regularly defeat men five times her size, or The Leader of the Four Horsemen of the Esophagus, and the commentator described her as a 'multi-food sensation'. She had recently demolished forty-eight dozen oysters at the Acme Oyster House in New Orleans, where we had eaten two dozen between us. She weighed ninety-eight pounds and held the chicken wing eating world record, twice beating the infamous Joey Chestnut, to eat 183 wings in twelve minutes.

But today was all about dogs. The ten-minute time slot started and Sonya got away to a flier, but was neck and neck with Julia Lee, her biggest rival, after five minutes. Sonya ending up defending her title 'smoking Julia in the final five' to eat forty-five long dogs in all, including buns. Second place only had thirty-three dogs, so it wasn't even close.

Then came the men's event. Joey Chestnut, twenty-eight at six feet one and 220 pounds, was looking for his sixth title. In a pre-match interview he said 'I'm ready. I'm hungry. I'm ready. It's all about the start. Got to get away to a good start. Need the early burps.' His main competitor was Matt 'Megatoad' Stonie, a man of Asian heritage. The Megatoad looked like an eater, but Joey had dominated the sport for the past five years.

A fat, bald man with a goatee beard was asked if anybody could beat Joey this year, who had eaten 309 dogs in five titles.

'If one of us gets in that zone,' he said. 'Then he can be beaten. I know I can beat him.'

Then Joey was interviewed.

'Anyone who thinks it's just eating is wrong,' he said. 'I

put a lot of training into this. It's all about practice and building up, building up tolerance. I break my body down and build it back up. It might sound arrogant, but I feel I'm smarter than the other eaters out there.'

'He earns every dog that he puts down,' another competitor said about Joey. 'He has the tools that you need to succeed. He has the capacity and he has the speed. And he has the mental element. That's all important. It's all hard work and dedication, like the best athletes out there. I compare him to Lance Armstrong or Mike Tyson.'

The announcer, Paul Page, then introduced the competitors.

'Destiny has arrived and it stands above us like a perfect blue sky,' opened Page. 'Now here are the eaters.'

Page listed out the achievements of the men as they came out on the stage, each with their own theme music being played.

'Here is Pat Bertoletti who won the recent chilli eating competition, which is ironic, because he considers himself a poultry expert.' AC/DC's Thunderstruck was blaring out of the speakers as Pat took his seat.

Another man was the wedge and fries champion. Eric the Red Devil was the ultimate shrimp and fried bread eater, whilst Adrian Morgan, wearing a T-shirt with the slogan 'I Came, I Ate, I Conquered', had eaten fourteen pounds of catfish, amongst other things. Boston had gone ninety-seven years without a dog champion, but the Megatoad was there to change all that.

'And now we have Crazy Legs Conti,' said Page. 'He holds the record for pancakes and beef brisket, but will always been known for the sixty cubic feet of popcorn that he was buried under before eating himself to freedom, which is why he's known as the 'Houdini of Cuisini'.'

The matzo ball eating champion of the world was a huge fat man named Eric Badlands, considered by many to be the number two eater in the world, with thirty-nine titles. Pepperoni, key lime pie, 275 jalapeno peppers, strawberry shortcake and ice cream were just a few of the foodstuffs he had devoured in record time.

Notorious B.O.B., whose favourite two words were 'meat loaf', had demolished twenty-three pounds of salmon chowder. A small Asian man who looked like he'd just fallen off a key ring had eaten seven pounds of deep fried asparagus in ten minutes. The world sushi champion, Eater X Tim Janus, had scooped in 171 pieces of sushi in six minutes. These boys made the fifty eggs eaten by Paul Newman in Cool Hand Luke look like child's play.

Finally it was time to introduce Joey 'Jaws' Chestnut. He needed no introduction, but by the time Paul Page had finished screaming, he was completely hoarse. Joey's impressive resumé is too long to list, but he ate 241 chicken wings in thirty mins in 2007, and once drank a gallon of milk in forty-one seconds.

The rules of the event were listed, stating that the entire dog and bun must be eaten. There was an automatic disqualification for a 'reversal of fortune'. There was a judge for each of the twenty or so contestants.

With the formalities over, the television went to a short commercial break advertising 'Major League Eating—The Game', which could be downloaded for $19.99.

Back to the tournament and it was time to get down to the business of eating. And then they were off. Very little chewing was going on. The men dipped their dogs into water to make them slide down easier. They were like machines. Some wore headphones that played psych-up music. The leader board tracked across the bottom of the television screen as did the 'dog count'. About seven per minute was needed to beat Joey's 2009 world record of sixty-eight in ten minutes. A bikini-clad bottle-blonde model stood behind each contestant, holding up numbered cards to signify the running tally of dogs consumed.

As expected, Joey got away to a great start and was four dogs to the good after four minutes. After six minutes he'd pulled out to six dogs in front.

'The half way point is where Chestnut traditionally takes over,' said Page. And he did. He was ten dogs in the lead after eight minutes. 'This is the point where Joey eats through the pain.'

When the ten minute bell went, Joey had won his sixth world title, tying his record of sixty-eight dogs.

'He's the greatest major league eater of all time,' screamed Page. 'He's taken out the Golden Mustard Belt yet again. I don't know what's pumping through my veins, but I am overcome right now.'

Joey looked remarkably composed with just a few beads of sweat on his forehead.

'I just feel sorry for the crowd,' Joey said into the microphone, amidst the cheers. 'As I wanted to give them a new record, but I had nobody really pushing me.' Second place had gone to Eater X with fifty-two and a quarter dogs.

'Incredible performance,' said Page. 'See you all next year.' And the show finished abruptly.

That afternoon the fun in Jackson continued. We witnessed yet another mock street shoot out, with characters walking down the street in their cowboy outfits, acting as they walked before even getting to the scene. One was in black and white striped overalls, with a ball and chain. 'I am a man of constant sorrow, I've seen trouble all my days,' he sang as he hobbled along.

We went for a drink at the Silver Dollar Bar. The Jackson Six N'Awlins Jazz Band was playing. They were very good. Lucy had a jalapeno margarita and I had a fruity IPA beer. I was starting to like the fruity beers. A man next to us ordered a burger and laboured over it for forty-five minutes, picking the bun up, scraping things off it, putting it back down and eating one chip at a time.

'Let's just say,' I said to Lucy. 'He wouldn't have been welcome at Coney Island today.'

The yearly fireworks in Jackson, acclaimed as some of the best in the state, were cancelled because of a forest fire threat, but we watched others on television in the bar, as the national celebrations continued in earnest. Fireworks and festivities were on every channel from all around the country, the most impressive in Washington. 'Glory glory hallelujah, his truth is marching on' was the main song being played.

We moved on for a quick drink at the Snake River Brewing Co., where the only good thing about the place was it name, before heading to the Million Dollar Cowboy Bar in the main street. We got asked for ID at the front door.

'Do you want mine too?' I asked Mr Mustang, the cow-poke doorman who was dressed all in black and wearing a wide-brimmed hat and sunglasses at 10pm.

'Yes,' he said. They never back down at that point.

'I'm probably older than you,' I said, handing him my driver's licence. 'Have you ID'ed yourself?'

He didn't respond, we paid the $3 cover charge, and walked into the big soulless bar that had saddles for seats. A four-piece country band came on and played songs from the good ones—Johnny Cash, Waylon Jennings, Hank Williams, Merle Haggard. It'd been a good day. But then an argument developed with Lucy about who held their guitars higher, Johnny Cash or the Beatles, or something as equally ridiculous.

We saw out the rest of the Fourth of July celebrations in silence.

37

IDAHO POTATOES

'You say potato, I say potahto…'

—**'Let's Call The Whole Thing Off', Louis Armstrong**

Men all around America stared at Lucy's breasts. It's happened all over the world for the past two years, but men, particularly middle-aged men, stare at her. They are drawn to her breasts. I watch the men and see them lock on and then stare, fixated, obsessed and mesmerised, regardless of the presence of me or their wives, as if nothing else in the world matters to them at that moment. The men of Idaho were no exception to the rule.

We were sitting in The Pioneer Saloon in Ketchum. The bar was all wood with a moose head on the main wall and a bison head over the door. There was a large elk as well and a bobcat. We were at the bar. There was a mirror on the other side of the bar.

'See that guy with the blue cap on?' Lucy said to me.

'Yeah,' I said, looking at him in the mirror. He was about fifty, unshaven and had unkempt hair. He wore a red lumberjack shirt and dirty jeans.

'He's staring at me. Has been for ten minutes. He just won't stop.'

'He matches the profile,' I said.

The man got up and walked past us, ogling Lucy as if oblivious to my presence. He even paused for a better look as he got in line with us.

'Filth,' Lucy said. 'Absolute filth.'

'I reckon there might be few of them in Idaho.'

We were in Ketchum for the final leg of my Ernest Hemingway world tour. I'd been to all of Hemingway's houses and haunts—Paris, Cuba, Spain, Italy, Africa, Peru, Key West, Chicago—and had made it to the last one, the place of his suicide. We'd driven five hours from Wyoming that day and visited Hemingway's grave in the Ketchum Cemetery. A notorious drinker, there were full bottles of wine and beer on his full length gravestone, as well as hundreds of coins. He lay next to his fourth wife, Mary.

Driving into the state, Lucy read out the preamble to the Idaho section from our guide book. As well as having more lakes than anywhere else in North America, it is home to Demi Moore, Evel Knievel and a large number of neo-Nazi white supremacists.

'What do neo-Nazis generally do these days?' Lucy said.

'I'm not sure about the neo bit, but I think they bash blacks and gays,' I said.

'Well, you might want to rethink those shorts.'

I was wearing my flowery-pink board shorts again.

'Yeah,' I said. 'I always seem to wear these at the wrong times.'

'I wouldn't worry,' Lucy said. 'I think the Nazis are right

up in the north, anyway. And it was years ago, it says here.'

We drove into a petrol station and I went straight to the toilet. I pushed open the door. Standing pissing into the toilet was a man. The room was a small one with one toilet and a sink. It was only meant for one person. The man had obviously forgotten to lock the door. He looked at me and I looked back. He was a skinhead and was covered in tattoos. He had steely blue eyes. I went to apologise, but decided not to speak. He looked away and finished as if I wasn't there. Then he pushed past me and left the bathroom.

'I just ran into one in the toilet,' I said to Lucy back out at the car.

'A Nazi?' she said.

'Pretty sure. And look at my shorts. I walked in on him in the toilet.'

'Look at those guys.'

Getting out of a nearby car was a group of three men who looked like the one I'd just encountered.

'Christ,' I said. 'I didn't have Idaho down as a danger state. I thought it was all about potatoes.'

We drove to Ketchum and were lucky to get a hotel room as there was not much accommodation available, owing to the bike riders' convention in town. There's always a convention. After a long day's drive, we thought we'd go and relax in The Pioneer Saloon. Still sitting at the bar after Slimy Blue Cap departed, I ordered a pint of Las Lagunitas IPA. Lucy drank red wine.

'Care for another one?' said the bartender as I finished my drink. His nametag said 'Declan'.

'Yes, please,' I said. 'It's good.' It was a fruity beer, with a bitter aftertaste.

He poured my drink. He was about forty-five and looked fairly normal.

'I hunt,' he said. 'And fish.' His comment came from nowhere. Perhaps he'd seen us looking at the stuffed animals on the walls.

'I ain't got no wife or kids,' he went on. 'So I hunt and fish.'

'Oh,' I said.

'Do you know,' he continued. 'To shoot a bison in Wyoming only costs $50. But if you're from out of state, it's five grand.'

'Oh.'

'Five grand,' he repeated. 'And a bear is only twenty bucks if you're from Wyoming.'

'That seems cheap,' I said.

'Mind you,' he said, ignoring my comment. 'There's no great honour in shooting a bison. It's like a cow. But I use every bit of it. The entire beast. I dress it, keep the cape, eat the lot.'

'Do you get bison in Idaho?'

'The odd one wanders over from Yellowstone,' he said. 'Will you be eating here tonight?'

'No,' I said. 'We read Desperados is good so we're going there.'

'It is good, but our tucker is real good too.'

'We're sort of set on Mexican,' I said.

'Fair enough. Fair enough, but have a look at our menu anyway,' he said, handing one to me and one to Lucy.

I looked at it for a few minutes. Idaho is famous for its potatoes. The state licence plate actually reads 'Scenic Idaho—Famous Potatoes'. The menu was laden with potato meals. Baked potato, cheese and bacon potato, Joe's Potato, baked potatoes with red peppers and lots of others.

'You got me,' I said to Declan. 'I'll have the buffalo burger.'

'Bam,' he yelled and pumped his fist. 'You won't regret it. The buffalo burger is good. Real good. So are our potatoes.'

'Why do you call them buffalo when they're actually bison?' I asked him.

'Well, I don't really know,' he said. 'Can't say I've ever thought about that.' It seemed nobody in America had.

'What brings you to Ketchum, anyway?' he said.

I told him we were travelling around the States for a few months.

'Where'd you fly in to?' he asked.

'Miami.'

'Ah, I'm from Jacksonville. Did you drive the 95?' Yanks refer to highways solely by the number.

'Yes,' said Lucy. 'We went the whole way up the east coast on the 95.'

'You got a car?' he asked.

'We do now,' I said. 'But we were on the bus there.'

'The Dog?' he asked.

'Yeah, we got the Greyhound all the way up to Boston.'

'Jesus,' he said and smiled. 'Are you okay? Any stab wounds?'

'It was no picnic, I can tell you,' I said. 'But I think they've just about healed.'

'Seriously?' Declan said. 'Check yourselves again. There'll be more. A guy had his head severed clean off on a Dog a while back.'

'The Dog, hey?' he said to himself as he went to serve another customer. 'Jesus.'

We didn't eat any potatoes in Idaho, famous or otherwise, but the buffalo burger at The Pioneer Saloon was excellent, as were the beers.

We set off the next day and a message came up on the dashboard display telling me that I needed to change the oil soon. I didn't know how to do that, so drove to a service station. There was a girl behind the counter who was in her mid-twenties. She was ugly and looked dumb.

'Hi,' I said. She just looked at me.

'I need to change the oil in my car,' I said. 'Is there anybody here I can talk to?'

She shook her head.

'Does anybody here know anything about cars?'

She shook her head again. It was really just a continuation of the first head shake.

'Is there a man here?'

'Not.'

'Does a man work here?'

'Not.'

'Do you speak English?' I asked.

She went to speak.

'Don't bother,' I said. 'It's a good service you provide here.' I walked back out to the car.

We got the oil changed at another place and kept driving. We drove all day. We saw a roadside marker in west Idaho stating that many stage coach robberies had occurred in the area in the 1880s, when it was a toll road. We saw dead deer and cattle grazing. We saw a dead skunk on the side of the road. We passed through the dirt hills that turned to pine trees as we crossed the Blue Mountains. We descended to the vast Oregon plains as we followed Highway 84 to the West Coast. We had crossed the entire state of Idaho and we didn't see a lake until we reached Oregon.

38

THE CHAIN GANG

'That's the sound of the men, working on the chain gang...'

— **'Chain Gang', Sam Cooke**

America is riddled with chains. Chains of restaurants, chains of petrol stations, chains of supermarkets, chains of hotels. They are everywhere. There's no doubt that the Americans are firm believers in economies of scale.

Nowhere are the chains more obvious than when driving the country's roads. As you approach each exit on the highway, and this happens every few minutes as there are hundreds of them, you see the chains advertised. They're displayed on four sets of signs by the side of the road. The signs are a few metres high and a few metres wide and are bright blue.

The first sign is usually reserved for the petrol stations, or gas stations, as the Yanks call them. I once asked someone where the nearest petrol station was and they had no idea what I was talking about. On that sign will be the names and logos of the petrol stations available if you take the exit. BP, Exxon, Phillips 66 and Texaco are the predominant ones.

The next sign, which appears a few hundred metres later, lists the fast food chains off the highway. It tends to be filled with McDonalds, Burger King and Subway—the big chains—but the smaller towns will list individuals as well. Somewhere in the middle of Minnesota, the big blue sign for food simply read 'Mike's'. There was space for eight other establishments, but at that time, Mike had the monopoly on the provision of food. The only reason we knew Mike was serving food was because it was the second sign, which is always for food, and the sign had the heading 'Exit 89—Food' written at the top. Despite the multitude of chains in America, a lot of individuals do have shops and restaurants. And they invariably put their name in the title. Wayne's Liquor, Fred's Beer and Wine, Bob's Burgers, Mike's Café, Rod's Steak House—that's the nature of the Yanks—you've got to get your name in there as a mark of pride and self-promotion.

The third enormous blue sign lists the attractions of the upcoming town. Every town, no matter how small, has an array of attractions. The main exit to Orlando, Florida lists Disney World, Universal Studios and SeaWorld. The exit to small towns will list things like the Cattle Museum or the Beef Jerky Factory.

But it's the fourth sign where the American chains really come into their own. It is headed 'Lodging' and is always filled with the usual suspects—Best Western, Travelodge, Motel 6, Holiday Inn, Days Inn, Quality Inn, Comfort Inn and Super 8.

It was the Super 8 chain that we generally sought out. We'd stayed in our first one in Savannah, Georgia and it was cheap and clean. You always knew what you were getting with Super 8. Every one, no matter where in the country, was exactly the same—two queen-sized beds, flat screen television, fridge, microwave, Wi-Fi Internet access and the taps with basin in the main room, outside of the bathroom. I always found that a little strange. Super 8 was the epitome of generic, but they were comfortable and cheap. When I say cheap, they were usually around $100 a night, and in some of the two-horse towns that we stayed in, I didn't really find it all that cheap.

Despite every room being identical, we were always happy when we saw the big tacky canary-yellow sign of the Super 8 on the side of the highway. And there were a lot of them. In parts of the Mid-West, they seemed to appear every five or ten minutes. In fact, Super 8 is the world's largest budget hotel chain, with 2,039 locations in America.

Naturally, like all American hotels, the breakfast was horrendous. After a few stays I didn't even bother going. It was an array of stale cakes and muffins, some cardboard-style cereal and some heavily-sweetened post-mix orange juice. You'd be better off with a drink of water and a look around.

And like all other hotels in the world, no matter what their class, Super 8 were 'committed to protecting the environment' and in order to save it, urging its guests to rehang towels instead of having them washed. What they were really committed to saving was their own money by reducing laundry costs. Of all the hotels we stayed at in America, and there were forty-one, only one took the environment seriously. It was the 320 Guest Ranch in Montana where you received $10 off your bar and restaurant bill for every day you requested no cleaner.

Most American hotels also allowed pets to stay in the rooms, and Super 8 was no exception. It usually cost an extra $20 a night. This is because Americans seldom leave the country. They just pack up the kids and pets and half the house into their ghastly Winnebagos and drive.

And like all hotels, the Super 8 had the absurd check-in/check-out time disparity of about four hours, check-in normally being at 3pm, whereas you had to be out of the room by 11am the next day.

No matter how many times I saw it, I could never get used to it. Every time we sped by a highway exit and saw the manifestation of the four big blue signs in the distance—the McDonalds, the Super 8, the Starbucks, the Burger King, the Exxon and whatever low-level attraction the town had fabricated—we were seeing corporate America in all its dire glory. And it wasn't a pretty sight.

But despite the garish sign and the über-generic nature, it was always a comforting feeling to wheel the bags into a Super 8 and wash off a long day's drive. We'd lie on the bed, turn on the television and watch episodes of Keeping Up With The Kardashians, that were repeated constantly all week in a never ending loop until the next show.

I'll give them that, when the Yanks are onto a good thing, they stick with it.

39

ESCAPE FROM ALCATRAZ

'In the streets of San Francisco, gentle people with flowers in their hair…'

—'San Francisco', Scott McKenzie

As we approached San Francisco, the fresh green pines of Washington and Oregon were replaced with golden brown grass and dryness. The country felt very Californian as we passed the Napa Valley and crossed the Mendocino County Line.

Then it was time for the usual ten-lane video game as we drove into Frisco, the cars dodging and swerving and swapping lanes at an accelerated pace. A Mustang Man cut in front of me. I almost clipped him, so I hit the horn hard. His personalised number plate was 'Kick'.

'Maybe he's a kick boxer,' Lucy said.

'Maybe,' I said.

A thick blanket of fog descended across the bay as we crossed the Golden Gate Bridge.

California is like a country unto itself. The neighbouring states seemed so much more sedate. As we crossed the state line we passed a Union Pacific coal train. A man with a back pack was running alongside the tracks as the engine chugged along. He picked up speed then leapt onto the train and clung to its side, a stow-away in the broad daylight.

Then there was a 4.3 magnitude earthquake in Fort Bragg. We'd only been thirty-five miles away. We didn't feel it, but there was definitely a lot more action in California.

On our way to San Francisco, we'd driven down the west coast and through the Avenue of the Giants, a forest of enormous redwood trees that were each wider than our car and looked like something out of a Robert Frost poem. We followed Highway 101, Ventura Highway, for 600 miles as it snaked along a canyon above the Smith River, winding through the pines and the morning mist.

California was the first place in America where we'd seen an abundance of personalised number plates. There are a lot of egos in the Golden State. And a lot of Mustang Men, just ones who see themselves as cool rather than tough. There were a lot more bikers as well, hogging the road and doing their absurd low wave of camaraderie.

Continuing down the Californian coast, we went through Orick, the town that paint forgot. All the shops and houses looked like they hadn't been touched for forty years. Anyone staying at the motels there, with their decrepit signs and rickety doors, is just asking to be killed. Just outside of Orick there was a hitchhiker beside the road. He came out of the woods with a guitar on his back, undoubtedly a resident of Orick just waiting to take someone back to his motel for an easy kill. There were actually a lot of hitchhikers in California, having not seen one in the whole of America. They are all of the same mould—long hair, unruly beard, dirty clothes, covered in tattoos and a guitar on the back. You only need one thing to pick them up, and that's a death wish.

California is the home of the free-spirited. We had lunch at Garberville. Garberville is a very cool town. At least, it thinks it is. As we parked, a long-haired man walked past us. He had the world 'karma' tattooed all the way down his arm. The Hemp Connection, Ganja Jesus and Stoner Jesus were three of the stores on the main street. Other shops had the marijuana leaf symbol painted on the entrance. I'm not entirely sure what that signifies, except that some pretty hip dudes reside inside and there's sure to be a chilled out vibe. There were also a lot of tattoo shops. The town was full of hippies and weirdos. All of California was. They think they're pretty cool in California, but in so doing, they take themselves a little too seriously.

On the way out of town we saw a middle-aged hippy couple selling tie-dyed sheets by the side of the road. The man was in a shirt that matched his multi-coloured products and the woman was one of those past-it types who thinks she's still got it, but never really had it in the first place. She had long grey hair. They always do, because they're either too groovy or too lazy to dye it, unlike the ridiculous sheets they sell.

The north of California behind us, we crossed the Golden Gate Bridge and landed in the heart of San Francisco. It was quickly apparent what a melting pot of cultures San Francisco is. There are thousands of Chinese, quite a few Italians, an array of hippies and try-hards, and there is always a smattering of Irish. Nowhere else in America, apart from perhaps New York City, is more diverse.

Our hotel was in Chinatown and was run by Chinese. Everything in Chinatown was run by Chinese. The woman at the check-in desk was angry and unhelpful, like she was doing us a favour. The simplest request was met with static like it was a personal slight. The Wi-Fi wasn't working, so I asked her to reset the router.

'No,' she said. 'It working.'

'It's not,' I said. 'We have two computers and an iPhone and none of them will work.'

'Can't do it. It working.'

'Just humour me and switch off the box will you please?' I said.

She didn't respond, but did as I asked and the Wi-Fi started working. She made no acknowledgement.

We walked out of the hotel.

'Jesus, it's like being in central Beijing,' I said. 'It's all so filthy.'

Litter was all over the ground and old Chinese women were trying to hawk street food. A group of Chinese men stood on a street corner, snorting and spitting indiscriminately, above them a sign that read 'No loitering when children are present'. Another twenty men were crowded around jumping and squawking like geese at two others who were playing cards under a tree, presumably for money.

'I'm not a big fan of some Chinese,' I said.

'My dentist is Chinese,' Lucy said. 'He's alright.'

'Well, there's bound to be a couple of good ones in twenty billion.'

Bruce Lee was brought up in the Frisco Chinatown, where virtually no English is spoken. I certainly didn't hear any, until I met Wayne that is.

I went into Wayne's Liquor to get a six-pack of Sierra Nevada beer. Wayne was Chinese.

'Hi Wayne,' I said.

'Herro,' he replied.

He came out from behind the counter and shadowed me around the store, as the Chinese tend to do. I haven't been able to work out if it's a sales technique or because they don't trust their fellow man.

'How much is the Sierra Nevada?'

'Wun or sees?'

'Six.'

'Ta dollaa,' he said.

I handed him the $10.

'Thanks Wayne,' I said. 'See you tomorrow.'

'Than you. Than you wewy much.'

Wayne was alright too.

Right next to Chinatown is North Beach, the Italian area. One street is Chinese and then the next is Italian. And it's like being in the centre of Italy. The main street, Cristoforo Colombo Corso, is filled with atmospheric restaurants that you don't ever want to leave, and the smell of garlic pervades the air.

We ate at Molinari's Deli. Its walls were lined with old-fashioned looking tins of olive oil and cured sausages hung from the roof. An old Italian man was singing Adele's *Someone*

Like You as he made me a roast beef and sun-dried tomato sandwich. The queue went out the door and down the street.

Then there was Haight Ashbury, the trendy area known as Hippy Row. Petite and colourful houses there, called painted ladies, start at almost $1 million and don't last on the market very long. The area is home to Jimmy Hendrix's old recording studio and house, as well as a host of cool shops like Day-dreamz Smoke, Head Rush Hash and Pipes, Wasteland, XGeneration, and Jammin N Haight. There are also tattoo shops for the café crew, an incense and African art shop, Palm and Spiritual Readings, Psychic and Tarot Readings, and pastel-coloured coffee houses. Slogans such as 'democracy is not a spectator sport' and 'politicians not allowed on premises' were painted on shop doors, as was the peace symbol, artistic graffiti and the word 'mojo'. Even the Ben & Jerry's shop had the subtitle of 'Peace, Love and Ice Cream'. Everyone was looking for a place to chill.

We went to a bar called Vesuvio on Jack Kerouac Alley. It was a good little bar with green murals on the outside and artistic people on the inside—the types who wear cardigans and horn-rimmed glasses and read newspapers while drinking white wine or cider very slowly. 'Beware of pickpockets and loose women' was one sign behind the bar, which was made famous by Kerouac in the 1960s. You could almost feel the ghosts of the Beat Generation while sitting at the bar, which was only a few doors down from City Lights, the bookstore known for publishing their writers.

But like its weather, San Francisco changes quickly. Soon after leaving Hippy Row is a region called Tenderloin, far and away the roughest looking area we'd seen in all of America. It's the red light district and where table dancing was invented in the States. I'd imagine the Greyhound station is there.

A cab driver told us that the area was named years ago because the cops didn't want to walk the beat there as it was too dangerous. To encourage them into the area, the butchers would give them free meat. The area still looked very dodgy. Gangs of homeless black men lurked on every corner, looking upon us like lions on gazelle as we drove past, just willing the car to break down.

'Don't come here after dark,' the cabbie said. 'It's as bad now as it was 150 years ago. It's very bad during the day and even worse after dark. If you're in Union Square, whatever you do, don't wander past Jones Street. Not that you'd have any reason to anyway, but don't.' Union Square is the upmarket shopping district that borders Tenderloin.

Apart from its multi-culturalism and diversity, San Francisco has everything—shopping, cuisine, personality and nightlife. Every night is like a Friday. All the bars and restaurants are full and there's a vibrancy of excitement in the air. We could hear the noise of bars and parties going all night on both a Monday and a Tuesday. Walking back into our hotel room one night, we heard very loud and vivid sex noises, moans and cries to God emanating from one of the rooms. There were at least two girls in there, such is the free-spirited nature of Frisco.

The cable car was invented in San Francisco in 1873, and we caught one down one of the many steep streets (Divisadero Street is the one made famous by Steve McQueen's car chase in Bullett). We got off at Fisherman's Wharf and walked around the shops of Pier 39, then had clam chowder in a bay-side Italian restaurant called Pompeii's Grotto. There was water on the cement outside and the smell of fish from the morning's trade. There are many clam chowder restaurants and stalls by the bay and the chowder we had was excellent—far better than in Boston.

In fact, Frisco is a bit like Boston, just bigger and better, but it does think it's a little cooler as well. We walked past a man who was playing air guitar as he skipped along, completely comfortable in his own ridiculous folly.

We went on a walking tour of the Golden Gate Bridge as a supposed celebration of its seventy-five year history. The bridge has been declared one of the Modern Wonders of the World and its design and construction are still lauded today. It is said to be possibly the most beautiful and certainly the most photographed bridge in the world. We contributed to the latter statistic. Whilst it is a suspension bridge, it is actually one of the safest places to be during an earthquake.

And one of the most popular for suicides. More people die by suicide at the bridge than at any other site in the world. With a fatality rate of 98%, only twenty-six people have been known to survive the jump. Over 1,500 haven't survived and jumps are still occurring on a two-weekly basis. There is even an emergency phone at the first key pillar with an official notice that reads 'There is hope. Make the call.'

It was freezing cold out there on the bridge. It was

shrouded in fog (it is usually shrouded in fog) and the bay wind cuts clean through you. San Francisco has an extraordinary climate. Down by the bay the conditions are arctic, even when it's sunny. Two minutes away up the hilly streets and it's bright and hot. And the temperatures hardly vary all year round.

But there is no place colder in San Francisco than Alcatraz Island, which sits in the middle of the bay, only a ten minute ride from the city. Only one official company is allowed to take people to the island and the boats are booked out three weeks in advance. I discovered this the day before we arrived, so we ended up paying $200 each for a package tour, instead of the usual $30.

We toured the disused jail by ourselves, with earphone commentary from former guards and inmates, which was as chilling as the wind that whistled around the complex, prowling for an entry. It almost felt as if the cell doors were going to slam shut at any moment.

The cells were lined up and small, but looked comfortable enough, even in the darkness of solitary confinement, known as the Hole. The administration area, the kitchen and the exercise yard all felt like they'd been inhabited the week before.

Apart from the freezing conditions in the cells, the worse thing for the prisoners would have been the view. Whichever way they looked, the striking city skyline and the torment of all it had to offer, lay before them.

We saw the cells of Al Capone, Machine Gun Kelly and Robert 'The Birdman' Stroud, as well as the cell where Frank Morris tunnelled through the air vent to escape with the two Anglin brothers in 1962. The trio were never found. Perhaps they grew tired of just staring at the view.

40

YOSEMITE AND THE VALLEY OF DEATH

'I looked outside of my window, there was fear in the pit of my heart. There was desert as far as the eye could see, blistering, dusty, and hard.'

—'Death Valley', Heart

We drove down the west coast of America, through the sand dunes and deserted beaches, along the famous Highway 1. After the upmarket beachside town of Carmel, where Clint Eastwood lives and was once mayor, we passed through John Steinbeck country—Monterey and the more gritty Salinas—made famous by his novels East of Eden, Tortilla Flat and Cannery Row. Then we headed east through the golden hills of California.

We stopped at a supermarket in a small roadside town. We bought some lunch, and as we were about to leave the car park, a man yelled out to us.

'There are some fresh strawberries over near that white van,' he said. I looked at him. He obviously didn't work at the supermarket.

'Just over there,' he said, pointing at a white van about thirty metres away. 'Feel free to go and get some. Won't cost you nothin'.'

Always keen for a freebie, we started walking towards the van.

'This looks dodgy,' Lucy said after a few seconds.

'Yeah, you're right,' I agreed. 'Abort. Abort.'

We turned and walked back to our car, much to the chagrin of the man.

'Go to the van,' he yelled. 'The strawberries are in the van.'

We got in our car. I could see that he was still yelling, but we couldn't hear him as we closed and locked the doors.

The next day we drove to Yosemite National Park and into its verdant valley of meadows, which at their edge displayed sheer cliff faces releasing waterfalls. The famous Tunnel View presented itself as we entered the park, then El Capitan, the giant granite cliff, rose above the valley, along with the Sentinel and Half Dome, two other granite monoliths.

Huge boulders sat amidst the pines as we climbed the Sierra Nevada to 10,000 feet, passing enormous blue mirrored alpine lakes. We passed above the pines to where patches of snow remained and the rocks looked like a desert in the sky, with only the occasional pine poking through the crevices.

Yosemite covers an area of over 760,000 acres. An ecologist's paradise, over 1,400 plant species occur in the park and the park's varied habitat supports over 250 species of animals. Typical wildlife that visitors are expected to see include the black bear, bobcat, cougar, grey fox, mule deer, mountain king snake, Gilbert's skink, white-headed woodpecker, brown creeper, spotted owl, a variety of bats, the golden-mantled ground squirrel, chickaree, fisher, Steller's jay, hermit thrush, northern goshawk, pika, yellow-bellied marmot, white-tailed jackrabbit, Clark's nutcracker, black rosy finch, Sierra Nevada bighorn sheep, great grey owl, willow flycatcher, mountain beaver and the Yosemite toad.

We didn't see any of that. Lucy had the binoculars at the ready and she was frustrated.

'There's been no wildlife at all here,' she said. 'Apart from that rat thing before.' A solitary rat had scurried across the road to the safety of a small bush.

We descended from the roof of the park, winding around the typically barrierless road, circling round and round like a corkscrew to the valley below. As we drove down, we could see the actual desert on the distant plain below, the preamble to Death Valley.

Crossing the lower desolate plain, the ground peppered with solidified black volcanic lava, a fork of lightning struck a hill in the distance and the rain came suddenly and hard. We could smell the rain on the dust as we drove and then, just as abruptly as it had begun, it stopped and the sun was bright.

We continued through the tiny desert towns of Big Pine and Independence. It had been a good day's driving, me singing along with Eighties anthems while Lucy played the air drums, but we were tired and we stopped for the night at Lone Pine.

We had trouble getting a room in Lone Pine because of the ultra-marathon convention on in town. I pulled into the driveway of the fifth hotel we'd tried and parked there while I checked if there were any rooms free. Lucy waited in the car, and as I came back out, a big and grizzly hairy biker and his woman were getting off their bikes.

'Any rooms left?' the biker yelled at me from two metres away.

'Don't know,' I said. 'I just got one.'

'No, I guess you didn't check for us, did you?'

'Well, I'm in room 1,' I said. 'So you should be fine.' A strange piece of information to volunteer.

Ten minutes later, I was out in the car park washing Mal.

The beauty about a hire car is that it can go through any terrain and at any speed, hitting anything you like along the way. Apart from the millions of bugs we had hit around America, driving in the Dakotas we must have killed ten small sparrow-like birds. They kept dive-bombing the car.

'I can't avoid these birds,' I'd said to Lucy. 'They're like kamikazes.'

'I don't know about that,' Lucy said. 'But these Dakota birds are pretty bloody stupid.'

The other good thing about a hire car is that you don't have to clean it. But we'd grown attached to Mal and he was filthy. Water was flooding across the car park as I washed the blood, guts and feathers from the front of the car with a powerful hose.

'It's about time you washed that car,' someone yelled at me. It was the biker again. His woman laughed an insidious laugh.

'Don't you wet my bike, ya hear,' he went on. 'I know what room you're in, remember?'

I laughed, then put my head down. When I looked up he had gone.

I finished washing the car and reparked it in its spot. As I walked back to my room, I saw that I had saturated a gleaming chrome and black leather Harley Davidson. I got to the room, drew the curtains and locked the door.

We set off early the next morning for Death Valley. The price for petrol at the final station before the park was $5.48 per gallon (two hours later in Nevada it was $2.99, the cheapest we saw in America).

A sign at the entrance to the park read 'Caution— Extreme Heat Danger'. Our guide book enumerated a number of heat-related dangers and emphasised the necessity to have at least five litres of water per person. We had 500ml between us.

A brochure for the park advised:

This is a harsh environment—any emergency can become life-threatening, especially in summer (we were in summer). *Heed the safety warnings in the park newspaper, including in relation to extreme heat and dehydration, unsafe driving, flash floods, and mine hazards. Do not depend on*

GPS navigation or cell phone use in the park: service may be non-existent or unreliable. Great extremes haunt this hottest, driest and lowest of national parks.

Death Valley's low moisture, intense sunlight, drying wind, and salty flats limit plant growth. It averages less than two inches of rain per year, but moisture evaporates at up to 150 inches. The kangaroo rat, an animal that can go for months without drinking, is one of the only mammals in the park, which is riddled with active earthquake lines.

The brochure went on to say that Californian gold-rushers attempted to pass through the area on their search for fortune in the West. Only one wagon made it through. One man died in the process and, upon leaving, his friend said, 'Goodbye Death Valley'. The name stuck.

We drove into the Valley. It was an inhospitable environment, just rocks and dust and dirt, speckled with cactuses. A vast and empty wasteland. Endless salt plains lined the road. Dust storms swirled on the distant plains, like mini tornados. The road wound and undulated through the rising and falling desert, 1,000 feet, then 2,000, 3,000 and back to 1,000. The temperature went from 55 to 110 degrees in thirty minutes of driving.

There was evidence of a flood from the day before. We could see where the water had driven its course through the dirt to create mud and pools on the road that were quickly drying. Hours earlier it would have been impassable.

Whilst the danger of Death Valley was vastly overrated, the plains on the ground below did look like the valley of Hell.

As we drove down, we passed an ultra-marathon runner. He was about sixty and was wearing a woollen jumper and long pants. He was running up the steep hill.

From the base of the valley we could simultaneously see the highest and lowest points in the contiguous USA— Mount Whitney at 14,491 feet and Badwater at 282 feet below sea level.

Then we had to get out. We started driving up the other side of the cauldron. It was a one-lane narrow road and the going was slow. We got stuck behind a Ford Mustang. I couldn't get past him. He was hogging the road and breaking sharply. I got right up behind him, putting the pressure on.

At the rim of the valley there was a look-out point. The view was breathtaking so we pulled over. So did Mustang Man.

'Why you following so close, man?' he said, standing with an aggressive posture, his hands on his hips.

'You were driving too slowly. There were plenty of places to pull over.'

'I don't pull over for nobody, ever, and I'll drive as slow as I like. You shouldn't be that close to me.'

'Well, if you can't handle the pressure, pull over.'

'You back off next time,' he said. 'Asshole.'

'Look,' I said. 'You're obviously a professional fuckwit, but how about taking the day off?'

He stepped a little closer. He was dressed all in black leather and looked a bit tougher than I had initially thought.

'Welcome to Death Valley,' he said. 'It's called that for a reason you know.'

Then he walked to the edge of the cliff and stared out, unmoved until we left.

41

VIVA LAS VEGAS

'Bright light city gonna set my soul, gonna set my soul on fire…'

—'Viva Las Vegas', Elvis Presley

We made it onto the Strip, Las Vegas Boulevard, via Frank Sinatra Drive. We were about to take Dean Martin Drive, but decided on Ol' Blue Eyes at the last second. The move paid off. We landed right next to our hotel, the New York New York. We'd seen it from a distance, the Statue of Liberty, almost a third of the size of the original, standing out the front like a sentinel. Then there were the towers of the hotel shaped like the Chrysler Building and the Empire State, a roller coaster full of screaming people snaking around them both.

We'd driven through the desert towards Las Vegas along yet another highway dedicated to the US military. This time the sign merely read 'We Honor You'. The sky was gun-barrel blue as thunder clouds formed above the distant grey hills. You could feel the cactuses on the dry ground yearning for the rain. Twenty miles out, we could see the heart of

Vegas, with all the glitzy hotels piled on top of each other. It all looked so out of place in the middle of the desert. At least five helicopters could be seen at any time flying over the city.

On the way in to Las Vegas, we stopped at the 'Welcome to Fabulous Las Vegas Nevada' sign on the outskirts of town. There was a queue of people waiting to get a photograph with the sign. A local man had taken it upon himself to take photos for people for money. That was fine, but what was annoying was his ushering of people and trying to control proceedings.

'Can I take a photo for you?' he yelled at us.

'No thanks,' I said. We stood there, waiting to get a clear opening without any other people in the frame.

'Well, you've got to run. You've got to get up there and get forward quick,' he said in an aggressive manner.

I stared at him. 'How about we play our own game, mate,' I said. 'And you play yours.'

'I'm sorry I asked,' he said.

'So am I.'

Inside the New York New York Hotel, the theme of the east coast continued. It was like being transported onto the streets of New York itself. There was a Broadway Street, a Hudson and a Greenwich, as well as an imitation subway station. Apart from all the gaming tables and slot machines, where fat middle-aged people sat and smoked and stared blankly, mindlessly pulling the lever of hope, there were indoor streets of bars and delis, all in the style of the Big Apple. And there were restaurants of every variety—Mexican, Japanese, Italian, French, Irish, and of course, burger joints. Greenberg's Deli served New York style sandwiches, and Times

Square Hot-Dogs served Nathan's hot-dogs, and or course, burgers. The Broadway Bar & Grill served meat and burgers. Fashion and souvenir shops dotted the landscape, as well as the ubiquitous Harley Davidson store.

After a brief morning session in the hotel gym, which overlooked the Strip and the desert in the background, I went to meet Lucy at the pool. The walk from the room was momentous, down corridor after corridor. It was like a rabbit warren. I finally found the elevator, noticed there was no thirteenth floor—a thirteenth was likely to spell bad luck for the punters—and rode down to the third floor, before walking a similar distance to another elevator that took me to the pool.

They say that New York is the city that never sleeps. But I've walked its streets mid-morning on a Sunday and nothing is open and there's not a soul in sight. The time of day in Las Vegas seems completely irrelevant. It is truly a city that never sleeps. You can get anything you want at any time of the day. It was only 10am, but the hotel was in full swing. People were eating sushi, the bars were packed, as were the gaming tables. It could have been 10pm. Of course, there were no clocks anywhere to alert people to the time. And there was no fridge in our room—got to keep people out of the rooms so they're more likely to gamble.

I finally made it to the pool. There was house-style music blaring and the sun lounges were nearly full. Waitresses in bikinis were taking drink orders and people were standing in the pool drinking. Three lifeguards sat on elevated towers, surveying the waste-deep water. They were dressed in the full Baywatch red outfits, complete with those red flotation devices and printed on the back of their shorts was 'Lifeguard'. I suspect they'd never had to go into the water to save anyone. They probably couldn't even swim.

I found Lucy lying next to the pool. She was wearing a striped coloured bikini, tortoiseshell Ray-Bans and a Boston Red Sox cap. I sat next to her.

'What took you so long?' she said, smiling.

'It's a rigmarole to get here. I left the room half an hour ago, I reckon. Much going on here?'

'There are a lot of heroes.'

'Yeah,' I said. 'That chap there is very fond of himself.'

Walking past us was a muscular man in his twenties. He was tanned, wore tight black shorts and was fully waxed, even under the armpits. On his stomach was a tattoo of a red lipstick kiss. He sauntered to the edge of the pool and eased himself in, very aware that he was being watched, and happy about it.

'God,' I went on. 'Look at the watch on that bloke.' He was a fat man and had long hair and a beard. He was covered in tattoos and his gold watch was the size of a small television.

'It doubles as a knuckle-duster,' Lucy said.

'He'll be in the Harley Davidson shop later on. And I see Willie Nelson's been good enough to join us.'

Next to Waxed Man was a seventy year old with long grey plaited hair and stubble on his face. He was wearing a cowboy hat.

'Good Lord, there are some tools here,' I said.

'And quite a lot of surgical enhancement,' Lucy said.

A bottle-blonde with enormous gravity defying breasts walked past us. She was wearing a bikini about three sizes too small.

I picked up the drinks menu. 'These drinks are expensive,' I said. 'And they have a very liberal interpretation of 'cocktail'. That's just a rum and coke and it's $15.' I was pointing at the Cuba Libre. I guess adding a twist of lime turned it into a cocktail.

'I expect to see you dancing in the pool later,' Lucy said. 'A couple of Bud Lights in your hands. Or better yet, some Bud Light Limes.'

I laughed. 'Can you hear those guys?' I said.

A few seats over was a group of six guys. They must have been in their early thirties. They were each holding a bottle of Bud Light.

'This is going to be a great weekend,' the ringleader said. He was wearing a thick gold chain around his neck, with a matching bracelet. He was slightly older than the rest. He had a baseball cap on backwards. 'Thank you all for coming,' he went on. 'Keep your cell phones on and have fun. Go big or go home. That's all I ask.'

'I wonder if any of us will get arrested?' said another, who had a slicked back mullet hairdo.

'Hey, man, what happens in Vegas, stays in Vegas, you feel me,' said a third, presumably pretending to be a rapper.

'True religion,' chimed another.

'Vegas, baby,' said the ringleader, then they all clinked bottles, slapped each other on the back and each took a slug of beer.

'Good one,' said Lucy.

'What's the point of the backwards cap?' I said. 'What tools. The ringleader looks like a CUB.'

'Cashed Up Bogan?'

'Yep. Nothing worse.'

The 'What happens in Vegas, Stays in Vegas' catchphrase is everywhere in the city. It can be heard being said at bars and is written on beer mugs and coasters. People are trying so hard to have the weekend of their lives. Trying so hard to be crazy.

As I was getting comfortable and starting to read Lucy's Vanity Fair magazine, two young men came and sat on the lounges next to me. The guy closest to me was covered in oil, had skin tight shorts on and couldn't have been more than six inches from my chair. He was clearly gay.

'That's sealed my fate,' I said to Lucy. 'I'll see you up in the room.'

At night we ate at Chin Chin, the sushi bar in the hotel. Lucy drank champagne and I had a large Tsing-Tao beer. The sushi was first rate and we sat up at the bar and chatted and laughed. We couldn't keep our eyes off each other. We then walked out onto the Strip for a look around. Our hotel was next to the MGM Grand and the Monte Carlo. We passed the Luxor, with its giant sphinx poised in front of it and the Roman-themed Caesar's Palace, which has an exact replica of the Trevi Fountain. The Paris Hotel was very prominent with its Eiffel Tower dominating the skyline. Nearby to it was The Flamingo, the famous pink neon resort built in 1946 and marking the beginnings of the Strip as it is known today. All the hotels were laced with neon. There's not a self-respecting establishment in Vegas that doesn't have neon all over it. We made it as far down as the Venetian. The Venetian is an incredible structure. On the outside there is a copy of the Rialto Bridge and an enormous replica of the Campanile of St Mark's Church. Inside the hotel there is a proper functioning canal, complete with gondolas that people ride while being serenaded by opera singing gondoliers. There is an almost life-sized Piazza San Marco and an imitation sky inside that gives the appearance of daytime, with clouds that look like they're moving. It is all remarkably realistic.

On the return to our hotel, we stood and watched the Fountains of Bellagio show, along with hundreds of other gasping tourists. Frank Sinatra's Luck be a Lady was playing loudly as a multitude of water bursts shot high into the air in varying directions, punctuating the song. It was impressive.

Every fifteen metres, both men and women handed out cards which read 'Girls direct to your door in 20 minutes' and a phone number. They wore shirts that said the same thing. On one corner was a man standing on a wooden box with a microphone. Next to him were two other men, disconnected looks on their faces, holding signs with 'Trust Jesus' on them. The man with the microphone was preaching to the crowd as they waited to cross the road.

'You must trust Jesus. Jesus is God. The Bible tells us this. You must trust him, listen to him or you will die painfully.'

He then focussed on two small children who were standing with their parents.

'You children,' he said. 'Your parents made you, so they own you. And God made us all, so he owns us all. Choose Jesus or you will burn. Choose paradise or go to Hell. Jesus is God. He was born to Mary by immaculate conception and he is God. Trust him.'

The kids turned away, as if from a bright light, and hugged into the legs of their parents.

The traffic lights changed and everyone crossed the road.

'Some compelling arguments there,' I said to Lucy. 'But they've really got to sort out this God and Jesus bullshit. I still don't follow the dichotomy. Isn't God the father of Jesus and Jesus the son, in which case Jesus wouldn't be God? God would be God, wouldn't he?'

'Who knows?' said Lucy. She'd heard it all before.

'And this immaculate conception business,' I went on. 'What a load of shit that is. I'd say a more likely explanation is that Mary was a complete slut and had been with every bloke in Bethlehem. She got pregnant, had no idea who the father was because there'd been so many, and pleaded it was immaculate and God put it there. Genius really. So unbelievable that the fools actually believed it.'

We got back to the hotel, having walked the length of the Strip and went onto the Casino floor for a gamble. There were hundreds of gaming tables dotted around an enormous playing area. The room filled with the sounds of coins dropping and video game style music from the slot machines. We decided on the Black Jack table. I bet and Lucy watched. I employed the 'Hi-Lo' method, a rudimentary card counting system that I had adapted slightly. I'd used it with success seventeen times straight in Australia, but it didn't work in Vegas—or perhaps I'd had a few too many beers and was having difficulty keeping count. Either way, I didn't win, so we tried the Roulette wheel instead. I've never won at Roulette so Lucy did the choosing. The place was awash with cigarette smoke, so it was always going to be quick, one way or another. We sat at a crowded table where two men in suits pretended they were high rolling big shots and yelled loudly and hugged each other every time they won. From a distance, anyone would have thought they were winning $1,000 a time, but it was actually $10. Lucy and I, betting on red or black, lost the first two spins. We switched to odds or evens— I couldn't be bothered with spreading fifty cents on numerous numbers across the board. Mind you, a woman who was doing that had a huge pile of chips in front of her and ours was rapidly dwindling. We then won a spin, then lost two more. We broke even a few times, then bet big and lost it.

The rest of our money gradually whittled away and at no time were we on top. Of course, we had a system. Everybody has a system, but you can't beat the house, that much I did know. Every real gambler dies broke.

Exhausted after a long day, we went back to our room on the forty-fifth floor. I had a beer in the bath and listened to a Johnny Cash album. While I looked up through the steam at the black marble walls, it dawned on me that it was nearly over.

I dried myself and then lay down on the palatial bed next to Lucy. The neon lights from the Strip shone through our window, giving the room a soft glow.

'Our dinner tonight at the sushi bar felt like a real date,' Lucy said. 'It felt like you'd whisked me away for a romantic weekend to Vegas. I liked it very much.'

So had I.

42

CITY OF ANGELS

'Are you a lucky little lady in the city of light…'

—**'L.A. Woman', The Doors**

Arriving into Los Angeles from the air, I could see what I'd heard about LA was true—it is a sprawling city, an enormous metropolis. We were flying over the house-jammed suburbs for twenty minutes. The next day we caught a bus from our hotel and it took forty minutes and didn't even take us all the way through Hollywood. The beaches were even further away than that. It is a big city. That much is true. Everything else I'd heard about Los Angeles was complete bullshit.

'LAX is such a busy airport that it's an absolute nightmare.'

We flew into the airport at night. There were a fair few people around, but it was manageable and we made it through the baggage reclaim and out the gate to a shuttle bus in a few minutes. The airport was clean, with plentiful shops and eateries. It looked like a good airport.

The shuttle took an hour and a half to take us to our Hollywood hotel. When we finally made it, the driver, who had annoyed me by dropping us off last, despite having to double back to do it, stood there in front of me, obviously waiting for a tip.

'I paid the gratuity on the Internet when I booked it,' I said. 'There was an option to do it.' I assumed there would be no way for him to know if I did or not. He was an Eastern European.

'No, you didn't,' he said. 'I get receipt. Wait.'

He went to the glove box then came back with my credit card receipt for exactly $30.

'Oh, that's strange,' I said, grabbing my bags and walking off. 'Thank you.'

I turned to look at him. He was still there and did not look impressed. He mumbled something in his mother tongue and huffed off back to the shuttle.

It wasn't just the fact that he dropped the other passengers off first that annoyed me. He'd been a moron of a driver as well, stopping at amber lights the whole way. Then we passed In-N-Out Burger. There was a queue of at least forty cars for the drive-through. They went the whole way through the car park and came out onto the street and blocked our path. Instead of using the horn and pushing past, he waited ten minutes for the queue to move before we drove on.

Either way, we'd not been in a cab or anything like it for over a month and it was hard to take. That's how long we'd had Mal. We'd driven 9,120 km with him and it was sad to bid him farewell. We bought a beer each to celebrate our relationship with Mal. We sat drinking the beers in the parking lot of the car hire company with Bruce Springsteen playing on the car stereo.

'Look at what you've done to me,' Lucy said as she took a sip of beer. She'd been converted to beer and Bruce.

I then kissed Mal goodbye and didn't look back. And the shuttle was a far cry from the valet parking in Las Vegas, where all you had to do was scan the ticket on a machine and the car would appear in less than two minutes, at no cost. Yes, it'd been good to have a car, but we were back to dealing with the public.

We checked into our forty-first and final accommodation for the tour. Breakfast the next day was almost passable. There was a man at breakfast with slicked back hair like a Wall Street banker.

'Thank you for opening your hotel and letting us film here,' he said to the manager, so that all could hear. 'It's been excellent to film here. A real pleasure.' Everyone in the room was looking at him. We were in a roadside Travelodge motel.

'It's impossible to get around. You'll be in cars or taxis the whole time, stuck in the horrendous traffic.'

We didn't catch a taxi in LA and we weren't stuck in traffic. There is a modern, clean and efficient metro system that serves the city and it is excellent, apart from the fact that the escalators run down and you have to walk up the steps. What's more, the barrier gates are always open and there are no ticket inspectors, so you can ride for free.

The metro took us to all the key places we wanted to go—the Kodak Theatre where the Academy Awards are held, a place to view the famous Hollywood sign, the Hollywood Walk of Fame where stars line the footpath with the names of celebrities on them, many of whom I'd never heard of, and Grauman's Chinese Theatre which features handprints of well-known actors. Hollywood Boulevard was an impressive street, laced with neon, and we saw no seedy edge to it. As expected, it was riddled with tourist souvenir stores.

There are also plentiful buses that criss-cross the city. They are useful, but not much fun. We caught one at night. We were the only whites on there, apart from a few drunks, one of whom was standing near to my seat running his fingers through his hair while his dandruff was falling on me. There was no passenger limit either. People were jammed down the aisle, squashed up against one another. A black woman was sitting near us. She had dreadlocks and, at a guess, was in her forties. There was a salesman of fake jewellery standing next to her, shaking an array of gaudy bracelets at her and another woman, who I don't think she knew.

'Don't look at him, don't make eye contact,' the black lady said to the other woman. She was referring to the salesman. 'He'll break you down and then you'll buy.'

The other woman didn't respond. The salesman kept shaking the bracelets, no expression on his face.

'And if he don't sell anything to you,' she went on. 'He'll steal your jewellery. He's got all these gold bracelets and shit and dangling them distracting you and then 'whoosh', yours is gone.' The old man could hear all this, but it didn't seem to be registering. The poor old bloke could barely stand up.

'Clean off. Gone,' she added for clarity.

Yes, the bus system is good, but it's better not to use it if you don't have to.

'LA is a disgusting concrete jungle.'

One day we went to the shopping area at Grove Road. It's an outdoor mall of boutique stores adjacent to trendy food outlets in a quaint Farmer's Market. Easy listening music is piped throughout the area. It's all very chic. And Hollywood Boulevard itself is a vibrant area. It's quite a good looking city generally and there's no more concrete than any other big city.

'It's full of smog. There's so much smog and pollution that it's hard to breathe and you can't see the Hollywood sign because of it.'

In our three days in LA we didn't see a cloud in the sky. There was no smog either. The air was clear and the sky blue. From a comfortable first floor vantage point on Hollywood Boulevard, we had an untrammelled view of the Hollywood sign and took pictures, along with the many Japanese tourists.

'It's too dangerous to go anywhere at night.'

LA is pretty much all blacks and Hispanics. Where we stayed in Hollywood it could have been a Colombian town. All the signs were in Spanish and all the people spoke Spanish.

We walked the streets at night, and apart from some homeless black men slumped in a gutter, far too drunk to cause any threat, we saw no problems on the street at all. Meanwhile, in tranquil Denver, Colorado, a man walked into a cinema with tear gas and an AR-15 assault rifle and killed twelve people and wounded fifty-nine others who were watching a *Batman* movie. The same night we were in a Los Angeles cinema watching *Savages*.

We did see one incident though. It happened at our hotel when we were checking out. We were sitting in reception, having been refused a late check-out, when a genuine Californian Mustang Man walked up to the front desk to check-in. He was in a vest top and army boots, but he didn't look all that tough. The little Indian man behind the counter advised Mustang that his room wouldn't be ready until the check-in time of 2pm. It was 1pm.

'What time is check-out?' asked Mustang.

'11am.'

'I've stayed in hundreds of hotels,' said Mustang. 'And I've never heard of that. Ever. I've even stayed at a Travelodge.'

'I've never not heard of that policy,' I said to Lucy.

'How are you going to resolve this?' said Mustang. He was getting irritated.

'Check-in is at 2pm,' said Indian. 'There's nothing I can do. You can call hotels.com and see the check-in time.'

With that, Mustang went berserk and started fist-slamming the counter.

'I made the fucking booking online,' he said. 'I shouldn't have to call anyone. Give me my room.'

Indian stood resolute. 'You're not getting a room now, sir,' he said. 'I have the right to refuse service. No room for you.'

'Get fucked,' screamed Mustang and stormed out. 'I hope you enjoy your stay in this terrible fucking excuse for a hotel,' he said to us on the way out, gesticulating wildly.

He walked over to five friends who were standing in the parking lot. They didn't look all that tough either, but one looked like a druggie and had an army cap on.

'I'd be surprised if there's not at least one gun in that car,' I said to Lucy.

A minute later, Mustang stormed back into reception.

'Listen, I want my room now,' he said.

'No room,' said Indian. 'I'm calling security.'

Ten minutes of car park posturing later and the five men

drove away, just before the very tough looking, well-armed security guard arrived.

'Well, that's disappointing,' I said.

'Very,' said Lucy.

'Mind you,' I said. 'He might be better off than us.' I pointed to a sign in reception that read: 'This facility contains chemicals known to the State of California to cause cancer and birth defects or other reproductive harm.'

'You see celebrities everywhere in Hollywood.'

We saw no celebrities on the streets of Hollywood or elsewhere in LA. We went to all the key shopping districts where they allegedly hang out, and even went to the In-N-Out Burger near to the Kodak Theatre. After starving themselves so they can fit into their skimpy dresses, apparently the actresses go there after the Academy Awards for a binge. We'd heard from a lot of people that In-N-Out Burger is excellent, far better than any other burger chain. Words like 'amazing' and 'incredible' have been used. We were excited about our visit. The place was packed and it was only 11.45am. All the tables were taken and people were standing in line to sit down. Surprisingly, there were only four burgers on the menu, but Lucy had the inside word. She ordered our burgers 'animal style', meaning that pickles and sauces and all the extras were added.

In a word, the burgers were terrible. They were just greasy Big Macs, but not as tasty.

When we were leaving, a camera crew came up to us and asked if they could interview me. Well, they asked Lucy first, but she didn't want to, so I subbed in.

'I want to ask you a couple of questions about In-N-Out Burger,' the interviewer opened with. She was quite young and her face was covered with acne, so I gathered it wasn't for the prime time news.

'Are you aware that under the drink containers there are Jesus crosses and some verse from the Bible?' she said.

'No, I wasn't.'

She then asked me my views on corporate policies like that.

'It doesn't really bother me,' I said. 'As long as they don't force it down your throat like the rest of America does.' She looked a little taken aback.

'But what I will say,' I went on, 'is that In-N-Out Burgers are crap.'

'I didn't see any religious stuff in the shop,' Lucy said afterwards. 'Did you?'

'No, but it's absurd. They have their Bible verse on the cups to make themselves feel better while they dish up cardiac-arresting grease to Average Joe who knows no better.'

Having seen no celebrities in the key areas, we went for a sure thing.

A man on Hollywood Boulevard had given us a ticket to be in the audience for a live recording of The Late Late Show With Craig Ferguson at CBS Studios. Ferguson is a Scottish comedian. We'd seen his show on TV in Mexico and had slated it to each other. But we thought it was something novel to do.

We made our way out to CBS and joined the long queue for the show.

'Why aren't these people at work?' I said to Lucy. It was 3pm on a Thursday.

'Probably out of work actors,' she said.

'It really galls me when people should be at work and

they're not.'

But it soon became apparent that most people in that line probably were out of work actors. A twenty-or-so-year-old guy next to us was there on an early date with a girl, maybe even their first date. He started dancing with her in the queue, twirling her and commentating as he did with sound effects, such as a 'shwooshing' noise as she spun, then 'bam' as they reconnected.

'You can't do this type of street dancing without sound effects,' he said to the poor girl, who looked uncomfortable. 'It just doesn't happen.'

As we were about to go in, a heavily made up sixty year old woman in bright clothing came up to me.

'Jackson Hole,' she said, referring to the logo on my T-shirt.

She was clearly drunk, but a nutcase as well. For no reason, she started talking about Las Vegas and I said we had just been there.

'Oh, I love Vegas,' she said, smiling. 'I wanted to do a duet with Barbra Streisand there once, but it didn't come off.'

She went to walk away. 'God bless,' I said, knowing it would elicit a reaction.

'God bless you, too.'

'And good luck,' I said.

She stopped and walked back. 'I don't need luck,' she said. 'God has blessed me and given me all the luck I need. He's got a plan for me.'

'I can see that,' I said.

She wasn't let in to the event.

We nearly weren't either. The ticket we'd been given had a notice on it which read: 'Dress smart casual, like what you'd wear to a movie date'. I was in board shorts and a T-shirt, with flip flops. Everyone else was at least in jeans.

'You can't come in dressed like that, sir,' said the security guard at the gate. He was a large black man. All the security guards in America are large black men. I think he had Tourette's syndrome as he was saying 'Sup? Sup?', presumably a contraction of 'what's up?', to every person who approached him.

'But the ticket says that you can wear what you'd wear to a movie date,' I said.

'You wouldn't wear that to a movie date.'

'I would,' I said. 'And the beauty of it is, we're actually off on a movie date straight after this.' And we were. I showed him the tickets. He smiled and shook his head and let us pass. A rare victory.

Up in the studio there were a lot of 'So, who wants to see a show today?' yelling sort of crap from a comedian sent in to warm up the crowd.

'If you think a joke of Craig's is not funny,' he said. 'Well fuck you, laugh anyway.'

'And one more thing,' he said, just before Ferguson came out. 'You must take your sunglasses off. Craig likes to make a personal connection with you and to do this he needs to see your eyes.'

Craig came out and did a piece to camera and then had some knighted English actor on the show that I'd never heard of. Craig himself was actually quite funny and it was a surprisingly enjoyable couple of hours.

And, although nobody outside of America, Mexico and a small town in Scotland has ever heard of Craig Ferguson, it counted as a Hollywood celebrity spot.

'Universal Studios is a waste of time and only for kids anyway.'

We went to Universal Studios for its 100th anniversary. That's not the reason we were there, it just happened to be the anniversary. So as to avoid the queues, we arrived at 7.45am for the 8am park opening. And it paid off. We didn't wait for a thing. We did a two minute survey interview when we arrived and got a 'front of line' pass for the Studio Tour. That saved us a seventy minute wait later in the day. The line for the tour weaved round and round metal guard rails and looked endless. Most people were waiting in the sweltering sun.

But first we went to the *Transformers* ride. It was the latest ride at the park and the most popular. Later in the day the waiting time reached up to two hours, but we got straight on. The park brochure described the ride as 'fusing photo-realistic 3D HD media and elaborate flight simulation technology with cutting edge physical and special effects, *Transformers* is the next generation immersive Theme Park attraction'. I had no idea what all that meant, but the ride was quite unbelievable and beyond my powers of description. It was worth the $80 park admission fee in itself (of course, the park cost far less for military personnel). We sat on a bench-like seat in a carriage and were buckled down with a rubber-covered metal bar. Everything went dark, and then it was on. The car hurtled its way through a maze of transformers smashing each other and crashing into things. The wind rushed through our hair and we were sprayed with water and covered in smoke, all the while deafened by the sound effects. It was like being in the middle of a very realistic violent cartoon. A little Asian kid next to me screamed for the entire ride.

Next, we went to the *Jurassic Park* ride to 'face off against living dinosaurs' including a plunge down a treacherous 84-foot waterfall. A woman at the gate told us that the water features were turned off and that we wouldn't get wet. The carriage wound its way through a jungle with fake dinosaurs and then along a river. We got soaked. As we fell over the waterfall drop, Lucy mimicked the Asian kid from the *Transformers* ride. The jolt back jarred my spine against the hard plastic seat.

'I didn't find the drop off all that scary,' I said to Lucy as we got off the ride. The digital photo of our carriage that was displayed at the exit proved otherwise.

The Revenge of the Mummy, billed as 'a terrifying thrill ride of ghastly creatures that uses Linear Induction Motors Technology to catapult riders at 45 miles per hour', was an indoor rollercoaster, and not merely a simulation. It didn't last long, but it was exhilarating.

The *Simpsons* ride was another virtual ride and detailed as 'highly aggressive'. It was and as we got off I started yawning, a telltale sign of motion sickness. We'd been on four bone-shaking rides in thirty minutes.

It was then time for a few shows. First up was the *Terminator*, a spectacle that required 3D glasses. There has been no advancement in 3D glass technology since its inception in the early 80s. In 1981 I saw a Cowboys and Indians movie in 3D with glasses from Pizza Hut. The glasses are exactly the same over thirty years later, except that they are made of plastic instead of cardboard and they're black instead of the one red and one blue lens of the predecessors. The show was rather average. Waiting to go in, we watched a large television screen telling people to clap and say 'oh yeah'. Everyone did.

302

'Herd mentality is an amazing thing,' I said to Lucy.

I was overheard by a fat woman in charge of crowd control, who must have interpreted my comment as troublemaking.

'Stay behind the line. You must not proceed beyond the line until you are told to do so,' she said.

'She should go back to Greyhound,' Lucy said.

Then at the first chance, the multitude of Asians came steamrolling over the line and into the auditorium. The Asians are nearly as bad as middle-aged women.

The next show was the *House of Horrors*. It was shithouse and not remotely scary, the *Special Effects Stage* was marginally better, the *Animal Actors* show was quite good with racoons, birds, dogs, cats and guinea pigs running around doing as they were told. The *Waterworld* show, which was the actual set for the 1995 movie, was entertaining with a lot of fire and blowing up and splashing. The front row of the stand was reserved for the handicapped. A big fat woman sat in one of those seats.

'She doesn't look handicapped,' Lucy said. 'She just couldn't be bothered walking up one step.'

'No, not handicapped,' I said. 'A fat, lazy bitch perhaps, but not handicapped.'

The *Studio Tour*, with Wild West and Mexican towns and old sets from *Jurassic Park* and *Jaws* and *Back to the Future*, as well as the actual street Wisteria Lane used for *Desperate Housewives*, was very impressive. They were filming an episode of CSI as we passed through, but we didn't see any actors.

In all, the park was excellent and well worth it. We'd been told that half a day was needed to see it in full. When it comes to fast sight-seeing, Lucy and I have no peer. To say we are lightning quick would be a gross understatement. But we didn't wait for any ride or show and were at the park for seven hours. You couldn't do it in less time than that.

On our final day in Los Angeles, we went to a diner near our hotel for one last American burger, then left for LAX. There was a hippy wanker playing his guitar on the balcony of his hotel room as we drove away—a fitting farewell.

Going through security at LAX, there was a young overweight woman in uniform greeting passengers with a countenance of death.

'Do not stand forward of the yellow line until you are called,' she yelled at us. We were next in the queue.

'I didn't even see the yellow line,' Lucy said to me.

'Me neither,' I said. 'And there's no sign saying that we have to wait behind it anyway.'

We passed security without exchanging words with the woman.

'She's probably been earmarked by Greyhound,' I said. 'They've got her in the draft for next season, but she's a bit young yet.'

'And not fat enough.'

'No,' I said. 'But she's certainly showing a lot of potential.'

We boarded the plane bound for London.

And then it was over.

43

TIME TO SAY GOODBYE

'But I'm in so deep. You know I'm such a fool for you. You got me wrapped around your finger...'

—'Linger', The Cranberries

It was over.

We'd flown from LAX back to London. A few weeks later I was back at the airport again and sat in the bustle of Terminal 5 at Heathrow. My mind was silent and a feeling of nostalgia filled me. I'd finished the trip. It hadn't ended the way I'd wanted it to, but I'd finished it. I had always been pretty good at doing things.

I'd had no contact with Lucy since we'd arrived in London. I phoned her. She answered.

'Well, that was a trip and a half wasn't it?' I said.

'Hello. Where are you?'

'Heathrow. I've got to board in a minute.'

'How are you? What are you doing?' She sounded surprised that I was back at the airport.

'It was an amazing trip wasn't it?'

'Yes it was. It was amazing for me, too,' Lucy said. 'Amazing.'

'We certainly gave America a bit of a nudge didn't we? Forty-five states isn't bad.'

'We did that. Maybe one day we'll do the other five.'

'Yeah maybe,' I said. 'I worked out that in cars, buses and trains, we drove for 25,000 kilometres in total, 15,000 of them ourselves in hire cars.'

'Really?' she said. 'And I'd say we spent 99% of our money on food and drinks.'

'Yeah,' I said. 'And we wasted the rest.'

Lucy laughed. I could picture her smiling that smile of hers. There was no better thing than her smile.

'It's hard to think we'll never be on another Dog together,' she said.

'I can't say I'll miss the Dog all that much, but it does seem sad in a way.'

'I'm sad,' said Lucy.

There was a short silence.

'I've missed you, Lucia,' I said, feeling awkward.

'I've missed you.'

'We sure did have some fun while it lasted,' I said.

'Where are you going to end up?'

'I don't know. I'm going to Australia now. I better go. So long, you lovely little creature. I really loved you. No hard feelings, okay? Good luck with everything,' I said. 'You'll do well. Regards to the felines.'

'I love you,' she said. 'Bye.'

I waited for the line to go dead. But the space held.

'Wait,' she said. 'Hold on a second.'

'Yes?'

'I was thinking,' she said.

'Yes?'

'You should write it all down so we don't forget it.'

'I won't forget it.'

'But so we've got a record of it all,' she said.

'I might just do that.'

A captivating novel—and its sequel—from
Hugo-nominated author Dominic Green

Mount Ararat, a world the size of an asteroid yet with Earth-standard gravity, plays host to an eccentric farming community protected by the Devil, a mechanical killing machine, from such passers-by as Mr von Trapp (an escapee from a penal colony), the Made (manufactured humans being hunted by the State), and the super-rich clients of a gravitational health spa established at Mount Ararat's South Pole.

www.fingerpress.co.uk/smallworld
www.fingerpress.co.uk/littlestar

Travelling the West Coast, USA?

**Designed specifically for an Internet-connected iPad,
this book has capabilities that ordinary travel books
don't even dream about.**

Jewel of the Left Coast showcases a town that's a hit with
visitors and long-term residents alike. With annotated field
trips to the Getty Museum, Beverly Hills, Sunset Strip and
downtown LA, detailed guides to shopping and spa services,
more than 100 links to restaurant reviews on Yelp, hotel
guides by neighborhood (including hotel photo slideshows)
and interactive maps, this book is your indispensable guide
to Santa Monica and its nearby attractions.

www.fingerpress.co.uk/santa-monica-jewel-left-coast

FOLLOW THE BAND -
A FAN'S-EYE VIEW OF USC TROJAN FOOTBALL

A multimedia celebration of the history and traditions of Trojan Football

USC Trojan fans and alumni who bleed cardinal and gold will love this "fan's-eye view" of Trojan Football.

Designed for the iPad, this innovative guide combines embedded videos, slideshows and panoramic photos with insightful details and fun facts.

www.fingerpress.co.uk/usc-trojans-football

Lightning Source UK Ltd.
Milton Keynes UK
UKOW01f2323241116
288515UK00005B/264/P